2012 The Real Story

Also By Jack L. Summers

Fiction

Caleb

The Deadly Practice

Lair of the Wolf

The Healer

The Cure

Non-Fiction

Warriors of the Faith

The Christmas People

Discovering the Monster Within

Higher and Faster

2012 THE REAL STORY

BY

JACK L. SUMMERS

TRAFFORD PUBLISHERS

Bloomington, IN 47403

Order this book online at www.trafford.com
or email orders@trafford.com

Most Trafford titles are also available at major online book retailers.

This book is a work of non-fiction, and is based on reference material obtained from the King James Version of the Bible and material readily available on the internet. Large portions of the text are from sources provided by Logos Publications, the educational arm of the Christadelphian faith, and used with their permission. The interpretation of this information is solely the authors

This book contains no graphic language, violence or mature scenes. Specific biblical material quoted should be appropriate for all ages but specifically early teen through adults.

Printed in the United States of America.

ISBN: 978-1-4269-7649-0 (sc)
ISBN: 978-1-4269-7650-6 (e)

Library of Congress Control Number: 2011912366

Trafford rev. 07/26/2011

 www.trafford.com

North America & international
toll-free: 1 888 232 4444 (USA & Canada)
phone: 250 383 6864 ♦ fax: 812 355 4082

To my son Scott
daughter and son-in-law Marcia and
Demetri
and grandson Leo
who are not alarmed by 2012

And to Pat
without whom nothing is possible

PREFACE

Much has been written about the year 2012. A simple web search will produce hundreds of thousands of hits, many of them concerning the Mayan Calendar, which will reach the end of its cycle in December of 2012, and the prophesies of Nostradamus, who some say prophesied the end of the world in the year 2012. In addition, a new motion picture entitled 2012 portrays in graphic detail the end of the world, we know it.

Astronomers and astrologists likewise see portents of comets or unknown asteroids colliding with the earth with cataclysmic results. Ecologists warn that global warming and the pollution of the atmosphere of the earth will destroy the world in the not too distant future. On the other end of the spectrum are those who predict the return to the earth of extraterrestrials that they assure us have been here before.

In response to these alarms, entrepreneurs have opened web sites selling dried food and other survival supplies to those who wish to plan to survive the horrific events that some predict will occur on December 12th, 2012. However, some of us are Christians. As Christians, our source of solace is the Bible, which we believe is mankind's only link to the Maker and Creator of the Universe. In that marvelous book is God's plan for the future. It is the purpose of this volume to examine the claims of the doom and gloom brigade, and compare them to God's plan.

This is not a simple task, because most of the Creator's plan is contained in prophetic language in books of the Bible that many Christians won't take the time to study and understand. Compounding the problem is the centuries of misunderstanding of the events in those prophecies that have clouded modern thought.

Since "experts" have debated many of these issues for decades, I understand that some who read this manuscript may disagree with its contents. After, all, some of the same criticisms that can be leveled at Nostradamus' prophecies can be leveled at this work. But, unlike those of Nostradamus, the end time prophecies in the Bible are logical, carry a unified message, and are marked by prophecies that were made in advance that have come true.

I am not a theologian. I was not schooled in any great religious institution of higher learning. But, I do possess two doctoral degrees, a keen enquiring mind, a thirst for history, and a fifty years experience with in depth Bible study. It is my plan to present what the Bible has to say about the end of the world in an understandable fashion.

This work would not be possible without the study material available from *Logos*, the educational arm of the Christadelphian faith. Much of the in depth Bible study quoted here is based on the pioneering work of the late H.P Mansfield and is used with the permission of *Logos*. Readers are encouraged to examine the wealth of reference material available from www.logos.org. au where material may be downloaded or purchased.

In the end, perhaps the reader will examine the evidence, vouch for its authenticity by double-checking the premises presented, and then decide if they need survival gear, or a church in their community. Either way, when you reread this on January 1, 2013, this interpretation should have more weight.

A simple caveat must be stated. Beginning in Chapter 10, certain passages of scripture are presented with significant discussion. These cannot be simply read as a novel. They are better used for in depth study and contemplation.

This work was inspired by the countless number of young men and women who have come to my attention who choose to believe the word of a civilization, however sophisticated in science and astronomy, whose approach to their god was to rip the living beating hearts from human beings. I hope that the time honored, history proven word of a loving and compassionate God will ease their anxiety.

CHAPTER 1

The Mayan Calendar

The Mayans started all the fuss over 2012 so this is the place to begin. Their civilization lived in a large area that included southern Mexico, Guatemala, El Salvador, Belize and the western areas of Honduras. It reached a zenith between the third and tenth centuries BCE, but by 1200 ACE, their society collapsed. No reason for the collapse has ever been determined. It remains an enigma.

When the Spanish appeared on the scene, they still encountered Mayans who spoke the language. Mayan cities, overgrown in the jungle by the vines of time, stood mute testimony to their former glory, but the natives who lived there then, had no knowledge of their existence or function. It is in part due to the mysterious disappearance of this great civilization that has added fuel to the theory that the recycling of the Mayan Calendar is a predictor of the end of civilization as the world now knows it.

It was nearly the end of the 18th Century before explores penetrated the dense Guatemalan rainforest and found the Mayan pyramids, temples, monoliths and plazas complete with picture and hieroglyphic writing. The Maya kept historical record in a fashion consisting of ideographic and phonetic elements. A number of these still exists on stone monuments that tell of the day to day events in their lives, records their calendar and describe astronomic events.

Diego de Landa, a Spanish priest, visited Mexico and was appointed the Franciscan provincial of Yucatan. In the manner of countless religious zealots throughout history, he set about to systematically destroy every important and valuable Mayan artifact and document he could find. While he was intrigued by the Mayans, he found their practice of ritual human sacrifice to be abhorrent. Single handedly, he changed what history had to teach us about the Mayans.

In July of 1562, de Landa found a cave containing sacred Mayan statues along with evidence of human sacrifice. The priest was so incensed at the perceived barbarism that he ordered the destruction of the five thousand idols in the cave. Perhaps his most heinous historic act was to burn the entire extensive library he found in the cave. Considering the number of idols, and the extent of the manuscripts, this was likely a major repository of Mayan knowledge consistent with a "Mayan Library of Congress."

This should be a lesson for the modern Christian. Even though de Landa felt he was doing "God's work" in eradicating what he believed to be "devil worship", one must always examine the consequences of the act and not allow emotion to rule the day. A mere three books survived the conflagration in the cave. Regrettably, the majority of Mayan history and knowledge was lost.

Still, history has treated the rampaging priest far more kindly than he deserves. In spite of his callused and savage treatment of the Mayan artifacts, his book, *Refacion de las cosas de Yucatán* published in 1566 remains the definitive text on the Mayan civilization. The book wasn't printed for over three hundred years, but when it was, it provided the tools to decipher a phonetic alphabet the made it possible to translate nearly one-third of existing Mayan hieroglyphs.

The Dresden Codex, named for the city of Dresden where the book was kept, must be included in any discussion of Mayan civilization. It is an unusual book filled with hieroglyphs which had defied translation. Ernst Førstemann, a German scholar who worked at the library, cracked the code of the Mayan calendar in 1889. This was the key to the interpretation of the myriad inscriptions on Mayan artifacts.

Førstemann discovered the Codex was actually a chart with complex astrological tables that calculated the length of a year to be 365.2420 days. It is a more accurate number than can be calculated by the Julian calendar that we use today. Mayan astronomers also predicted the solstices and the equinoxes as well as the orbits of solar system planets, the cycles of Venus and Mars, and other celestial phenomena. Remember, this was far in advance of Western Civilizations attempt to do the same things. The *Popol Buh* and *Chilam Balam* are books that were written shortly after the Spanish first arrived. These books and codices combined with the discoveries in the jungle demonstrate clearly that the Mayan civilization rivaled the Greek and Egyptians in knowledge, science and architecture and was likely as old or older.

The Mayan Calendar

Mayan life was intricately involved with time. It was also an era when humankind struggled to understand the strange forces of the universe that dictated their daily lives. They knew the sun rose in a particular direction and set in another. They could chart its course and predict its solstices. But, why did the sun do those things? What caused drought? What caused floods, terrible storms or crops to fail? There must be someone or something out there controlling the process. In an attempt to aid their understanding, as with nearly every primitive civilization ever studied, this force was personified. The result was a religion.

If there is a religion, someone has to be in charge. These were the priests. They were consulted for advice concerning religious, civil and agricultural matters. Time was so critically important in their day-to-day lives that children were named for the date on which they were born. Thus, time intertwined with religion, and to answer these questions, the priests consulted their sacred calendars.

Mayan math was relatively simple using only three symbols, a shell-shaped glyph for zero, a dot for one and a bar for five to represent units from zero to nineteen. For example, the number thirteen would be two bars and three dots.

The presence of a mathematical zero, was a concept the Mayans understood and was extraodinary for its time. When Christ lived, and for centuries after, the Romans were ignorant of its existence, yet the Mayans were using a shell as its symbol. It was a familiar tangile object used to represent an abstract symbol. They also used metrical calculation and place numeration which was clever for a culture that didn't use the wheel.

Despite their many calendars, Mayans marked the passage of time with three parallel cycles. The first time cycle was a sacred calendar call the Tzolkin. It used the numbers one through thirteen and a sequence of twenty named days. It is similar to the named days of the week that we use. 5-Chikchan would paralled our Sunday the 5th. 6-Kimi would correspond to Monday the 6th. Despite calculating the year as the familiar 365 days, their time measurment was different, and every 260 days the numerical/ name combinations would recur. Then the calendar would begin again.

They used a numbering system based on twenty. Many believe they counted using their fingers and toes. Thirteen apprears to be an important number to Maya and it fits with the growth cycle of the moon. The moon is not visible when it is new, and when it is full remains so for two full days. This fits a thirteen day growth cycle. The length of Tzolkin could be related to the 273 day or nine month gestation period of a human fetus. Perhaps the 260 days is the time between when a woman suspects she is pregnant until she actually gives birth. Of course this is reasonable but speculative.

Haab is the agricultural calander, and it consists of 18 months of 20 days each. Another five day month, considered a month of insecurity and bad luck is called Uayeb. A combination of the two calanders produces a 365 day year. The calander was used to track seasons, and solar events that occur on roughly the same day each year. There is evidence that Mayan were aware of the quarter day discrepancy, but there is no knowledge that they ever did anything about it. The two clanaders started every 260 and 350 plus 5 days, but every 52 years they coincide.

The Tzolkin and the Haab ran concurrently, and to go back to any given date, 52 years or 18,980 days would pass, because both 365 x 52 and 260 x 73 when added equals the same 18,980 days. The Tzolkin would require 73 revolutions and the Haab 52, so that every 52 calendaar years of 365 days the same date would reoccur. A Mayan date, say 21k (the position of the day in the Tzolkin) 0 Pop (the position in the Haab) it would take 52 years for that date to recurr.

The Mayans expected that the world would end at the completion of this 52 year cycle. Like many modern cults who have predicted the end of the world and retired to a mountain top to await the inevitable. In the Valley of Mexico, all fires were extinguished, pregnant women were locked up lest they turn into wild animals, children were pinced to keep them awake so they wouldn't turn into mice, and all pottery was shattered in preperation for the end of the world.

In an attempt to plead for the gods to grant the Mayans another 52 years of existence, a special night time ceremony was held. A procession, led by the priests, wound its way throught the night across a causeway to the top on an extince volcant that juts from the basin floor of Mexico, today called the Hill of the Star, above Ixtapalapa. They scouererd the stars, and waited for the Seven Sisters, the constellation of Pleiades to cross the center of the heavens. If that occurred, it would proclaim an additional fifty-two years of human existance.

At the exact moment of this occurrence, the priest would make a single slash in a previously selected victim and extract the still beating heart. In the cavity where the heart had been, the priest used a fire drill to kindle a new flame. Torches were lit from the flame and it was carried across the lake to the temple in Tenochititlan, and from ther to the other villages and farms around the lake. This was called the New Fire Ceremony and was embraced by nearly all Mesoamericans. This might be considered similar to the apprehension felt by some Christians or doomsday prophets at the end of the recent Millennium. However, the Mayan world didn't end, and likely would not have even without the human sacrifice.

The Mayans thus connected their "end of the world prophecy" with a natural occuring peneomenon, the movement of a known constellation. Unless one believes that human sacrifice influences the forces of the universe, this practice must be considered flawed.

The modern Western calendar was introduced in Europe in 1582. Based on the Gregorian calendar, it calculate the earth orbit to be 365.25 days. This proved to be 0.0003 of a day per year too long, but was amazingly accurate for scientists living so long ago. On the other hand, the Mayans derived their calanders from the Olmecs who date back roughly 3,000 years. And, they did it withought the insturments used in the 16th centruy to produce our modern calendar. Despite that, they calculated a year that was only 0.0002 days too long, a more accurate prediciton than their instrument rich successors in Europe. The Olmecs had the Long Count calander, but whether they created it, or received it from an even earlier culture is not known.

The Long Count Calander

The Mayan's had a third calander. It is known as the "long count" and is a continuous recording of days that cycles every 5,000 years, or so. The current version began in 3,114 BC. By adding the 2010 years that have transpired since then, we are in the 5,124th year of the cyle. So, it will end very soon. A typical Mayan date would be as follows: 12.18.16.2.6.3 Cimi 4 Zotz. 4 Zotz is the date in the Haab calander while Cimi is the Tzolkin date. The other numbers, 12.18,16.2.6.3 represent the Long Count date. A kin, or day is the last number of the Long Count going from left to right. The Long Count cycle is 13 Baktuns, or about 5,126 years where the number 13 might represent the growth of the moon from new to full. In Mayan mythology, every Long Count cycle is a world age in which the gods attempt to create pious and subservient creatures. The origins of these myths are lost in the mists of history.

The first age marks the creation of the earth. This creation contained both living beings as well as living vegetation. However, these creatures were were mute and could not pay homage to the gods. At the end of the cycle they were destroyed.

In the Second and Third Ages, the gods created the humans of mud and then wood, but the gods were still not satisfied and wiped them out. The current age in which we live it the fourth and final age. Why it has been determined to be the final age is not clear, except for the prediction of the end of the age in 2012. This is the age of the modern, fully functional human beign. Perhaps these ages referred to the changes of evolution. Is so, Mayan experts wonder what will occur when the current age expires in December of 2012.

It must be pointed out that this philosophy is based on the same logic that suggested the world would end at the end of the 52 year cycle of the other calendars. Is it reasonable to assume that this logicis more accurate?

Mayan Prophecies Concerning 2012

According to Joseph Robert Jochmans, "The Hopi and Mayan elders do not prophesy that everything will come to an end. Rather, this is a time of transition from one World Age into another. The message they give concerns our making a choice of how we enter the future ahead. Our moving through with either resistance or acceptance will determine whether the transition will happen with cataclysmic changes or gradual peace and tranquility. The same theme can be found reflected in the prophecies of many other Native American visionaries from Black Elk to Sun Bear."

The Mayans prophesied that from 1999 we have 13 years to realize the changes in our conscious attitude to stray from the path of self-destruction and instead move onto a path that opens our consciousness to integrate us with all that exists. Many might suggest that the path to self destruction by earthlings started long before 1999. They felt that our Sun, called Kinich-Ahau, every so often synchronized with the enormous central galaxy. And from this central galaxy received a "spark of Light" which causes the Sun to shine more intensely producing solar flares as well as changes in the Sun's magnetic field. In Mayan lore, this occurs every 5,112 years. They add that this causes a displacement in the earth's rotation, thus producing great catastrophes.

They also believed the universal processes, like the 'breathing of the galaxy' are cycles that are unchangeable. The change that occurs is the consciousness of man that passes through it. Each change means that the subsequent civilization will be more perfect than the last.

According to the Mayan calculation their civilization began on 4 Ahau, 8 Cunku or 3113, B.C. The completion of one cycle from that time ends on December 21, 2012. They say the powerful synchronizing light from the center of the galaxy will change the polarity of the sun. This produces a great cosmic event that would propel mankind into a new Golden Age.

In the last Mayan cataclysm, a flood destroyed mankind, leaving only a few survivors. They believe that knowing the end of the cycle will allow them to prepare to embrace the perfection of the new age. This is not unlike the Biblical story of Noah. Indeed evidence of universal flooding is found all over the world. Furthermore, geologists agree with the Biblical account that in the beginning the earth was covered with water.

Their first prophecy talks about 'The Time of No-Time', a period of 20 years, which Mayan's call a Katún. The last 20 years of the Sun's cycle of 5,125 years. This cycle is from 1992—2012. During these times, solar winds become more intense and can be seen on the Sun. This would be a time of great realization and great change for mankind. And it would be mankind's destructive contamination of the planet that would contribute to these changes. According to the Mayans, these changes would happen so that mankind comprehends how the universe works so we could advance to superior levels, leaving behind superficial materialism and liberating ourselves from suffering. These are noble sentiments, but ones to which mankind is totally impervious.

According to the Mayans seven years after the start of Katún, which is to say 1999, the world would enter a time of darkness which would force us to confront our own conduct. They say that this is the time when mankind will enter "The Sacred Hall of Mirrors". There, we will look at ourselves and analyze our behaviors with ourselves, with others, with nature and with the planet in which we live. Supposed, this will be a time in which all of humanity, by individual conscious decisions, decides to change and eliminate fear and lack of respect from all of our relationships.

The prophecies state that the start of this period would be marked by a solar eclipse on August 11, 1999, known to them as 13 Ahau, 8 Cauac, and would coincide with an unprecedented planetary alignment, the 'Grand Cross' alignment. This would be the last 13 years of the Katón period. The last opportunity for our civilization to realize the changes that would occur at the moment of our spiritual regeneration.

For the Mayans, everything is numbers and the time of the 13 sacred numbers started in August 1999. They predicted that along with an eclipse, (On August 11, 1999, a total eclipse of the Sun, with an eclipse magnitude of 1.029, occurred and because of the high density populated in the areas of the path, there is little doubt that this was the most-viewed total solar eclipse in human history; although some areas in the path of totality (mainly in Western-Europe) offered impaired visibility due to adverse weather conditions) the forces of nature would act like a catalyst of changes so accelerated and with such magnitude that mankind would be powerless against them.

Also, that our technologies on which we rely so much would begin to fail us. We would no longer be able to learn from our civilization in the way that we are organized as a society. They said that our internal, spiritual development would require a better place along with a better way to interact with more respect and compassion.

The first prophecies were attained by their study of our Sun. The Mayans discovered that the entire solar system moved. That even our universe has its own cycles, repetitive periods which begin and end like our day and night.

These discoveries lead to the understanding that our solar system rotates on an ellipse that brings our solar system closer and further from the center of the galaxy. In other words, according to the Mayans, our Sun and all of its planets rotate in cycles in relation to the center of the galaxy or Hunab-Kú, the central light of the galaxy.

It takes 25,625 years for our solar system to make one cycle on this ellipse. One complete cycle they called a galactic day. The cycle is divided into two halves similar to our day and night. The half closest to the central light, is our solar system's 'day' and the half furthest away is its 'night'. Each day and each night lasts 12,800 years. That is to say, the central galaxy is the Sun for our entire solar system.

According to the Mayans, every grand cycle has its minor cycles that carry the same characteristics. One galactic day of 25,625 years is divided into five cycles of 5,125 years. The first cycle is the galactic morning, when our solar system is just coming out of the darkness to enter the light.

The second cycle is the mid-day, when our solar system is closest to the central light. The third cycle is the afternoon, when our solar system begins to come out of the light. The fourth cycle is the late-night., when our solar system has entered its furthest cycle from the central light. And the fifth and last cycle is night before dawn, when are solar system is in its last cycle of darkness before starting again. This is the cycle we are ending now.

The Mayan prophecy says that in 1999, our solar system began to leave the end of the fifth cycle which started in 3113 B.C. and that we find ourselves in the morning of our galactic day, exiting darkness and on the verge of being in plain day of our central galaxy in 2012. They say that at the beginning and end of these cycles, which is to say, every 5,125 years, the central sun or light of the galaxy emits a ray of light so intense and so brilliant that it illuminates the entire universe. It is from this burst of light that all of the Suns and planets sync. The Mayans compare this burst to the pulse of the universe, beating once every 5,125 years. It is these pulses that mark the end of one cycle.

Interestingly, probes of deep space by the Hubble telescope have shown we are not the center of the universe, and that our universe is billions of light years in size. In none of the Hubble images is there any hint of an enormous source of central galactic energy.

This brings us back to what the Mayans call 'The Time of No Time'. It is a short, intense, evolutionary period, inside the grand cycles where great changes take place to thrust us into a new age of evolution as individuals and as mankind.

As individuals we will be required to make decisions that will affect us all. If we continue on this negative path of hate, an eye for an eye, destruction of nature, of fear and egoism, we will enter straight into the time of destruction and chaos, and we will disappear as the dominant race of this planet.

This is reminiscent of Christ's words in Matt 24:6-7 And ye shall hear of wars and rumors of wars: see that ye be not troubled: for all these things must come to pass, but the end is not yet. For nation shall rise against nation, and kingdom against kingdom: and there shall be famines, and pestilences, and earthquakes, in divers places.

On the other hand, if we become conscious and realize that we all form part of a great organism, and that we should respect one another and be grateful to our planet, then we will move directly into positive growth, our Golden Age. Our planet, the Sun and the Galaxy are awaiting our decision. It is up to us what will happen in this time of change. Whether we go through a time of suffering and destruction or we find ourselves united in one positive consciousness moving closer to our next stage, the choice is ours. If this is the case, based on past human interaction, our planet is indeed doomed.

The Mayan civilization was indeed a spectacular one, and their science and technology is extremely advanced for their time on the world stage. However, their predictions are based on an astrological data set that cannot be verified. The fact that they predicted the 1999 solar eclipse is of no surprise, since all of their calendars have been predicting eclipses for a long time. They present an interesting story that seems easy to believe, if one had nothing stronger to believe in. Unfortunately, many people do not. Fortunately for Christians, they do.

CHAPTER 2

Nostradamus

The other player on the 2012 stage of gloom and doom is the legendary psychic and prophet, Nostradamus. Born in Saint-Rémy-de-Provence in the south of France in December 1503, Michel de Nostredame was the son of a grain dealer who was also a prosperous home-grown notary. His family was originally Jewish, but had converted to Catholicism during the previous century. Nothing is known about his childhood, but at the age of fifteen he entered the University of Avignon to study for his baccalaureate.

Little more than a year later, he was forced by the plague to leave. In 1529, after some years as an apothecary, he entered the University of Montpellier to study for a doctorate in medicine, but was promptly expelled when it was discovered that he had been an apothecary, which was a 'manual' trade expressly banned by the university statutes. He then continued work as an apothecary, and created a "rose pill" that was widely believed to protect against the plague. In 1531 he was invited by Jules-César Scaliger, a leading Renaissance man, to come to Agen. There Nostradamus married a woman whose name is still in dispute (possibly Henriette d'Encausse), but who bore him two children. In 1534, his wife and children died, presumably from the plague. Apparently, the Rose Pill was not as effective as originally advertised. After their death he continued to travel, passing through France and possibly Italy.

He settled down in 1547 in Salon-de-Provence, where he married a rich widow named Anne Ponsarde Gemelle and eventually had six children—three daughters and three sons. After a further visit to Italy, he began to move away from medicine and towards the occult. He wrote an almanac for 1550, for the first time Latinizing his name to 'Nostradamus', and was so encouraged by its success that he decided to write one or more annually.

Taken together, they are known to have contained at least 6338 prophecies (most of them failed predictions), as well as at least 11 annual calendars, all of them starting on 1st January and not, as is sometimes supposed, in March. He then began his project of writing 1,000 quatrains, which form the supposed prophecies for which he is famous today. Feeling vulnerable to religious fanatics, however, he devised a method of obscuring his meaning by using "Virgilianised" syntax, word games and a mixture of languages such as Provencal French, Greek, Latin and Italian. For technical reasons connected with their publication in three installments, the last 58 quatrains of the seventh century, or book of 100 verses, were never published.

The quatrains, written in a book titled *"Les Propheties"*, received a mixed reaction when they were published. Some people thought Nostradamus was a servant of evil, a fake, or insane, while many of the elite thought his quatrains were spiritually inspired prophecies. Soon nobility came from all over to receive horoscopes and advice from him, though he normally expected *them* to supply the birth charts on which they were based.

Catherine de Médicis, the queen consort of King Henry II of France, was one of Nostradamus' admirers. After reading his almanacs for 1555, which hinted at unnamed threats to the royal family, she summoned him to Paris to explain them, as well as to draw up horoscopes for her royal children. At the time he feared that he would be beheaded, but by the time of his death in 1566, she had made him Counselor and Physician in Ordinary to the King.

By 1566 Nostradamus's gout, which had painfully plagued him for many years and made movement very difficult, finally turned into dropsy, or in today's jargon congestive heart failure. At the beginning of July, after making an extended will and a much shorter codicil, he is alleged to have told his secretary Jean de Chavigny, "You will not find me alive by sunrise." The next morning he was reportedly found dead, lying on the floor between his bed and a makeshift bench.

Some biographical accounts of Nostradamus' life state that he was afraid of being persecuted for heresy by the Inquisition, but neither prophecy nor astrology fell under their pervue, and he would have been in danger only if he had practiced magic. In fact, his relations with the Church as a prophet and healer were always excellent. His brief imprisonment at Marignane in late 1561 came about purely because he had published his 1562 almanac without the prior permission of a bishop, contrary to a recent royal decree.

Nostradamus was familiar with recent Latin printed editions of a variety of esoteric writings as well as his acquaintance with astrology. Recent research suggest that most of his prophetic work was a paraphrase of collections of ancient end-of-the-world prophecies, including those from the Bible, and supplemented their insights by projecting known historical events and identifiable anthologies of omen-reports in the future.

Thanks to these facts, his work contains many predictions involving ancient figures like Sulla, Marius, Nero, Hannibal and others, as well as descriptions of "battles in the clouds" and "frogs falling from the sky." He confidently expected, at that time, that the world would end either in 1800 or 1887, although 2242 remained a possibility depending on the system he used for the calculation. Perhaps his logic was that if he made enough predications, one of them might come true.

Nostradamus had a plethora of historic sources to draw on such as Livy, Suetonius, Plutarch, and a range of other classical historians, as well as from the chronicles of medieval authors such as Villehardouin and Froissat. Many of his astrological references, by contrast, are nearly word for word quotes from *Livre de l'estat et mutations des temps*, written in 1549/50 by Richard Roussat. His planetary tables, on which he based the birth charts he couldn't get out of writing, are easy to identify as unoriginal, and as was usually the case, the charts were wrong.

His major prophetic source appears to be *Mirabilis liber* of 1522, which contained a range of prophecies by Pseudo-Methodius, the Tiburtine Sibyl, Joachim of Fiore, Savonarola and others. His Preface has 24 biblical quotations all but two of which are in the exact same order as Savonarola. He also included material from Petrue Crinitus's *De honesta disciplina* of 1504, which included extracts from Psellus's *Da daemonibus,* and the *De Mysteriis Aegyptiorum* (Concerning the mysteries of Egypt), a book on Chaldean and Assyrian magic by Iamblichus, and a 4th century neo-Platonist.

Nostradamus claimed in 1555 to have burned all the occult works in his library, it is impossible to know exactly what books were destroyed in that fire. The fact that they were described to have burned with an unnaturally brilliant flame suggests many of them were vellum manuscripts which were routinely treated with saltpeter.

Since most of his work was based on library research, it is doubtful that he used trance states, other than contemplation and meditation. In letter 41 of his collected Latin correspondence, last published by Jean Dup be, he described his process. Popular legend that he used flame or water gazing or both at once is based on a casual reading of his first two verses which liken his efforts to the Branchidic or Delphic oracles. In his dedication to King Henri II, he describes, "emptying my soul, mind and heart of all care, worry and unease through mental calm and tranquility."

His works are as follows:

The Prophecies: This is a collection of his major long-term divinations and was first published in 1555. A further 289 prophetic verses followed in 1557. In 1558 a third edition of 300 new quatrains were supposedly printed but only fragments of them remain. Due to the printing practices of the time, no two volumes are exactly the same.

The Almanacs: By far the most popular of his works, were published yearly until his death. Frequently, he published two or three almanacs in a single year. The ones he called *Almanacs* were very detailed predictions, while the more generalized ones were published under the names *Prognostications* or *Presagers*.

Translation of Galen is an alleged translation of Galen's early work.

Traitè des fardemens is basically a medical cookbook filled with material "borrowed" from other sources. It also contained his formula for treating the plague. The therapy, which included bloodletting, didn't work. It likewise describes formulas for compounding cosmetics.

Orus Apollo is a manuscript in Lyon Municipal Library where more than 2000 original document relating to Nostradamus reside under the aegis of Michel Chomarat. It is the supposed translation of an ancient Greek work concerning Egyptian hieroglyphs based on later, Latin versions, all of which are incorrect. They were not accurately translated until Champllion did it in the 19th century.

As is apparent from his publication, Nostradamus' reputation as a prophet is largely one manufactured by his modern-day supporters who use his words after the fact in events that have already happened, or are so imminent that they are bound to happen. This is called "retroactive clairvoyance. The only forward translated quatrains are very general like a war will start or a fire will occur.

Some believe Nostradamus was not being prophetic when he wrote, but simply commenting on controversial events of his time and using metaphors and cryptic verbiage to avoid persecution for his views.

His prophecy that "a great and terrifying leader would come out of the sky" in 1999 and 7 months "to resuscitate the great King from Angoumois" is over-stated. The phrase *d'effraieur* (of terror) does not occur in the original printing. There the word is *deffraieur* (defraying, hosting). Since Nostradamus projected past events into the future, this probably refers back to the restoration to health of the captive Francis I (Duke of Angoulême) following a surprise visit to his cell by his host, Charles V, who was, in 1525, the Holy Roman Emperor. Five planets were in the same astrological sign on both those dates.

The majorities of the quatrains are disaster related like plagues, earthquakes, wars, floods, invasions, murders, droughts, battles and include nearly every disaster imaginable. They concern individuals, groups, single towns or a collection of towns. Each is presented in the context of the end of the world. A number of luminaries of his day, including Christopher Columbus, collected end time prophecies.

His writings are frequently misquoted, at times to "prove" he predicted some current dramatic event. The claim is always that he predicted what just happened. Since the Internet, many erroneous postings are listed proving Nostradamus' prowess, and enhancing his reputation. This one was circulated on the internet after September 11.

> In the city of God there will be a great thunder
> Two brothers torn apart
> While the fortress endures Chaos
> The great leader will succumb
> The third big war will begin when the big city is burning

The first four lines were indeed written before the attacks by a Canadian graduate student, in a research paper including the poem as an illustration as how the validity of prophecies can be exaggerated. He raised the points:

Why is New York City called The City of God? Great thunder could apply to any disaster. Two brothers? Many things come in pairs. The great leader will succumb is so ambiguous it is meaningless. The fifth line was added by an anonymous Internet user and is obviously a forgery because Nostradamus' quatrains were all four-line verses. Besides, Nostradamus never referred to a "third big war."

It seems hard to escape the conclusion that Nostradamus did not predict 9/11. No quatrain even bears a passing resemblance to the events of that day. Perhaps Nostradamus should have been more specific if he expected us to think differently. After all, what use is a quatrain as a prediction if it is so vague that it cannot be attributed to an event even afterwards?

No discussion of Nostradamus and the end time prophecies would be complete without consideration of the *The Kolbrin Bible. It* is a 2-part, 11-book secular anthology. The first six books or the "Egyptian texts" were written by Egyptian academicians following the Hebrew Exodus. The last five books or "Celtic texts" and were penned by Celtic priests after the death of Jesus.

Several accounts describe an object in orbit around our sun called the "Destroyer," which the Celtic authors call the "Frightener." According to recently translated Sumerian texts, this object (also known as Nibiru or Planet X) is in a 3600-year orbit around our sun, and *The Kolbrin Bible* warns us of its imminent return and of yet another Biblical tribulation.

Many believe The Kolbrin Bible offers historical proof of what his followers call the "Nostradamus Comet," and connect it to the bearded star he mentions his prophecies. In *Les Propheties* C2:Q43 he writes:

> During the appearance of the bearded star.
> The three great princes will be made enemies:
> Struck from the sky, peace earth quaking,
> Po, Tiber overflowing, serpent placed upon the shore.

Could Nostradamus have possessed an ancient copy of this wisdom text in his secret library? Perhaps, but what is known for certain is that the historical accounts contained in this ancient wisdom text are purported to be urgent messages from the past, to the present. Proponents of the theory believe this because these accounts were not recorded by those seeking to ensure the legacy of a battlefield victory. They also claim that the previous flybys of the Destroyer were faithfully recorded by those who survived the global cataclysms, thousands of years ago.

This theory has spawned unwarranted fear and anxiety in people around the world and been the impetus for a worldwide industry to sell survival information and supplies. Reasonably, with modern telescopes both on the earth as well as the Hubble Telescope in space, the galaxy is being scrutinized at a level undreamed of a few decades ago. It is likely that such a comet, large enough to do that much damage in three short years would already be visible.

Regardless of the facts, Nostradamus will continue to have his followers, and as long as there is an internet, he will continue to be both glorified and vilified.

CHAPTER 3

Planetary Alignment

It seems that every decade or so, humanity is warned by gloom-and-doom soothsayers that a planetary alignment will take place in the near future and cause havoc on the Earth, the premise of the motion picture *2012*. Of course, it is not *astronomers* who give these warnings, rather, zealots (astrologers and psychics) who frequently have very limited knowledge of the night sky or the solar system in general. Indeed, John Gribbin in the late 1970's wrote a book entitled The Jupiter Effect which predicted the end of the world would occur in 1983 due to a once in a millennium planetary alignment. Obviously, the world didn't end in 1983!

However, alignment can be used in two different ways for planets. The first way is typically what people first imagine when they hear the phrase *planetary alignment*, that is, if viewing the solar system from over the Sun's North Pole, the planets form a straight line from the Sun outward. In this scenario as viewed from the Sun, the planets would fall on top of one another on the sky. One would see the planet Mercury and all of the other planets would be hidden behind Mercury. This is the type of alignment that will be discussed here. And, although modern astronomy tells us Pluto is not really a planet, it will be considered one for this discussion since it has been used in all former planetary disaster models.

The second type of alignment is one in which the planets follow a straight line traced out on the sky. Since the bright planets lie in virtually the same plane, because their orbital planes all lie within a few degrees of the Earth's orbital plane, they will always appear to follow a straight line on the sky if you extend the line far enough. This "straight line" is called the ecliptic, which is represented as a great circle on the sky with the Earth at the center of this circle. After all, we are the center of it all are we not?

The Geometry of Alignments:

First of all, it is impossible for all the planets to form a straight line out from the Sun or viewed superimposed on each other in the sky. Each planetary orbit is tilted slightly, or sometimes not slight at all in the case of Pluto, with respect to the Earth's orbit. That orbit is a plane that can be traced out on the night sky as a line completely around the sky and is called the ecliptic. These zealots confuse the term planetary alignment with the more accurate words that should be used, planetary configuration or a loose grouping of the planets in the sky.

Actually an event that occurred in 1983 in which the planets would be within 96° of each other in the sky. They were not in a straight line as most people would misinterpret with the term *alignment*. To have all of the planets on the same side of the Sun and virtually all within the same quadrant (*i.e.*, 90°) happens approximately once every 200 years—rare as far as humans are concerned, but not rare as far as the solar system is concerned.

The last series of planetary configurations or perhaps more accurately called multiple planetary conjunctions occurred in the year 2000. Did the Earth tilt over? No. Did tidal forces trigger earthquakes? No. Did the polar ice caps melt? No. Were we even be able to *see* the conjunctions? Not really.

Planetary Configurations in the Year 2000

This section must begin with an apology. The information to explain this subject is extremely technical, and has been simplified as much as possible without teaching a course in advanced astronomy. In fact, the subject is not absolutely necessary to this discussion. However, if one desires to wade through them, they will tell the reader a great deal about what to expect when the subject of planetary configuration is discussed concerning the end of the world. For those interested in that challenge, consult Appendix Two.

In short, close planetary configurations have happened many times in the past and note that the Earth still exists. Feel better now? Of course you do. Crackpots (*i.e., astrologers and psychics sensational T.V. shows, movies and survival gear merchents*), it would seem, have a much stronger influence on our minds than our bodies.

CHAPTER 4

Bye Bye World

If the 2012 Gloom and Doom Society continues on course to alert the world about the end of life as we know it, interested and alarmed citizens will generate more than enough energy for debate. The debate will fall into a number of basic camps, but perhaps the two largest divisions will simply be the religious group and the non-religious group. The former will attempt to analyze the information as it relates to their particular concept of a deity, while the latter will either discard the idea as folly or begin making preparations to survive the cataclysm.

While the ideal of surviving the cataclysm is inviting, if there is indeed some sneaky heavenly body, big enough to cause a catastrophe of this magnitude, on a collision course with the earth, surviving the horrors of a nuclear winter will be too daunting for most. If those who theorize that such a disaster eliminated the dinosaur era on earth are correct, then mankind has little chance of survival. Also, if that was indeed the case, it cannot be the same theoretical 36,000 year orbit asteroid, since unless some laws of the universe have been suspended or rearranged, if it hit the earth eons ago, it can't do it again. This is a major hole in the theory for this to be the event that ushers in a new era from the Mayan perspective.

As to the Mayan Calendar, there is no real historic evidence to date the cycle of their disasters. However, according to their lore, the last one that significantly changed humankind was a flood. The Christian account of Noah and the Ark and the great flood that destroyed the world is indeed similar, but the period of that event, as calculated by Christianity, does not fit the 5,112 year Mayan cycle.

Indeed, end time prophecies date well back into recorded history. These are listed in appendix one.

Appendix one is by no means a comprehensive list. Obviously, humanity has not been too successful at predicting the end of time as we know it. Despite the countless timetables to destruction, the world is still here. But, the Bible has a well organized plan for what will come, and the assurance that no one, not even Jesus, knows when that will be. Christians should find it easy to ignore the hoopla concerning 2010. For those who need more convincing, read on.

CHAPTER 5

God Who?

The best way to answer this question is to look at poles on the subject. The Opinion Dynamics Corporation conducted a telephone poll in the evenings for FOX News service on September 23-24, 2003. They sampled 900 registered voters nationwide and reported an error margin of ± 3 percentage points.

Fully 92 percent of Americans say they believe in God, 85 percent in heaven and 82 percent in miracles. Though belief in God has remained at about the same level, belief in a devil has increased slightly over the last few years, from 63 percent in 1997 to 71 percent today.

The poll also showed that about a third of Americans believe in ghosts (34 percent) and an equal number in UFOs (34 percent), and about a quarter accept things like astrology (29 percent), reincarnation (25 percent) and witches (24 percent).

There is a gender gap on many of these subjects. Women are more likely than men to believe in almost all topics asked about in the poll, including 12 percentage points more likely to believe in miracles and eight points more likely to trust there is a heaven. The one significant exception is UFOs, with 39 percent of men compared to 30 percent of women saying they accept the existence of unidentified flying objects.

In this survey, young people are much more likely than older Americans to believe in both hell and the devil. An 86 percent majority of adults between the ages of 18 to 34 believe in hell, but that drops to 68 percent for those over age 70. Similarly, 79 percent of young people believe in the devil compared to 67 percent of the over 70 age group.

Republicans are more likely than Democrats to say they believe in God (by eight percentage points), in heaven (by 10 points), in hell (by 15 points), and considerably more likely to believe in the devil (by 17 points). Democrats are more likely than Republicans to say they believe in reincarnation (by 14 percentage points), in astrology (by 14 points), in ghosts (by eight points) and UFOs (by five points).

Overall, most Americans think religion plays too small a role in people's lives today (69 percent), with only 15 percent saying it plays too large a role and seven percent saying "about right." The poll finds over a third (37 percent) say they attend church, synagogue or other place of worship at least once a week, 13 percent almost every week, 12 percent about once a month and 19 percent seldom attend. Three percent attend on holidays and 15 percent never attend.

The Washington Post reported the results of the think tank, based on one of the largest polls of Americans' religious beliefs ever conducted, with 36,000 adults interviewed. They found that 92 percent believe in God or a universal spirit—including one in five of those who call themselves atheists. More than half of Americans polled pray at least once a day.

However, Americans aren't rigid about their beliefs. Most of those studied, even many of the most religiously conservative, have a remarkably nonexclusive attitude toward other faiths. Seventy percent of those affiliated with a religion believe that many religions can lead to eternal salvation. And only about one-quarter of those surveyed believe there is only one way to interpret their religion's teachings.

"Even though Americans tend to take religion quite seriously and are a highly religious people, there is a certain degree of openness and a lack of dogmatism in their approach to faith and the teachings of their faith," said Gregory Smith, a research fellow at the Pew Forum on Religion and Public Life.

A belief in God or a higher spirit is pervasive. Even Americans who describe themselves as atheist or agnostic have a robust sense of a higher power: Twenty-one percent of those who describe themselves as atheists expressed a belief in God or a universal spirit, and more than half of those who call themselves agnostic expressed a similar conviction.

Smith said some people may identify with the term *atheist* or *agnostic* without fully understanding the definition, or they have a negative view of organized religion, even though they believe in God.

For many Americans, God is a vivid presence. About one-third of the people surveyed said they receive answers to their prayer requests at least once a month and say they have experienced or witnessed a divine healing of an illness or injury.

The report found that almost one in five Christians speaks or prays in tongues—ecstatic worship or prayer using unintelligible speech—from time to time, with 9 percent speaking in tongues weekly. At Greater Mount Calvary Holy Church in the District, a Pentecostal church, worshipers say that they speak in tongues frequently and that it brings them closer to God.

On the political front, the Pew report found that across the faiths, those who pray more are more politically conservative. Among Jews who pray daily, 36 percent are politically conservative—more than twice the percentage of those who pray less often. Among evangelical Christians, 56 percent who pray daily are politically conservative compared with 40 percent who pray less often.

The report also found agreement among the most and least faithful on hot-button issues. It confirms that those who attend church and pray frequently are most likely to oppose abortion and believe that homosexuality should be discouraged. Less of a divide was found on other issues. More than 60 percent of Americans, for example, want the government to do more to help the needy and support stronger environmental laws. And majorities in most religions believe that the United States should concentrate on problems at home.

It would appear, from the results of these two polls that roughly eight or nine out of ten Americans believe in God. It also appears that in a majority of self-identified Christians, that there is no strong tie for most of them to the tenants of their religion, leaving room for a variety of interpretation of their religion's dogmas. This is indeed understandable, because statistical research shows that ***less than 10% of professing Christians have ever read the entire Bible*** (Heartland World Press).

Thus, the church as a whole is Biblically illiterate! Yet, the remaining 90+% somehow feel that they have the right to foist their beliefs on non-believers even though they don't know what they're talking about!

This is one reason, and likely the major reason that so many Christians can become pawns in an end of the world scare. Perhaps if the average Christian knew more about God's plan for mankind, they could feel more optimistic about the future. And, why is that? Because they have never read or studied the Bible, the only written communication we have from God. Why don't more people read the

Bible? Because parts of it are difficult to understand, (not impossible, just difficult), and because the true religion of the original teaching of Jesus Christ to the twelve apostles has become so filled with superstition, myth, and misunderstanding, that the underlying, unshakeable theme of the scriptures is lost.

In a survey by George Gallup, founder of the polling firm behind the survey and a prominent American evangelical, he was appalled by the results. Only one third of the respondents knew who gave the Sermon on the Mount (Jesus). Billy Graham was a popular alternative! One quarter were not aware of the event commemorated by Easter, (the crucifixion and resurrection of Jesus Christ); and Twelve per cent were under the impression that Noah was married to Joan of Arc! The survey also found that sixty per cent of respondents were unable to name five of the Ten Commandments. George Gallup, concluded that it confirmed the United States as 'a nation of biblical illiterates'.

The stringent measures taken by American politicians to avoid offending anyone by removing religion from the American way of life might help explain some of the results, but it is doubtful if the result would be better if the survey were conducted in the United Kingdom, Canada, Australia or any other English-speaking nations.

Printing, selling and giving away Bibles, as the Gideon Society have done for years, will ensure an increasing stock of books. But, if all those Bibles are left on the shelf they will have no impact on their owners. The content of a book cannot be absorbed by osmosis.

If you were buying something for yourself there's a fair chance that you would be glad to get a recommendation from someone who already had one. So here are some opinions about the Bible that could help you make up your own mind about this very special book.

Testimonials:

> *The Bible is not only a book which I can understand; it is also a book which understands me.*
>
> —Emile Caillet

> *Scripture is like a pair of spectacles which dispels the darkness and gives us a clear view of God.*
>
> —John Calvin

No man is uneducated who knows the Bible and no one is wise who is ignorant of its teachings.

—Samuel Chadwick

This book outlives, out loves, out-lifts, outlasts, outreaches, outruns, and outranks all books. This Book is faith producing. It is hope awakening. It is death destroying. And those who embrace it find forgiveness of sin.

—A.Z.Conrad

Read it to be wise. Believe it to be safe. Practice it to be holy. Robert
—C. Cunningham

Read it through; pray it in; live it out; pass it on.

—George Gritter

Others will tell you why reading the Bible is important.

Disregard the study of God and you sentence yourself to stumble and blunder through life, blindfolded, as it were, with no sense of direction and no understanding of what surrounds you.

—J. I. Packer

I have but to say, the Bible is the best gift God has given to man. All the good Saviour gave to the world was communicated through this book. But for it we could not know right from wrong. All things most desirable for man's welfare, here and hereafter, are to be found portrayed in it.

—Abraham Lincoln

Priests, atheists, sceptics, devotees, agnostics and evangelists are generally agreed that the Authorised Version of the English Bible is the best example of English literature that the world has ever seen.

—William Lyon Phelps

We have adopted the convenient theory that the Bible is a Book to be explained, whereas first and foremost it is a Book to be believed . . . There is a world of difference between knowing the Word of God and knowing the God of the Word.

—Leonard Ravenhill

I have heard a few Greek scholars say that when they first read Plato, they found it a mirror for their souls. That may be. But they never found in Plato salvation from their sins, nor a sinless Redeemer, nor the absolute assurance of eternal life and of resurrection after death. Only the Bible offers you that.

—Wilbur Smith

The Bible does not argue for the existence of God. It reveals Him.

—Roy E. Swim

The man who doesn't read his Bible has no advantage over the man who has no Bible.

—Albert M. Wells, Jr.

What the Bible does [in the lives of people] makes what it says believable.

—Kenneth L. Wilson

I am sorry for the men who do not read the Bible every day. I wonder why they deprive themselves of the strength and the pleasure.

—Woodrow Wilson

Because the Bible is a book from God it gives us its own recommendation as well, for there is nothing more vital in life than finding out what God offers, and what He wants us to do. So, from the very beginning, the Bible communicates His message and tells us what He has done, what He will do, and why. Its opening words present us with a self-existent God – one who has always been, and who will always be, and He is revealed as a purposeful Creator, who knows what he is doing and who will see it through to its intended end. And from its opening words on, the Bible makes it clear that it is a book about God which comes from God:

Over 250 times we read about the *"Word of the Lord,"* as God communicates His gracious purpose. But, none of that will matter to us unless we read God's Word. It can only be a special book to us if we make it special in our own lives. The apostle Paul once said this to a young man who had worked alongside him and learned much from him:

> *"But as for you, continue in the things which you have learned and been assured of, knowing from whom you have learned them, and that from childhood you have known the Holy Scriptures, which are able to make you wise for salvation through faith which is in Christ Jesus. All Scripture is given by inspiration of God, and is profitable for doctrine, for reproof, for correction, for instruction in righteousness, that the man of God may be complete, thoroughly equipped for every good work"* (2 Timothy 3:14-17).

That's what the Bible can do for us, if we let it. However, it will do nothing just sitting on the shelf gathering dust! And don't just open it occasionally, to see if there's anything worthwhile that you might chance across. That's not how you would treat any other book: it deserves to be read right through, from cover to cover: The important thing is to be disciplined and determined. Set aside a few minutes every day and patiently work your way through, perhaps starting with a gospel and then sampling an Old Testament book like Genesis, keeping a note of what you have read and ticking books off your list, one at a time.

God has a message for each of us in His Word, the Bible, and it is important that we seek it out and then live accordingly.

CHAPTER 6

Is God Real?

Just because the Bible says there is a God, Is there? This question about the existence of God has been asked by mankind since the beginning of time as we know it. Our primitive ancestors hid cowering in caves each night wondering if the sun would return the next day. Lacking insight into the concept of God, they personified the forces of nature and worshipped them. When crops failed, floods roared or earthquakes rumbled, they blamed a force they could not understand and tried to curry that force's favor through rituals and sacrifice.

Today, we look at the advancement of science, the explosion of knowledge and the sophistication of our culture and use the intellect that made it all possible to challenge the concept of God. We are led to believe that at some point in the remote past, a "Big Bang" occurred which brought this highly complicated universe into existence. What those who would remove God from the equation don't know is what force triggered the "Big Bang" in the first place.

The world is filled with scientific "laws." There is the law of gravity; the laws of motion; the laws of physics in general. Dictionary.Com lists some twenty-two definitions for the word law. Definition number 15 applies to the discussion here. It has two sections. Section A reads; A statement or relation or sequence of phenomena invariable under the same conditions. Section B states, a mathematical rule.

Notice, these are "laws" because observation has shown that given the same set of circumstances each time, the same outcome will be achieved. The simple question is what force created the circumstances to make this scenario valid? The same argument can be proposed for the laws of mathematics. Those who wish to believe that everything just happens, consider the following facts about our immediate universe.

A. The earth rotates at 1000 mph at the equator. If, for instance, it was, only 100 mph then day and night would be ten times longer and all vegetation would be destroyed by the excessive sunlight (2400 hours per day). Likewise, the prolonged darkness would cool the earth's surface at night to levels that would change the climate of the earth.

B. The sun has a surface temperature of 12,000 F. If the earth was 50% nearer to the sun then we would all roast to death. If we were 50% further away, then we would all freeze to death.

C. The Moon is 240,000 miles away from the earth and controls the tides. If it were only 50,000 miles away, then great tidal waves would flood the earth, twice daily.

D. The earth travels around the sun at 66,000 miles per hour. If this speed could be effectively reduced then the length of our seasons would be affected. We could conceivably have winters that lasted for a hundred years, making life as we know it, impossible.

We return to the question. What established the positions of the heavenly bodies so precisely? What determined the speeds at which they should revolve and pursue their paths through the heavens? Are we to believe that this was some random chance equivalent to the thousand monkeys with a thousand typewriters writing the great American novel?

These are only a few instances of the countless circumstances necessary for life as we know it, to exist on the earth. Yet wonderfully and marvelously they all come together to enable life to continue. It seems logically that it would be more difficult to believe that the universe could have happened by accident than it would be to believe that there was some Supreme Force behind it all.

Dan Brown, author of *The Di Vinci Code*, created a worldwide hubbub with his work. Fundamentalists condemned it. Preachers and evangelists railed on it from pulpits throughout the world. Representatives from nearly every major religion felt obligated to tell the world that Jesus was really a lifelong bachelor and never had any children, legitimate or otherwise.

They all ignored two small points. One, Mr. Brown began his tale by telling anyone interested enough to look at the preface that his was a work of fiction. Fiction, by definition, is a made up story. And, he told the readers that to make things more interesting, he was going to use real places, facts and occurrences to make the book better reading. This technique has produced countless classic books of historic fiction where the presence of real historic figures, battles or incidents have increased the enjoyment of the fictitious work for its readers.

But, if we look at one of the facts from *The DiVinci Code* concerning the concept of PHI, beginning on page one-hundred fifty, we can see another of these strange "laws" of mathematics and nature that suggests lurking in the background of the "law" is a Force to be reckoned with.

The term PI is likely more familiar to the reader than is PHI. PI, as even an elementary mathematician will tell you, is the ratio of the circumference of a circle to its diameter or the number 3.141592 etc., usually rounded to 3.1416. It is not the same thing as PHI, a mathematical expression that has fascinated mathematicians for 2,500 years.

Some of the greatest mathematical minds of all ages, from Pythagoras and Euclid in ancient Greece, through the medieval Italian mathematician Leonardo of Pisa and the Renaissance astronomer Johannes Kepler, to present-day scientific figures such as Oxford physicist Roger Penrose, have spent endless hours over this simple ratio and its properties. But the fascination with the Golden Ratio is not confined just to mathematicians. Biologists, artists, musicians, historians, architects, psychologists, and even mystics have pondered and debated the basis of its ubiquity and appeal. In fact, it is probably fair to say that the Golden Ratio has inspired thinkers of all disciplines like no other number in the history of mathematics. PHI is the number 1.618, sometimes called the "golden ratio." In mathematics and the arts, two quantities are in the golden ratio if the ratio of the sum of the quantities to the larger quantity is equal to the ratio of the larger quantity to the smaller one. The golden ratio is an irrational mathematical constant, approximately 1.6180339887.

Other names frequently used for the golden ratio are the golden section (Latin: *sectio aurea*) and golden mean. Terms encountered include extreme and mean ratio, medial section, divine proportion, divine section (Latin: *sectio divina*), golden proportion, golden cut, golden number, and mean of Phidias.

At least since the Renaissance, many artists and architects have proportioned their works to approximate the golden ratio, especially in the form of the golden rectangle, in which the ratio of the longer side to the shorter is the golden ratio, believing this proportion to be aesthetically pleasing. Mathematicians have studied the golden ratio because of its unique and interesting properties.

PHI is based on the famous mathematical Fibonacci sequence which is 1-1-2-3-5-8—13 etc. The importance of the sequence of numbers is that they are a progression in which each term is equal to the sum of the two preceding terms. The golden ratio is the limit of the ratios of successive terms of the Fibonacci sequence, or any Fibonacci-like sequence. If a Fibonacci number is divided by its immediate predecessor in the sequence, the quotient approximates ; e.g., 987/610 ≈ 1.6180327868852.

These approximations are alternately lower and higher than PHI, and converge on PHI as the Fibonacci numbers increase, and: Furthermore, the successive powers of PHI obey the Fibonacci recurrence.

Although this is more than the reader every wanted to know about PHI, the concept is fascinating, and is so constant that its use appears in ancient as well as modern architecture, painting, book design, perceptual studies, music, nature, mathematics, geometry, pentagrams, Ptolemic theory, pyramids and triangles. Though further discussion of the number is outside the scope of this discussion, interested readers will find much more about this fascinating number with a simple computer search.

In *The Di Vinci Code*, Dan Brown points out the following uses of the number.

a. Female honey bees always outnumber males in a honey bee colony, but when the number of female bees is divided by the number of male bees the number is PHI.

b. In the chambered nautilus, a cephalopod mollusk that pumps gas into its chambered shell to adjust its buoyancy, the ratio of one of the spirals that comprise the chambers to the next is PHI.

c. Sunflower seeds grown in opposing spirals. The ratio of each spirals diameter to the next is PHI.

d. Di Vinci was the first to recognize PHI in human anatomy. The distance from the tip of your head to the floor, divided by the distance from your bellybutton to the floor is PHI. The distance from your shoulder to your fingertips divided by the distance from your elbow to your fingertips is PHI.

e. Art work by Michelangelo, Albrecht Durer, Da Vinci, and many others, demonstrating each artist's intentional and rigorous adherence to the Divine Proportion in the layout of his compositions. Brown's character Langdon unveiled PHI in the architectural dimensions of the Greek Parthenon, the pyramids of Egypt, and even the United Nations Building in New York. PHI appeared in the organizational structures of Mozart's sonatas, Beethoven's Fifth Symphony, as well as the works of Bartok, Debussy, and Schubert. The number was even used by Stradivarius to calculate the exact placement of the f-holes in the construction of his famous violins.

We return once again to the question that started it all. Is the content of the universe, these so called "laws" of science some pure galactic accident of unbelievable proportions, or is there a greater intelligence out there? The latter view would appear to be the most rational thing to believe. That driving force behind everything in the universe some of us believe is God.

Some would suggest that our concept of God is the result of extraterrestrial beings as popularized by L.Ron Hubbard's book *The Late Great Planet Earth*. Others point to the alignment of earth made objects that only make sense from the sky, crop circles and a host of other phenomenon as proof of such visits. Does visitation to earth by extraterrestrials validate or invalidate the concept of God?

We have had extraterrestrials with us since the garden of Eden. The Hebrew word applied to the creator of the earth in Genesis is the Hebrew word *Elohim*. It is a pleural word that most often is translated as angels. A careful reading of the creation story in Genesis shows clearly that the beings actually doing the work of creation were God's emissaries, the angels.

Angels destroyed Sodom and Gomorrah on orders from God (Gen 19:1); "And there came two angels to Sodom at even; and Lot sat in the gate of Sodom: and Lot seeing them rose up to meet them; and he bowed himself with his face toward the ground;. They even walk among us even today. Heb 13:2 "Be not forgetful to entertain strangers: for thereby some have entertained angels unawares".

These angelic creatures are different from both God and Christ, as shown by one of the most compelling arguments for the Christian in predicting the end of the world. In Matthew 24:35—36 Christ states, "Heaven and earth shall pass away, but my words shall not pass away. But of that day and hour knoweth no man, no, not the angels of heaven, but my Father only. If Jesus didn't know when the end of time was coming, and the angels didn't know either, then man's attempt to make the prediction is a folly of ego that is doomed to failure.

Oh, and by the way, if you read the Bible, you might be amazed to discover that angels don't have wings. Wings are the artistic interpretation of Renaissance painters and have been embellished by song writers and idol makers for centuries but in point of fact have no basis in scriptural truth. The reader is challenged to find a single example of a winged angel in scripture. There are winged creatures in the Bible, but they are not angles.

Modern astronomy has proved the existence of literally billions of planets in the universe. It is strictly human to believe that the Creator made them all simply for our amusement. Although there is no way to prove it, it seems perfectly reasonable that humans are not the only things in God's creation.

These are but miniscule examples of reasons to believe in a God. God is worshiped in many ways by different people. Arabs, Indians, Buddhists, Druids etc. all worship some form of a higher being. Some believe in no God at all, yet list Atheist as a form of religion for legal purposes. As Christians, we worship Yahweh, the God of the Hebrews, and his son Jesus Christ, who we consider to be the savior of the world. We feel our beliefs have a firm foundation because Yahweh left us a Divine Roadmap called the Bible.

Since we have this roadmap to justify our faith, why then should we adhere to the idea that a Mayan native, who believed that if they presented the beating heart of a sacrifice to their supreme being to insure the continuation of their lifestyle could predict the end of the world as we know it?

CHAPTER 7

God's End of Time

The Bible is a remarkable document. If more people who consider themselves to be Christian would spend more time reading it and studying it, they would have less angst when things like 2012 come along. Scripture tells us the story of the earth; how it was populated; how God introduced Himself to us, and how He chose a people through which to reveal Himself to the world.

It chronicles the trials and tribulations of the Chosen People, their refusal to recognize His plan when He sent His son to explain it to them. It follows the development of Christianity, and even outlines the end of the world as we know it and the perfect society that will follow our current fleshly existence.

That's great you say, but that's what 2012 is about. Not quite. Remember Mark 13:32 But of that day and that hour knoweth no man, no, not the angels which are in heaven, neither the Son, but the Father." Christians need fear nothing after reading this verse. If Jesus himself didn't know, I doubt that the Mayans did. But, the Bible gave us a number of hints as to what the time of the end would be like, the end itself, and the glorious Millennial Kingdom that will be set up afterwards. It would be impossible to tell the entire story in a single manuscript, but a summary of particular passages might prove fruitful.

First, where are these hints of God's plan? To answer that question, we must try to capture the concept of God in terms we might understand. Many people, even those who are not Christian are familiar with the creation story. Scientists tell us it couldn't have happened the way it did in seven days time. For those of us who believe in an omnipotent God, if He so chooses to create in that fashion, seven days is plenty of time. Then does the modern science explanation bother the student of Scripture? Not at all.

Consider this. We see a dark planet shrouded in a mist. A new sun is born in the universe and light cleaves the darkness and draws the mist up in clouds. As we have already discussed, that sun is exactly the right distance from the earth to allow the development of the first life, vegetation. Then life begins in the sea and crawls forth from the water. Soon the planet is teeming with animal life. Nope, this paragraph didn't come from *Scientific American*; it came from the Bible, Genesis chapters one and two. It fits what science tells us happened.

But, what science can't tell us is what caused the "Big Bang"? What or who ordered that sun into being or positioned it exactly the proper distance from earth. Christians believe it was God. As for the week long time frame, consider this: "Ps 90:4 For a thousand years in thy sight are but as yesterday when it is past, and as a watch in the night." or "2 Peter 3:8 But, beloved, be not ignorant of this one thing, that one day is with the Lord as a thousand years, and a thousand years as one day."

Genesis tells us: Gen 1:1 "In the beginning God created the Heaven and the earth." Note there is a period at the end of this verse. Next comes Gen. 1:2 "And the earth was without form, and void; and darkness was upon the face of the deep. And the Spirit of God moved upon the face of the waters." Now, tell me how many days years or millennia transpired between those two sentences. If God willed it, it could be a literal day. But, if He chose to wait, as modern science suggests He did, it could have been eons. Science shouldn't frighten the thinking Christian nor Christianity the thinking scientist.

We could continue this interesting discussion and show that the lower animal life appears roughly in the order that science tells us it was created. Then man comes along. We are told in Genesis 1:26 "And God said let us make man after our image." Note the word "our" in the sentence. In the creation story, when the word God appears, it is nearly always the Hebrew word. *Elohim*, which as stated means angel or angels. God himself didn't do the actual work; it was the angels working under His direction. The word image is the Hebrew *tselem* that translates *shadow*. This creature was to be a shadowy image of the angels.

What does this have to do with the end of time? Well, after the great sin of Eden, the serpent is punished for tempting Eve. Gen 3:14 "And the Lord God said unto the serpent, Because thou hast done this, thou art cursed above all cattle, and above every beast of the field; upon thy belly shalt thou go, and dust shalt thou eat all the days of thy life:" Note that it was the serpent, and not some other mythical creature who was punished.

And further, Gen. 3:15 And I will put enmity between thee and the woman, and between thy seed and her seed; it shall bruise thy head, and thou shalt bruise his heel:" The serpent is punished with a fatal wound. His head would be bruised (from the Hebrew *shuwph* to break, bruise or cover, but *he* would receive only a bruised heel. Who is he? This is the first reference to Jesus Christ, who would eventually strike a fatal blow against sin, represented by the tempter in the creation story.

Where do the angels come in? In the Messianic Psalm we read, "Ps 8:4 What is man, that thou art mindful of him? and the son of man, that thou visitest him? 5 For thou hast made him a little lower than the angels, and hast crowned him with glory and honour." The "son of man" is the term often used in scripture for the Lord Jesus. On earth, he was a little less than angels. Remember what he said to the crowd in the garden of Gethsemane after he had healed the ear of the servant that had been cut off by one of his followers, most likely Peter, "Matt 26:53 Thinkest thou that I cannot now pray to my Father, and he shall presently give me more than twelve legions of angels?"

Still being a man of flesh and blood, Jesus didn't want to use his power to defeat them all himself, but he could call on all the help he needed from his Father. This same Jesus, as we shall see, after his glorification, will return to the earth more powerful than the angels, and with an army of immortals to establish a millennial kingdom of peace and justice. That's when the world as we know it will truly end.

CHAPTER 8

How Will God Do It?

The Bible clearly outlines God's plan for mankind. Unfortunately for us, part of that plan is couched in prophetic language that makes it difficult to understand. It is beyond the scope of this work to discuss all the scriptures and give all the proofs that accompany that plan so let's take a summary look at things.

We have already discussed Eve's encounter with the serpent in Eden, and that it hints to the coming of one who will destroy sin. The remainder of the Old Testament is the story of mankind's primitive development and the rampant sin that comes with totally free will.

To bring order to the chaos of the word, that had forgotten its creator, God approached a man named Abraham and gave him the following instructions: Gen 12:1 "Now the Lord had said unto Abram, Get thee out of thy country, and from thy kindred, and from thy father's house, unto a land that I will shew thee: 2 And I will make of thee a great nation, and I will bless thee, and make thy name great; and thou shalt be a blessing." Why? Acts 15:14 "Simeon hath declared how God at the first did visit the Gentiles, to take out of them a people for his name." God visited the Gentile world of Ur, and called out a family that would eventually be the Jewish nation, God's chosen people. Through them, he would show the world who he was. He later expressed that love, told the Israelites the plan He had for them when he called them out of Egypt.

A major part of God's plan was to send a personal representative to his wayward people in one final attempt to help them believe and trust in Him. Matt 2:6 "And thou Bethlehem, in the land of Judah, art not the least among the princes of Juda: for out of thee shall come a Governor, that shall rule my people Israel." Almost everyone knows who was born in Bethlehem. Jesus' mother was a mortal woman, who later had other children with her mortal husband Joseph. But the father of her firstborn, Jesus, was the mortal image of God Himself. Thus, Jesus was mortal, but with divine lineage. At age thirty, he began a three-year ministry that changed the world.

His ministry was to the Jews. He reminded them of their divine calling and the nature of their God. They refused to accept his message, plotted against him, and later put him to death. All this was part of the master plan. Jesus rose from the dead and gave his disciples final instructions before he went to be with his father. Among the last things he said was, John 14:3 "And if I go and prepare a place for you, I will come again, and receive you unto myself; that where I am, there ye may be also." Peter later confirmed it as he watched Jesus ascend into heaven. Acts 1:11 Which also said, Ye men of Galilee, why stand ye gazing up into heaven? This same Jesus, which is taken up from you into heaven, shall so come in like manner as ye have seen him go into heaven."

What is the meaning of this cryptic exchange? Throughout the Old Testament, in prophets like Isaiah, Ezekiel, Zephaniah, Zechariah, Haggai and many others, the reason for that exchange is outlined in prophetic language. Therein lays the problem.

In these prophetic books, people are referred to as grass or trees, nations as seas, and wars as thunders and lightening. Study of these works, though tedious at times, will allow the student to understand all the prophetic nuances in them. These books also chronicle history. When combined with the Apocalypse better known as the Book of Revelation, which we shall see in time is an historical document, a clear picture of what will transpire comes through. What it does not give us is the exact date and time.

To summarize:
1. God allows mankind to use the power of free will.
2. In time, mankind will push itself to the point of annihilation.
3. Universal war will sweep the globe.
4. Israel will be on the verge of extinction.
5. Christ will return to earth and raise the righteous dead.
6. The first judgment will be done in the Sinai desert.
7. With an immortal army, Christ will march from the Sinai.

8. He will demand the unconditional surrender and obedience of all nations.
9. Those who comply will join him; those who refuse will be destroyed.
10. Mortals who survive will become part of a perfect society.
11. A universal religion based on Jewish rituals will be established in Jerusalem.
12. Christ will rule for 1000 years as a King-Priest.
13. Immortals raised from the dead will be priests and teachers of the law.
14. Mortals will come annually to the great Temple in Jerusalem to worship.
15. During this time, sin will be non-existent.
16. At the end of the millennium, free will once again will be introduced.
17. A revolution against the ruling King-Priest will occur.
18. The immortals will destroy opposition to God once and for all.
19. The kingdom will be turned over to God.
20. The story ends, leaving what we will do for the rest of eternity up to the imagination. To discuss all these points in detail would require a number of volumes of thousands of pages each and a complete study of the entire Bible. Others, like John Thomas in *Elpis Israel* (available from Logos) has already done that. Besides, and a subject of that magnitude is obviously beyond the scope of this discussion. Instead, let's look at a few of the references briefly to assist in proving the point that God has a plan. He's in control, and will execute that plan.

CHAPTER 9

Is Christ the Real Deal?

There have been a number of influential prophets throughout history. Mohammed, Buddha and Confucius come readily to mind. Of course there are many others. What makes Jesus Christ different? First, he had a divine father: Luke 1:26-35 "And in the sixth month the angel Gabriel was sent from God unto a city of Galilee, named Nazareth, To a virgin espoused to a man whose name was Joseph, of the house of David; and the virgin's name was Mary. And the angel came in unto her, and said, Hail, thou that art highly favored, the Lord is with thee: blessed art thou among women. And when she saw him, she was troubled at his saying, and cast in her mind what manner of salutation this should be. And the angel said unto her, Fear not, Mary: for thou hast found favor with God. And, behold, thou shalt conceive in thy womb, and bring forth a son, and shalt call his name JESUS. He shall be great, and shall be called the Son of the Highest: and the Lord God shall give unto him the throne of his father David: And he shall reign over the house of Jacob for ever; and of his kingdom there shall be no end. Then said Mary unto the angel, How shall this be, seeing I know not a man? And the angel answered and said unto her, The Holy Ghost shall come upon thee, and the power of the Highest shall overshadow thee: therefore also that holy thing which shall be born of thee shall be called the Son of God."

The second separator from other prophets is the fact that Jesus was executed by the Roman authorities. John 19:16-19 "Then delivered he him therefore unto them to be crucified. And they took Jesus, and led him away. And he bearing his cross went forth into a place called the place of a skull, which is called in the Hebrew Golgotha: Where they crucified him, and two other with him, on either side one, and Jesus in the midst. And Pilate wrote a title, and put it on the cross. And the writing was, JESUS OF NAZARETH THE KING OF THE JEWS."

After his death on the cross he was laid to rest in a borrowed tomb: John 19:38-42 "And after this Joseph of Arimathaea, being a disciple of Jesus, but secretly for fear of the Jews, besought Pilate that he might take away the body of Jesus: and Pilate gave him leave. He came therefore, and took the body of Jesus. And there came also Nicodemus, which at the first came to Jesus by night, and brought a mixture of myrrh and aloes, about an hundred pound weight. Then took they the body of Jesus, and wound it in linen clothes with the spices, as the manner of the Jews is to bury. Now in the place where he was crucified there was a garden; and in the garden a new sepulcher, wherein was never man yet laid. There laid they Jesus therefore because of the Jews' preparation day; for the sepulcher was nigh at hand."

Three days later he rose from the dead never to die again, something no one else, Mohammed, Buddha or Confucius, has ever done: John 20:1-9 "The first day of the week cometh Mary Magdalene early, when it was yet dark, unto the sepulcher, and seeth the stone taken away from the sepulcher. Then she runneth, and cometh to Simon Peter, and to the other disciple, whom Jesus loved, and saith unto them, They have taken away the Lord out of the sepulcher, and we know not where they have laid him. Peter therefore went forth, and that other disciple, and came to the sepulcher. So they ran both together: and the other disciple did outrun Peter, and came first to the sepulchral. And he stooping down, and looking in, saw the linen clothes lying; yet went he not in. Then cometh Simon Peter following him, and went into the sepulcher, and seeth the linen clothes lie, And the napkin, that was about his head, not lying with the linen clothes, but wrapped together in a place by itself. Then went in also that other disciple, which came first to the sepulcher, and he saw, and believed. For as yet they knew not the scripture, that he must rise again from the dead."

Even the men who worked with him every day were amazed to find the tomb empty. It took "Doubting Thomas" to confirm the resurrection. John 20:24 But Thomas, one of the twelve, called Didymus, was not with them when Jesus came. The other disciples therefore said unto him, We have seen the Lord. But he said unto them, except I shall see in his hands the print of the nails, and put my finger into the print of the nails, and thrust my hand into his side, I will not believe. And after eight days again his disciples were within, and Thomas with them: then came Jesus, the doors being shut, and stood in the midst, and said, Peace be unto you. Then saith he to Thomas, Reach hither thy finger, and behold my hands; and reach hither thy hand, and thrust it into my side: and be not faithless, but believing. And Thomas answered and said unto him, My Lord and my God."

According to the encyclopedia, prophecy is defined as : 1. the foretelling or prediction of what is to come. 2. something that is declared by a prophet, esp. a divinely inspired prediction, instruction, or exhortation. But, the proof of the prophecy is in the fulfillment. As definition one states, it foretells what is to come. If the event or situation prophesied doesn't come or happen, the utterance falls into the category of educated, or sometimes off the wall, guess.

Prophecy must be an important topic since of the 23,210 verses in the Old Testament, 6,641 are prophetic in nature or 28.5% of the entire book. The New Testament contains 7,914 verses, of which 1,711 or 21.5% is prophecy. Thus 27% or nearly one-third of the entire Bible is prophetic scripture. Appendix Three contains a partial list of scriptural references concerning the Messiah. Suffice it to say, if the Bible is to be used as the reference source, Christ has to be the real deal.

CHAPTER 10

The Bible as History

To prove the point that the Bible can lead us to a rational look at future events, it is reasonable to look at history through Biblical prophecy in the book of Daniel. History in prophecy, particularly as it relates to the end of time does not begin with Daniel, but that book, coupled with the Revelation and areas of Ezekiel are the most pertinent. So let's give Daniel a go. The prophecy begins in Babylon when Nebuchadnezzar was king.

This king is also referred to as Nebuchadrezzar, a more exact spelling of his name according to the Aramaic *nabu-kudduriusur*. His father Nabopolassar seized the opportunity of Assyria's decline to assert Babylonian rule and was assisted by Cyaxares of Media. He then married the young Nebuchadnezzar to the daughter of Cyaxares. This alliance with the young general's skill was a complete success.

Nineveh was overthrown, the Assyrian empire collapsed and the spoils divided between the rising empires of the Medes and Babylonians. Egypt powerfully asserted its rule over parts of Assyria. In an attempt to prop up the failing Assyrians, or to plunder the remaining Assyrian territory if that failed that Pharaoh Necho marched to Carchemish.

His defeat in 605 BC was one of the most historic events in ancient history. Egypt was crushed and Necho chased back to the borders of the country leaving Nebuchadnezzar as ruler of the entire Middle East. In BC 604, the king died and his son ruled. Nebuchadnezzar developed a dynasty that lasted seventy years, and he reined 43 of those years himself.

As was the Babylonian custom, defeated nations were robbed of their leadership by deporting the young leaders to exile in Babylon. But, not just any youth. Daniel 1:4 gives specific guidelines as to the people to be deported. As will be the standard in this and subsequent discussions, the bold print will be the words of scripture, the discussion following the author's, and is based on the pioneering work of H.P. Mansfield.

VS4 Children [The Hebrew word here is *yeladim* and means youths. They would be inexperienced and easier to mold. Daniel was likely about 17 years of age. He would have seen Josiah's reforms, heard Jeremiah speak and most likely knew Ezekiel who calls him by name. This was quality number two for the captives who would be taken to Babylon. The first qualification was given in the previous verse where the word for Children=*beniy*=sons means they would all be males] **in whom was no blemish,** [Third qualification they had to be physically sound.] **but well favoured,** [Number four, good appearance and pleasant deportment.] **and skilful in all wisdom,** [Fifth, they had to be smart. Daniel was known for his wisdom. Like Moses, who learned the way of the Egyptians, but was not influenced by it, so would Daniel in Babylon, rightly discerning Yahweh's will in the midst of Babylonian intellectualism.] **and cunning in knowledge,** [Not just book-learning, they had to have common sense and analytic skills.] **and understanding science,** [To be able to sift through and analyze and interpret data.] **and such as had ability in them to stand in the king's palace,** [They had to be good enough to be members of Nebuchadnezzar's court.] **and whom they might teach the learning and the tongue of the Chaldeans.**

Who were the Chaldeans and to what extent could they be learned? The original word is *Kasdoyoh* and means wanderers. Ancient Chaldea was in southern Babylon in the area of Sumar. According to Unger, "the Chaldeans were a warlike, aggressive people from the mountains of Kurdistan." Apparently they were Haldians (or Khaldians), the inhabitants of Urartu, that is, Ararat or Armenia.

The ancient Chaldeans are mentioned in Babylonian inscriptions. They began to appear in Assyrian notices in the reign of Ashurnasirpal II (883 BC—859 BC), though their existence as a people goes back well beyond 1000 BC When Tiglath-pileser III (745 BC—727 BC) became king of Assyria he conquered Babylon. Here the Chaldeans and roving Aramaean tribes were constantly disturbing the native king.

In 731 BC Ukinzer, who came from one of the Chaldean cities, made himself king of Babylon. However, he was deposed by Tiglath-pileser III in 728 BC, who ascended the throne of Babylon and ruled under the name of Pul. Pul was followed on the Assyrian throne by Shalmaneser IV (726 BC—722 BC). He was in turn succeeded on the throne of Babylon by Merodach-Baladan, a Chaldean. Merodach-Baladan was conquered by Sargon but continued as king until 709 BC, when the latter became king of Babylon as well as of Assyria.

At the time of Hezekiah (702 BC), Merodach-Baladan, son of Baladan, ruled in Babylon. It was not until about 625 BC that Chaldean power began to assert itself over Assyria. Nabopolasser at that time rebelled against Assyria and established the new Babylonian Empire. He reconstructed the city of Babylon.

In the fourteenth year of his reign (612 BC) with Cyaxares the Mede and the Scythian king he captured Nineveh and laid it waste (cf. Nah 3:1-3). In 605 BC he was succeeded by his son Nebuchadnezzar II. Under Nebuchadnezzar, the youth of Judah and Jerusalem were carried captive to Babylon, and the Chaldean armies overran the Fertile Crescent, with Nebuchadnezzar making the Babylon of his day the most splendid city of antiquity (cf. Dan 4:30).

Nebuchadnezzar was succeeded by his son Evil-Merodach (562 BC—560 BC), who was murdered by his brother-in-law Neriglissar (560 BC—558 BC). The next king, Labashi-Marduk, reigned only three months and was succeeded by the usurper Nabonidus, whose son Belshazzar (Dan 5) was coregent until the fall of the Chaldean Empire in 539 BC"

From 625 on they controlled Babylon and it became the intellectual center throughout Asia. Astronomy was founded as an exact science by them and for 260 years they kept meticulous astronomical records. One of their astounding contributions was determining that a year was 365 days, 6 hours, 15 minutes and 41 seconds long: a calculation that measures within 30 minutes of what the most modern instruments can measure. Evidently, the Mayans didn't have a lock on amazing measurements. Astrology also flourished and Babylon was home to magicians, sorcerers, diviners and occultists. It was so prevalent it was elevated to a religion. The Hebrew captives were taken to the very center of this worship. Daniel 1:17 relates Daniel's education. He and his Hebrew companions, Hananiah, Mishael, and Azariah, better known as Shadrach, Meshach, and Abed-nego their Babylonian names, of fiery furnace fame, were forced to attend the Babylonian university against their will.

Despite this, they accepted the fate that Yahweh had decreed, yet remained faithful to His will. The result was that Daniel (whose name was also changed but we'll still call him Daniel) became one of the foremost scholars of his time with the God given gift of prophecy and dream interpretation, a skill that also saved his ancient relative Joseph's bacon.

At the end of their studies, they had a final exam before the king and his court. After a grueling oral exam, the king pronounced them the smartest men in his court, and Daniel the smartest of the smart. Chapter one concludes by telling us that Daniel served as the court sage and guru until the rule of Cyrus some 70 years in all.

Chapter Two of Daniel details the strange dream of Nebuchadnezzar concerning a colossal figure the king dreamed of and the angst it caused him. Only Daniel, with his God given power to interpret the dream could ease the king's mind. That the events Daniel described to the king are in the future is revealed:

VS28 But there is a God in heaven that revealeth secrets, and maketh known to the king Nebuchadnezzar what shall be in the latter days. [This has great significance. It states that there is a latter-day manifestation of the image in addition to the world events it symbolizes.] Daniel then describes the king's fearsome image It was important to the king due to the other prophesies concerning Babylon.

VS29 As for thee, O king, thy thoughts came into thy mind upon thy bed, what should come to pass hereafter: [The young king, recently given control of Babylon and having won major victories on the battlefield was of a religious bend, and stopped to contemplate what it all meant. He probably thought his kingdom would last forever.

Then he had the troubling dream that Daniel would relate in detail. Israel's prophet Jerimiah had already confirmed the eventual downfall of Babylon, and Daniel would confirm it. <Isa 13:19 And Babylon, the glory of kingdoms, the beauty of the Chaldees' excellency, shall be as when God overthrew Sodom and Gomorrah.> <Jer 51:37 And Babylon shall become heaps, a dwellingplace for dragons, an astonishment, and an hissing, without an inhabitant.> <Jer 51:43 Her cities are a desolation, a dry land, and a wilderness, a land wherein no

man dwelleth, neither doth any son of man pass thereby. 44 And I will punish Bel in Babylon, and I will bring forth out of his mouth that which he hath swallowed up: and the nations shall not flow together any more unto him: yea, the wall of Babylon shall fall.>] **and he that revealeth secrets maketh known to thee what shall come to pass.** [Added to emphasize the future nature of the events of the prophecy.]

VS31 Thou, O king, sawest, and behold a great image. [Likely a warlike image demonstrating Gentile power.]

This great image, whose brightness was excellent, stood before thee; [The metals were so highly polished that the image glowed.] **and the form thereof was terrible.** [It represented the kingdom of the flesh built on violence and bloodshed and that made its appearance terrible to behold. <Hab 1:7 They are terrible and dreadful: their judgment and their dignity shall proceed of themselves. 8 Their horses also are swifter than the leopards, and are more fierce than the evening wolves: and their horsemen shall spread themselves, and their horsemen shall come from far; they shall fly as the eagle that hasteth to eat. 9 They shall come all for violence: their faces shall sup up as the east wind, and they shall gather the captivity as the sand.>]

VS32 This image's head was of fine gold, [Fine gold suggests the best quality. Since the heavier metals were on the top, the image was top heavy and therefore vulnerable.] **his breast and his arms of silver,** [Less valuable than gold, it prompts Daniel to call this kingdom inferior to the gold kingdom.] **his belly and his thighs of brass,** [A further deterioration in the metal chain.]

VS33 His legs of iron, his feet part of iron and part of clay. [The deterioration of the metals continues until only clay is left creating an easily broken base.]

VS34 Thou sawest till that a stone was cut out without hands, [That is with no human help. The alter representing Christ was made of such a stone. <Ex 20:24 An altar of earth thou shalt make unto me, and shalt sacrifice thereon thy burnt offerings, and thy peace offerings, thy sheep, and thine oxen: in all places where I record my name I will come unto thee, and I will bless thee 25 And if thou wilt make me an altar of

stone, thou shalt not build it of hewn stone: for if thou lift up thy tool upon it, thou hast polluted it.> <Heb 13:10 We have an altar, whereof they have no right to eat which serve the tabernacle.> The stone of Israel will eventually triumph as is shown throughout scripture.] **which smote the image upon his feet that were of iron and clay, and brake them to pieces.** [Note these prophetic statements describing the future role of the Messiah. <2 Sam 22:43 Then did I beat them as small as the dust of the earth, I did stamp them as the mire of the street, and did spread them abroad.> <Ps 18:42 Then did I beat them small as the dust before the wind: I did cast them out as the dirt in the streets.> Compare them to the work of the stone.]

VS35 Then was the iron, the clay, the brass, the silver, and the gold, broken to pieces together, [The passage anticipates the latter formation of a confederacy of powers, (described in Ezekiel 38 that will be subsequently address) based on the symbols in the image. The image, which is now in antagonistic parts, will be confederated for the prophecy to fulfill.

The dream says the feet were smitten, *then* the iron, clay, brass, silver and gold follow, showing the breakup of the power of the ten kingdoms would preceded the breakup of the other parts. The Lord speaks to this prophecy as well. <Matt 21:43 Therefore say I unto you, The kingdom of God shall be taken from you, and given to a nation bringing forth the fruits thereof 44 And whosoever shall fall on this stone shall be broken: but on whomsoever it shall fall, it will grind him to powder.] **and became like the chaff of the summer threshingfloors;** [The judgment of Armageddon is likened to a threshing of nations. <Mic 4:11 Now also many nations are gathered against thee, that say, Let her be defiled, and let our eye look upon Zion 12 But they know not the thoughts of the LORD, neither understand they his counsel: for he shall gather them as the sheaves into the floor 13 Arise and thresh, O daughter of Zion: for I will make thine horn iron, and I will make thy hoofs brass: and thou shalt beat in pieces many people: and I will consecrate their gain. unto the LORD, and their substance unto the Lord of the whole earth.> <Joel 3:12 Let the heathen be wakened, and come up to the valley of Jehoshaphat: for there will I sit to judge all the heathen round about. 13 Put ye in the sickle, for the harvest is ripe: come, get you down; for the press is full, the fats of the overflow;

for their wickedness is great. 14 Multitudes, multitudes in the valley of decision: for the day of the LORD is near in the valley of decision.> <Ps 1:4 The ungodly are not so: but are like the chaff which the wind driveth away.>] **and the wind carried them away, that no place was found for them:** [Following the destruction of the Gogian confederacy at Armageddon, the Catholic countries of Europe will re-group under the beast, <Rev 17:12 And the ten horns which thou sawest are ten kings, which have received no kingdom as yet; but receive power as kings one hour with the beast. 13 These have one mind, and shall give their power and strength unto the beast.> and prepare to resist the demands of the King of Jerusalem. <Ps 2:10 Be wise now therefore, O ye kings: be instructed, ye judges of the earth. 11 Serve the LORD with fear, and rejoice with trembling. 12 Kiss the Son, lest he be angry, and ye perish from the way, when his wrath is kindled but a little. Blessed are all they that put their trust in him.> Without waiting for them to move, Christ will attack to "rebuke the nations far off." < Mic 4:3 And he shall judge among many people, and rebuke strong nations afar off; and they shall beat their swords into plowshares, and their spears into pruninghooks: nation shall not lift up a sword against nation, neither shall they learn war any more.> His army will be Israel after the flesh officered by the resurrected saints re-formed into a sharp new instrument to thresh the nations. <Isa 30:27 Behold, the name of the LORD cometh from far, burning with his anger, and the burden thereof is heavy: his lips are full of indignation, and his tongue as a devouring fire: 28 And his breath, as an overflowing stream, shall reach to the midst of the neck, to sift the nations with the sieve of vanity: and there shall be a bridle in the jaws of the people, causing them to err.> <Isa 41:15 Behold, I will make thee a new sharp threshing instrument having teeth: thou shalt thresh the mountains, and beat them small, and shalt make the hills as chaff. 16 Thou shalt fan them, and the wind shall carry them away, and the whirlwind shall scatter them: and thou shalt rejoice in the LORD, and shalt glory in the Holy One of Israel.>] **and the stone that smote the image became a great mountain, and filled the whole earth.** [Mountains are symbolically empires. <Jer 51:24 And I will render unto Babylon and to all the inhabitants of Chaldea all their evil that they have done in Zion in your sight, saith the LORD. 25 Behold, I am against thee, O destroying mountain, saith the LORD, which destroyest all the earth: and I will stretch out

mine hand upon thee, and roll thee down from the rocks, and will make thee a burnt mountain.> <Isa 2:2 And it shall come to pass in the last days, that the mountain of the LORD's house shall be established in the top of the mountains, and shall be exalted above the hills; and all nations shall flow unto it. 3 And many people shall go and say, Come ye, and let us go up to the mountain of the LORD, to the house of the God of Jacob; and he will teach us of his ways, and we will walk in his paths: for out of Zion shall go forth the law, and the word of the LORD from Jerusalem.> As the last reference illustrates, this kingdom will cover the world.]

The Image Prophecy

It is helpful to recognize the threefold purpose expressed in the Image prophecy. First the obvious application of the vision presents an outline of world history. Four Gentile world powers are represented by four different metals, (Babylon, Medo-Persia, Greece and Rome) to successively dominate the world but to be finally absorbed by the Kingdom of God (Ch. 2:44). Second, it shows what will come to pass in the latter days (Ch. 2:28). This requires a confederacy of the modern nations existent upon the territory dominated by these ancient empires.

Third and greatly significant, the prophecy foreshadowed the decline of national government, from the golden era of absolute autocracy under Nebuchadnezzar to the clay Socialism and Communism of the later days as required the statement of Ch. 2:43 The dramatic fulfillment of the prophecy in all three particulars shows that the greatest confidence can be placed in the prognostication of Scripture.

In vindication of the prophecy, history reveals the emergence of the four world powers and then an epoch of divisiveness among nations answering to the toes of the image. Despite its recent setbacks, the Russian power today is gradually incorporating within its influence a confederacy of powers answering to the requirements of the Image-prophecy. The decline of world government is obvious as Socialism, Communism and Islamic States rise, answering to the clay of the image.

Having told the king what he saw in his dream, Daniel now interprets the dream for the king:

2:38 Thou art this head of gold. [Thou means the dynasty of Nebuchadnezzar. The accepted dates of his dynasty, (and there is reason to doubt the dates though not the length of the rulers) are as follows. Nebuchadnezzar as head 606-643 reigned 43 years first as regent then as king. Evil-Merodach his son reigned 2 years. Neriglissar his son in law, reigned 4 years. Laboresoarched Negiglissar's son reigned 4 months. Nabonidus &Belshazzar reigned 20 years.

As the head of gold, Nebuchadnezzar was an outstanding incarnation of human pride and power; though subsequently humbled by the revelation of Divine wisdom and strength. His power was limited, however, to 70 years. <Jer 25:11 And this whole land shall be a desolation, and an astonishment; and these nations shall serve the king of Babylon seventy years. 12 And it shall come to pass, when seventy years are accomplished, that I will punish the king of Babylon, and that nation, saith the LORD, for their iniquity, and the land of the Chaldeans, and will make it perpetual desolations.> Exactly 70 years later, Babylon fell to the Medo-Persian empire. In the 19th year of Nebuchadnezzar's reign, the Temple in Jerusalem was destroyed and 70 years later, Darius commanded that it be rebuilt. <Ezra 6:3 In the first year of Cyrus the king the same Cyrus the king made a decree concerning the house of God at Jerusalem, Let the house be builded, the place where they offered sacrifices, and let the foundations thereof be strongly laid; the height thereof threescore cubits, and the breadth thereof threescore cubits;>.

In the 23rd year of his reign the last deportation occurred from Israel. <Jer 52:30 In the three and twentieth year of Nebuchadrezzar Nebuzar-adan the captain of the guard carried away captive of the Jews seven hundred forty and five persons: all the persons were four thousand and six hundred.> and 70 years later in the 6th year of Darius the Temple was finished. <Ezra 6:15 And this house was finished on the third day of the month Adar, which was in the sixth year of the reign of Darius the king.>

Hence 70 years separated the king's triumphs and the trials of Israel in dispersion. The head of gold answers to the lion with the man's heart in Daniel 7:4. It represents Babylon, which existed upon the territory of modern Iraq. How can it be incorporated in an image of the latter days as required in this chapter? (vs. 28,35). Both Iraq and Babylon the great must be linked into Gog's sphere of influence. This requires a religious-Communist confederacy as predicted by Daniel in chapter 8. Under the king, Babylon became the golden city for a golden age. In an inscription found by archeologists the king declares, "The walls of the cell of Merodach must be made to glisten as the sun. The halls of his temple must be overlaid with shining gold, lapis lazuli and alabaster. And the chapel of his lordship overlaid with gold. Nebuchadnezzar was fittingly the head of gold since he brought all the glory to Babylon and ruled with autocratic absolutism, answering to no one.]

VS39 And after thee shall arise another kingdom inferior to thee, [This was Medo-Persia who replaced Babylon in 536 BC. It is the bear of Daniel 7:3 and the ram of Daniel 8:3. Silver is a fitting image for the Medo-Persian empire since Herodotus records they collected their taxes in talents of silver.

Although represented by an inferior metal the Medo-Persian Empire outstripped Babylon in territory conquered and lasted 207 years compared to Babylon's 70. Then why is it represented by a metal inferior to gold. It was because their kings were bound by their own decrees and could not change them even if they wanted to do so. This is illustrated in the 6th chapter of Daniel when Darius tries to save Daniel from his own decree and is unable to. Nebuchadnezzar would have tolerated no such limitations to his rule. He could reverse his own decisions at will. No House of Legislature stood between the king of Babylon and his exercise of power as it did in Medo-Persia.] **and another third kingdom of brass,** [Brass or copper is the metal of Greece. Prior to the establishment of the Grecian Empire, Greece or Javan was noted for this metal. <Ezek 27:13 Javan, Tubal, and Meshech, they were thy merchants: they traded the persons of men and vessels of brass in thy market.> Later copper was incorporated into the armor of their warriors so they were described as "brazen coated Greeks." Both Daniel and the King would have known this.

In 334 BC, at the battle of Granicus, Alexander the Great defeated the numerically superior forces of Persia and in the following year, at Issus, the victory was completed and the Grecian Empire dominated world affairs. Elsewhere in Daniel's prophecy the leopard Dan. 7:6 and the he-goat 8:4 are used as symbolic representation of Greece.] **which shall bear rule over all the earth.** [Alexander the Great of Macedonia conquered most of the known world of his time, even invading India, though he subsequently withdrew his forces to the Indus River where he reportedly, "wept because there were no more worlds to conquer. He died at age 33.]

VS40 And the fourth kingdom shall be strong as iron: [The silver and bronze images were said to arise, "after thee," suggesting they would include Babylon. The iron power, Rome, never conquered Babylon or extended into Persia, so Daniel's description conforms to history.

Rome was know for its iron breastplates and swords it preferred. Gibbon, a historian who was a Biblical non-believer states in, *The Decline and Fall of the Roman Empire,* "The arms of the Republic sometimes vanquished in battle always victorious in war, advanced with rapid steps to the Euphrates, the Danube, the Rhine and the ocean;" and the images of gold or silver or brass that might serve to represent the nations of their kings were successively broken by the iron monarchy of Rome.

The legs of the image answer to the two-fold division of the empire, the ecclesiastical head in Rome and the civil administration set up in Constantinople, (Istanbul) by Constantine in 326 BC. Slowly over the next few Roman Emperor's the division became well defined.

In 476 the Western empire fell to the Barbarians and are represented by the toes of the image. In AD 800 they were replaced by the Holy Roman Empire unleashing a millennium of terror on Europe. The Eastern Empire remained independent until 1453 when Constantinople succumbed to the Ottomans and the Turkish Empire replaced it. Later in the prophecy the two legs of the Image are represented by the horns of the west (Dan 7:8) and the east, (Dan 8:9).]

forasmuch as iron breaketh in pieces and subdueth all things: and as iron that breaketh all these, shall it break in pieces and bruise. [The two words break and bruise used in this passage are significant. Break, *daqaq*, means to cause to crumble. To break in pieces. Bruise, *re'a* means to spoil by breaking, i.e. to make of no account. Rome did this both ecclesiastically and politically. Its power was great and it outlasted all the others. What it did in the past, the kingdom of God will do more completely in the future, break its enemies into pieces.]

VS41 And whereas thou sawest the feet and toes, [The entire Image will stand on two feet in latter-day manifestation. The feet comprise the latter-day revival of the two legs of the Image.] **part of potters' clay, and part of iron,** [Ancient iron was made by heating the ore then beating out the clay by hammering. If the clay impurities were not removed, the resultant metal was slag, a mixture of iron and clay, and speaks to the imperfect efforts of man to weld humanity into a strong alliance of peace and unity.

Clay is often used to represent man. <Job 33:6 Behold, I am according to thy wish in God's stead: I also am formed out of the clay.> <Isa 64:8 But now, O LORD, thou art our father; we are the clay, and thou our potter; and we all are the work of thy hand.>

The rust of iron is typical of the defilement of the flesh which it represents. Accordingly, the use of iron tools in the construction of altars and of Solomon's Temple were treated as defiling. <Deut 27:5 And there shalt thou build an altar unto the LORD thy God, an altar of stones: thou shalt not lift up <u>any iron tool</u> upon them.> <Josh 8:30 Then Joshua built an altar unto the LORD God of Israel in mount Ebal, 31 As Moses the servant of the LORD commanded the children of Israel, as it is written in the book of the law of Moses, an altar of whole stones, <u>over which no man hath lift up any iron</u>: and they offered thereon burnt offerings unto the LORD, and sacrificed peace offerings.> <1 Kings 6:7 And the house, when it was in building, was built of stone made ready before it was brought thither: so that there was neither hammer nor axe <u>nor any tool of iron heard in the house</u>, while it was in building.>] **the kingdom shall be divided;** [Ten kingdoms were formed from the ruins of the Western Empire, The Huns, Vandals, Visigoths, Burgundians, Gepidae, Lombards, Franks, Suevi, Alani and Bavarians. We must remember however that in scripture, 10 is used to represent a whole as divided, or something that is complete, so a literal ten kingdoms cannot be assumed. It also is used as a multiplier for large unspecified numbers. <1 Sam 29:5 Is not this David, of whom they sang one to another in dances, saying, Saul slew his thousands, and David his ten thousands?> <Ps 3:6 I will not be afraid of ten thousands of people, that have set themselves against me round about.> Used in the same way it represents Western Europe divided.] **but there shall be in it of the strength of the iron, forasmuch as thou sawest the iron mixed with miry clay.** [Two distinct cultural elements, Barbarian and Roman mixed. In the latter days it will be Catholicism and Communism, which will include the Muslim states.]

VS42 And as the toes of the feet were part of iron, [In 476, the last Roman Emperor, Romulus Augustus was deposed by Odoacer the Visigoth and the Empire came to an end, only the toes remaining. Manh attempts have been made to define ten literal kingdoms but at no time were there 10 distinct nationalities existing on the territory at the same time. Remember 10 means complete and not necessarily a rigid number. The prophecy could thus predict the empire was completely divide up and this is exactly what happened.] **and part of clay,** [Some kings would be strong, others weak.] **so the kingdom shall be partly strong, and partly broken.** [The same would be true of the nations themselves, and the history of Europe follows this precisely.]

VS43 And whereas thou sawest iron mixed with miry clay, they shall mingle themselves with the seed of men: [They are the toes or kings of vs. 44. Men here is from the Chaldean *enosh* a term used for the lowest form of man. Hebrew has several words for man. *Adam* speaks to man as far as his nation is concerned. The Hebrew *Ish*, relates man and his abilities. *Enosh* is man in his weakness. Daniel thus describes the gradual decline in human government form the autocratic dictatorship of Nebuchadnezzar to the time, in the later days when governments will have to defer to the lowest strata of society in order to rule. We are essentially there today.] **but they shall not cleave one to another, even as iron is not mixed with clay.** [Despite weapons of mass destruction that threaten the fabric of the world, mankind has no ability to form any lasting peace.]

VS44 And in the days of these kings [Those described in verse 43] **shall the God of heaven set up a kingdom, which shall never be destroyed:** [The same God that placed Nebuchadnezzar on the throne will set up his own kingdom that will not be destroyed as the Image kingdoms would be.] **and the kingdom shall not be left to other people,** [There will be no reason to leave this kingdom to others because its rulers will be the immortal, resurrected saints of God.] **but it shall break in pieces and consume all these kingdoms, and it shall stand for ever.** [All power will be broken and consumed as was the Image and Christ will rule the world. <Mic 4:13 Arise and thresh, O daughter of Zion: for I will make thine horn iron, and I will make thy hoofs brass: and thou shalt beat in pieces many people: and I will

consecrate their gain unto the LORD, and their substance unto the Lord of the whole earth.> <Luke 20:18 Whosoever shall fall upon that stone shall be broken; but on whomsoever it shall fall, it will grind him to powder.> <Isa 60:12 For the nation and kingdom that will not serve thee shall perish; yea, those nations shall be utterly wasted.> <Zech 14:9 And the LORD shall be king over all the earth: in that day shall there be one LORD, and his name one.> <Mic 4:7 And I will make her that halted a remnant, and her that was cast far off a strong nation: and the LORD shall reign over them in mount Zion from henceforth, even for ever.>]

VS45 Forasmuch as thou sawest that the stone was cut out of the mountain without hands, [This is the Kingdom of God of which Christ is the nucleus. <Isa 28:16 Therefore thus saith the Lord GOD, Behold, I lay in Zion for a foundation, a stone, a tried stone, a precious corner stone, a sure foundation: he that believeth shall not make haste.> The mountain from which it was cut is the flesh. <Jer 51:25 Behold, I am against thee, O destroying mountain, saith the LORD, which destroyest all the earth: and I will stretch out mine hand upon thee, and roll thee down from the rocks, and will make thee a burnt mountain.> The Kingdom's residents were "taken out of the Gentile nations of the flesh to become an immortal Israel. And it was done without the hand of man.] **and that it brake in pieces the iron, the brass, the clay, the silver, and the gold;** [The order of metals here suggests the king saw the metals of the Image broken and scattered on the ground.] **the great God hath made known to the king what shall come to pass hereafter:** [That is from the time of Daniel to the establishment of the Kingdom of God.] **and the dream is certain, and the interpretation thereof sure.** [The information was revealed by Yahweh and is above reproach.]

VS46 Then the king Nebuchadnezzar fell upon his face, and worshipped Daniel, [The king recognized the divine revelation from Daniel and gave him homage as was custom to do to great men in that time. When the saints in the age to come reveal their great Good News to a sinful world similar homage will be paid to them. <Isa 45:14 Thus saith the LORD, The labour of Egypt, and merchandise of Ethiopia and of the Sabeans, men of stature, shall come over unto thee, and they

shall be thine: they shall come after thee; in chains they shall come over, and they shall fall down unto thee, they shall make supplication unto thee, saying, Surely God is in thee; and there is none else, there is no God.> <Rev 3:9 Behold, I will make them of the synagogue of Satan, which say they are Jews, and are not, but do lie; behold, I will make them to come and worship before thy feet, and to know that I have loved thee.>] **and commanded that they should offer an oblation and sweet odours unto him.** [This would be an act of worship and Daniel would never have allowed it.]

VS47 The king answered unto Daniel, [The king is responding to Daniel. What did he say? He apparently told the king that he would not be worshiped and that God alone who gave the Revelation should be so honored. Thus he is answering the unrecorded act of faith by Daniel.] **and said, Of a truth it is, that your God is a God of gods,** [Chaldean here is *Elah of Elahin* corresponding to the Hebrew, *Eloah of Elohim*, the mighty one of the mighty ones. In acknowledging Daniel's God as such, the King acknowledged that the God of the Hebrews who manifested his power through the angel host of heaven is the God of Truth.] **and a Lord of kings,** [Chaldean here is *Marey Malchin* or dictator of kings. Nebuchadnezzar recognized Yahweh as such with this significant title.] **and a revealer of secrets,** [This is *Galeh Razin* a further title of Yahweh, and is derived from a word meaning to unveil. Christ said to reveal such secrets one had to be his friend. <John 15:15 Henceforth I call you not servants; for the servant knoweth not what his lord doeth: but I have called you friends; for all things that I have heard of my Father I have made known unto you.>

The king went to great lengths to ascertain the secret that the Divine nature revealed to him in his dream. Should Christians today do less to comprehend the revelations of Christ to us. <Rev 1:3 Blessed is he that readeth, and they that hear the words of this prophecy, and keep those things which are written therein: for the time is at hand.>] **seeing thou couldest reveal this secret.** [The king recognized the dream as true and this provided confirmation of Daniel's doctrine concerning the God he worshipped. In fulfillment of the type the setting up of the kingdom at Christ's return will provide confirmation of the Gospel.

The next chapter of Daniel describes the famous story of the fiery furnace that likely even the casual Bible reader will know, but

Chapter four brings another strange dream to the king and Daniel's interpretation. The interpretation of the dream predicts a period of insanity for the might monarch lasting a full seven years which came to pass. The dream is as follows:

VS9 O Belteshazzar, master of the magicians, [This title, repeated in Ch. 5:11 shows how far Daniel had been promoted. The magicians, also called Magi. It is significant that among Babylon's army at the siege of Jerusalem was one entitled Rab-Mag, < Jer 39:3 And all the princes of the king of Babylon came in, and sat in the middle gate, even Nergal-sharezer, Samgar-nebo, Sarsechim, Rab-saris, Nergal-sharezer, Rabmag, with all the residue of the princes of the king of Babylon.> which means Chief of the Magi.

Daniel, as master of the wise was able to influence the wise men of Babylon and this apparently continued during the Persian domination of Babylon a seen in Dan 6:2. This explains why the Magi came seeking the lord at Christ's birth. They studied the heavens and when they saw the star, linked them with Daniel's messianic prophesies (Dan. 9:24-25) and sent men on the long and difficult journey to enquire into the matter.] **because I know that the spirit of the holy gods is in thee, and no secret troubleth thee,** [In this verse gods is the Chaldean *Elahin*, mighty ones and is equivalent to the Hebrew *Elohin*. Though he did not see the entire picture, the king knew Daniel spoke for the true God of the universe. So, he had the greatest confidence in Daniel's ability to interpret the dream.] **tell me the visions of my dream that I have seen, and the interpretation thereof.** [This is a clumsy translation and requires an ellipsis. Tell me the *meaning of* the visions of my dreams.]

VS10 Thus were the visions of mine head in my bed; I saw, and behold a tree in the midst of the earth, and the height thereof was great. [Similar symbolism is noted in Ezekiel 31 when Assyria is likened to a Cedar of Lebanon. < Ezek 31:3 Behold, the Assyrian was a cedar in Lebanon with fair branches, and with a shadowing shroud, and of an high stature; and his top was among the thick boughs.> The kingdom of God was also likened to a tree by Jesus. < Matt 13:31 Another parable put he forth unto them, saying, The kingdom of heaven is like to a grain of mustard seed, which a man took, and sowed in his field:

32 Which indeed is the least of all seeds: but when it is grown, it is the greatest among herbs, and becometh a tree, so that the birds of the air come and lodge in the branches thereof.> The tree in this dream is Babylon in all its blossoming glory.]

VS11 The tree grew, and was strong, and the height thereof reached unto heaven, and the sight thereof to the end of all the earth: [Describing the glory and the extent of Babylon.]

VS12 The leaves thereof were fair, and the fruit thereof much, and in it was meat for all: [The king saw a tree that reached from earth to heaven and whose branches covered the world. It represented the desire of Nebuchadnezzar himself as predicted by Isaiah. < Isa 14:13 For thou hast said in thine heart, I will ascend into heaven, I will exalt my throne above the stars of God: I will sit also upon the mount of the congregation, in the sides of the north: 14 I will ascend above the heights of the clouds; I will be like the most High.>] **the beasts of the field had shadow under it, and the fowls of the heaven dwelt in the boughs thereof, and all flesh was fed of it.** [As noted, beasts and fowls represent nations subjugated by the widespread influence of the Babylonian Empire.]

VS13 I saw in the visions of my head upon my bed, and, behold, a watcher and an holy one came down from heaven; [This watcher was an angelic messenger come to be certain nothing is left to chance concerning the will of Yahweh.]

VS14 He cried aloud, and said thus, Hew down the tree, and cut off his branches, shake off his leaves, and scatter his fruit: [As the tree representing Babylon is lopped and pruned, the king learns that nations are limited as to their time and extent of dominance by Yahweh.] **let the beasts get away from under it, and the fowls from his branches:** [This foreshadows the dissolution of the Babylonian Empire.]

VS15 Nevertheless leave the stump of his roots in the earth, [Stump or *iqqar*, not the above ground stump, but the root stock beneath the ground. After its political power was gone, the influence of Babylon would spring anew in apostate Christendom, to be revealed as the

Babylon the Great of *The Apocalypse.*] **even with a band of iron and brass,** [The band of iron protected the Babylonian roots. The metals represent Greece and Rome. Babylon the great became divided into Greek and Roman Catholicism.

When the Turks came to Constantinople in 1453, the city became an Islamic center with mosques replacing churches. Greek Catholicism was driven to Moscow, where the "third Rome" was founded. Unfortunately, the Pagan teachings of Babylon were imprinted on the church in the days of Constantine and were openly incorporated into the theology of both Roman Catholic and Greek Orthodoxy.] **in the tender grass of the field;** [Grass is prophectic flesh and therefore people. < Isa 40:6 The voice said, Cry. And he said, What shall I cry? All flesh is grass, and all the goodliness thereof is as the flower of the field:> Among the superstitious people of Babylon the Great, paganized Christianity found acceptance.] **and let it be wet with the dew of heaven,** [Dew is doctrine or teaching. < Deut 32:2 My doctrine shall drop as the rain, my speech shall distil as the dew, as the small rain upon the tender herb, and as the showers upon the grass:> Heaven is frequently used to describe the ruling powers in prophetic scripture. That is the case here. The doctrine of the Pagan church dropped on the grass, and they drank it up.] **and let his portion be with the beasts in the grass of the earth:** [The king would play his part in the Divine drama and be reduced to a place among the cattle in the field.]

VS16 Let his heart be changed from man's, and let a beast's heart be given unto him; [The king's malady would symbolize the moral decay of the kingdom. Combined with the dream of the Image they represent both the political and moral bestiality that will symbolize Babylon the Great.] **and let seven times pass over him.** [Israel was warned that if they were disobedient as a people, they would suffer seven time of trouble. < Lev 26:18 And if ye will not yet for all this hearken unto me, then I will punish you seven times more for your sins. <Lev 26:21 And if ye walk contrary unto me, and will not hearken unto me; I will bring seven times more plagues upon you according to your sins.> <Lev 26:24 Then will I also walk contrary unto you, and will punish you yet seven times for your sins.> <Lev 26:28 Then I will walk contrary unto you also in fury; and I, even I, will chastise you seven times for your sins.>

These seven limits appear to mean an extended Passover. < Lev 26:43 The land also shall be left of them, and shall enjoy her sabbaths, while she lieth desolate without them: and they shall accept of the punishment of their iniquity: because, even because they despised my judgments, and because their soul abhorred my statutes.> Since the seventh day was the Sabbath, there is an apparent connection to the rest the land would enjoy.

The Sabbath principle appears in Jeremiah, when he predicts the 70 years of Babylonian captivity. < Jer 29:10 For thus saith the LORD, That after seventy years be accomplished at Babylon I will visit you, and perform my good word toward you, in causing you to return to this place.>

Under the yolk of the oppressor, the land rests from war and strife. < 2 Chron 36:21 To fulfill the word of the LORD by the mouth of Jeremiah, until the land had enjoyed her sabbaths: for as long as she lay desolate she kept sabbath, to fulfil threescore and ten years.>

The seven times of this prophecy is an extension of the sabbath principle. A time in Jewish reckoning is a year or 360 days. Seven times this number is 2520 days and on prophetic reckoning of a year for a day, < Ezek 4:6 And when thou hast accomplished them, lie again on thy right side, and thou shalt bear the iniquity of the house of Judah forty days: I have appointed thee each day for a year.> 2520 years.

Nebuchadnezzar besieged Jerusalem in the years 606-603 BC, so that 2520 years from that date would be 1914-1917. In 1917 the Turks were driven out of Jerusalem and the Jews invited to return. The termination of that period triggered an epoch that will not stop until Gentilism is overthrown and the Kingdom of God established.

The dream thus has two fulfillments. Nebuchadnezzar suffered an attack of Lycanthrope and acted like a beast. And, since the end of the 2520 years, the nations have acted more like beasts in their own national form of the disease. The pride, wantonness and bestiality of man is turning the world into a mad house.]

VS17 This matter is by the decree of the watchers, [These watchers are the angels or Elohim. Some of these watchers came down to earth to observe the apostate conduct of the flesh in Babel and after a conference decided to confuse the language. < Gen 11:5 And the LORD came down to see the city and the tower, which the children of men builded.

6 And the LORD said, Behold, the people is one, and they have all one language; and this they begin to do: and now nothing will be restrained from them, which they have imagined to do. 7 Go to, let us go down, and there confound their language, that they may not understand one another's speech.>

Others visited Sodom. < Gen 18:21 I will go down now, and see whether they have done altogether according to the cry of it, which is come unto me; and if not, I will know.> They are the eyes of Yahweh. < Zech 4:10 For who hath despised the day of small things? for they shall rejoice, and shall see the plummet in the hand of Zerubbabel with those seven; they are the eyes of the LORD, which run to and fro through the whole earth.> <Heb 1:14 Are they not all ministering spirits, sent forth to minister for them who shall be heirs of salvation?>] **and the demand by the word of the holy ones:** [Yahweh is holy and all the members of his family are holy as well. <Lev 19:2 Speak unto all the congregation of the children of Israel, and say unto them, Ye shall be holy: for I the LORD your God am holy.] **to the intent that the living may know that the most High ruleth in the kingdom of men,** [The kingdom of men here is singular. Everything not with God is lumped under the kingdom of the flesh or the kingdom of Satan.] **and giveth it to whomsoever he will,** [This was a lesson Nebuchadnezzar had learned the hard way. Despite his power, pomp and earthly majesty, he was but a tool of the almighty.] **and setteth up over it the basest of men.** [Basest from the Hebrew lowly. Literally, it means the lowest one of men. The statement has reference to one individual who will ultimately be set over mankind, the Lord Jesus. In revealing the ultimate purpose of Yahweh to the king, Daniel was suggesting if the king wished to continue to reign, he would have to emulate those characteristics. He must be entirely submissive to the will of Yahweh. His purpose ultimately is to set up in power over the kingdom of men, one that has been set at naught by men. The Lord Jesus.]

VS18 This dream I king Nebuchadnezzar have seen. Now thou, O Belteshazzar, declare the interpretation thereof, forasmuch as all the wise men of my kingdom are not able to make known unto me the interpretation: [The wise men of the king were unable to solve the riddle, just as the wise men of today are unable to solve the problems of the world. The basic principles of the scriptures are beyond them.

<1 Cor 1:21 For after that in the wisdom of God the world by wisdom knew not God, it pleased God by the foolishness of preaching to save them that believe.> Previously, the wise men had boasted in Chapter 2 that if they knew the dream they could interpret it. Their boast proved hollow.>] **but thou art able; for the spirit of the holy gods is in thee.** [The king recognized that Daniel spoke by divine inspiration, but since he called the prophet by his Babylonian name Belteshazzar suggesting he thought Daniel was influenced by Babylonian gods as well.]

VS19 Then Daniel, whose name was Belteshazzar, was astonied for one hour, and his thoughts troubled him. [The prophet had come to know the king very well and realized some of his good points. He understood the dream immediately, and the calamity that was about to befall the king. Compassion for the king sealed his lips for a short time, as Rotherham translates this. The king could see the concern on the prophets face.] **The king spake, and said, Belteshazzar, let not the dream, or the interpretation thereof, trouble thee.** [Realizing the dream was an ill omen, the king, never lacking in courage, encouraged Daniel to let him have the bad new.] **Belteshazzar answered and said, My lord, the dream be to them that hate thee, and the interpretation thereof to thine enemies.** [Lord here is from the Chaldean *Marey* that means to dominate or Dictator. The dream foreshadowed such humiliation and shame for Nebuchadnezzar that Daniel could only wish it upon the king's enemies.]

VS 20 The tree that thou sawest, which grew, and was strong, whose height reached unto the heaven, and the sight thereof to all the earth; [The tree that the king saw in his dream represented the Babylonian Empire strong and virile. Its thick massive trunk reached unto heaven and its wide spreading branches provided ample shelter for all birds and animals. It was the admiration of mankind.]

VS21 Whose leaves were fair, and the fruit thereof much, and in it was meat for all; under which the beasts of the field dwelt, and upon whose branches the fowls of the heaven had their habitation: [The king had been given the world, literally. He was warned that his great power had come from God. Twice he had been given a warning and twice he had heeded it. As his power increased, he overlooked this fact and grew in arrogance and pride before God and man. Thus he had to be humbled and restrained.]

VS 22 It is thou, O king, that art grown and become strong: for thy greatness is grown, and reacheth unto heaven, and thy dominion to the end of the earth. [Speaking of Nebuchadnezzar, Isaiah notes the aspirations of the king not only to dominate the earth but to act in the name of the Babylonian gods against the high places of Jerusalem, thus challenging God. <Isa 14:13 For thou hast said in thine heart, I will ascend into heaven, I will exalt my throne above the stars of God: I will sit also upon the mount of the congregation, in the sides of the north:> This is an allegory of the rise of Babylon the Great in the future. A modern day king of Babylon will arise to again challenge the God of heaven. <Rev 17:15 And he saith unto me, The waters which thou sawest, where the whore sitteth, are peoples, and multitudes, and nations, and tongues. 16 And the ten horns which thou sawest upon the beast, these shall hate the whore, and shall make her desolate and naked, and shall eat her flesh, and burn her with fire. 17 For God hath put in their hearts to fulfil his will, and to agree, and give their kingdom unto the beast, until the words of God shall be fulfilled. 18 And the woman which thou sawest is that great city, which reigneth over the kings of the earth.>]

VS23 And whereas the king saw a watcher and an holy one coming down from heaven, and saying, Hew the tree down, and destroy it; yet leave the stump of the roots thereof in the earth, even with a band of iron and brass, in the tender grass of the field; and let it be wet with the dew of heaven, and let his portion be with the beasts of the field, till seven times pass over him; [The command to the angel to "hew down the tree" shows that the rise and fall of nations is supervised and governed by God. To the end, He works thru the angels of heaven. <Ps 103:20 Bless the LORD, ye his angels, that excel in strength, that do his commandments, hearkening unto the voice of his word. 21 Bless ye the LORD, all ye his hosts; ye ministers of his, that do his pleasure. 22 Bless the LORD, all his works in all places of his dominion: bless the LORD, O my soul.> The command to proclaim judgment against Babylon was evidently issued by Michael the Archangel into whose hands the affairs of Israel were particularly placed. <Ex 23:20 Behold, I send an Angel before thee, to keep thee in the way, and to bring thee into the place which I have prepared. 21 Beware of him, and obey his voice, provoke him not; for he will not pardon your transgressions: for my name is in him.> <Josh 5:14 And he said, Nay; but as captain of the host of the LORD am I now come. And Joshua fell on his face to the earth, and did worship, and said unto him, What saith my lord unto his servant?> <Dan 10:21 But I will shew thee that which is noted in the scripture of truth: and there is none that holdeth with me in these things, but Michael your prince.>]

VS24 This is the interpretation, O king, and this is the decree of the most High, which is come upon my lord the king: [This was previously discussed.]

VS25 That they shall drive thee from men, and thy dwelling shall be with the beasts of the field, and they shall make thee to eat grass as oxen, and they shall wet thee with the dew of heaven, [The king had become pompous and callous to the rights of his people. For it, he was to be reduced to beastly behavior. So it will be at the time of the end, when the nations will be led by beastly leaders. This dream obviously occurred quite some time after the events of the first three chapters when the king was well ensconced on the throne.] **and seven times shall pass over thee,** [See the prior discussion on this period of 2520 prophetic years or days.] **till thou know that the most High ruleth in the kingdom of men, and giveth it to whomsoever he will.** [See notes vs. 17. Eventually all the nations, here represented by the king, must make this same declaration.]

VS26 And whereas they commanded to leave the stump of the tree roots; thy kingdom shall be sure unto thee, [The king was promised that once he was humbled he would be restored to his healthy state. Foreshadowing the nations of the end, those that are humbled and confess that Jesus is the Christ and submit to his rule, they too will be lifted up from their bestiality.] **after that thou shalt have known that the heavens do rule.** [He would acknowledge this.]

VS27 Wherefore, O king, let my counsel be acceptable unto thee, and break off thy sins by righteousness, and thine iniquities by

shewing mercy to the poor; [This statement suggests the king had considerable sins to answer for. <Dan 5:20 But when his heart was lifted up, and his mind hardened in pride, he was deposed from his kingly throne, and they took his glory from him:> This caused him to flout the instruction he received earlier from the prophet. History confirms the harshness in the rule of Babylon at this time.] **if it may be a lengthening of thy tranquillity.** [It is suggested in this verse that the king could escape the judgment by changing his ways and acknowledging the power of Yahweh. Unfortunately, the exhortation was not heeded by Nebuchadneaazr.]

The unfortunate king did not heed the warnings of the prophecy and began an extended period of insanity that lasted seven year. But the dream also reveals an interesting prophetic time line that has been brilliantly summarized by H.P. Mansfield as follows:

A SUMMARY OF NEBUCHADNEZZAR'S SEVEN TIMES OF INSANITY

The seven times represent seven years of 360 days, 2520 in all. The period relates both to the king personally and to Babylon prophetically. What happened to the king foreshadowed the destiny of the city and the empire he established. Though historic Babylon was completely destroyed, it was replaced by mystical Babylon: Babylon the Great of *The Apocalypse.* The religious influence of Pagan Babylon continued in papal Babylon as well as in her harlot daughters. <Rev 17:5 And upon her forehead was a name written, MYSTERY, BABYLON THE GREAT, THE MOTHER OF HARLOTS AND ABOMINATIONS OF THE EARTH.>

As a prophecy, the Tree-dream supplements the Image-dream. In the Image the deterioration of human governments was dramatically exhibited descending to the Communist clay of the feet. In the tree-dream the moral decline of rulers and people was shown. Taken together they show the drastic decline of governments, rulers and people: that the nations would act with bestial insanity. The king was shown the course of history, but not told when it would be consummated by the establishment of the Kingdom of God. That omission is supplied in the dream vision of Daniel 4 by the reference to "seven times."

A band of Iron and brass protected the lopped tree. Babylon was not finally crushed but continued to dominate in a different way, through religion. Paganism of Babylon was superimposed on other nations and ultimately incorporated into so-called Christianity. In 1054 the Great Schism took place and so-called Christianity was dived into the Roman and Greek Catholic churches. The influence of Babylon remained protected by the bands of iron (Rome) and brass (Greek)

The symbolism of the intoxicating religion of ancient Babylon is reproduced to illustrate that of Paganism. Of the former, Jeremiah declared. <Jer 51:7 Babylon hath been a golden cup in the LORD's hand, that made all the earth drunken: the nations have drunken of her wine; therefore the nations are mad.>

Thee cup in the hand of the Papal Babylon the Great has likewise affected the nations. <Rev 17:4 And the woman was arrayed in purple and scarlet colour, and decked with gold and precious stones and pearls, having a golden cup in her hand full of abominations and filthiness of her fornication: 5 And upon her forehead was a name written, MYSTERY, BABYLON THE GREAT, THE MOTHER OF HARLOTS AND ABOMINATIONS OF THE EARTH.> <Rev 18:3 For all nations have drunk of the wine of the wrath of her fornication, and the kings of the earth have committed fornication with her, and the merchants of the earth are waxed rich through the abundance of her delicacies.> This intoxicating folly will induce the nations to rise against Christ at his coming. <Ps 2:1 Why do the heathen rage, and the people imagine a vain thing? 2 The kings of the earth set themselves, and the rulers take counsel together, against the LORD, and against his anointed, saying,> What stupidity. The madness of nations will be accentuated by the wine of Babylon "at the time of the end," and will cause such a state of inebriation as will be incurable by man.

Seven times or years according to the lunar dating of the Bible comprises 2,520 days and on the prophetic basis of a day for a year 2,520 years. What are the commencing and terminal dates of that epoch? W. H. Carter wires: "Some students have suggested that as both the Tree and the Image, were concerned with the Kingdoms of Men, the count should be from the 1st of Nebuchadnezzar; but it will be found that in so reckoning the period does not reach forward to the end of the kingdom, as seems fitting. Moreover, the seven times were to pass over the not the tree but the 'stump'."

He suggests the following figures:

Nebuchadnezzar's 1ˢᵗ year: BC 603 terminates 117-18

Babylonian domination of Judah begins BC 603 Nebuchadnezzar's 38the year; 7 years of madness begins. BC 545-terminates 1956-57

1ˢᵗ Year of Darius the Median following the conquest of Babylon (534-533) terminates 1986-87 AD by Cyrus the Persian.

Cyrus decree issued BC 532 BC terminates 1988-89 AD.

The first of these terminal dates saw an event of greatest significance in regard to the fulfillment of God's plan. The Balfour Declaration was proclaimed in 1917 inviting Jews to return to Palestine and establish a national home.

The second in 1957 saw the development of an event equally dramatic. The Rome Pact was signed laying a foundation for the ECC or Common Market. This has divided Europe into two parts answering to the Image, though as yet the feet is not formed nor are they standing upright.

In 1988 the US attack on Libya drew the US, Great Britain and Israel closer together, an alliance that must subsequently come to pass. These dates could possibly be the beginning of the latter days. Once again it is necessary to point out that no timetable, however beguiling, can predict the establishment of the Kingdom of God. Jesus didn't even know when that would be done when he walked the earth. The latter days may be a few years of our time or centuries. In any event, prophecy suggests we are in the "latter days."

The fifth chapter of Daniel again tells of a significant Biblical event the famed "handwriting on the wall." This phrase endures to the present day and signifies an event which will surly happen. Without realizing it, many people, Christians and non Christians alike, affirm the presence of Biblical prophecy. A new king, Belshazzar, son of Nebuchadnezzar sits on the throne and the disembodied hand that writes on the wall presents him with a reason to consult the Hebrew sage, Daniel. Let's look at the prophecy and its historic significance.

VS25 And this is the writing that was written, [Once the hand was removed, all eyes turned to the four simple words.]**MENE, MENE, TEKEL, UPHARSIN.** [The words mean numbered, numbered, weighed and divided. No difficulty attached to reading the words. Now Daniel tells the king what it means.]

VS26 This is the interpretation of the thing: MENE; [The word is doubled. Why? Because of the certainty of the vision. When Joseph interpreted Pharaoh's dream it was doubled because, <Gen 41:32 And for that the dream was doubled unto Pharaoh twice; it is because the thing is established by God, and God will shortly bring it to pass.> and the same is true here.] **God hath numbered thy kingdom, and finished it.** [Daniel had already explained that Yahweh could do this. Dan. 2:21. Paul's exposition deals with the same subject.<Acts 17:25 Neither is worshipped with men's hands, as though he needed any thing, seeing he giveth to all life, and breath, and all things; 26 And hath made of one blood all nations of men for to dwell on all the face of the earth, and hath determined the times before appointed, and the bounds of their habitation;> The days of Babylon had been numbered, and they were at an end.]

VS27 TEKEL; [The word means weighed and is from a common root with the word Shekel and means to weigh or balance a thing. Here, it signified the time of judgment had been irrevocably set. The punishment would fit the crime.] **Thou art weighed in the balances, and art found wanting.** [Their actions had been weighed and the kingdom of Babylon was found unsatisfactory.]

VS28 PERES; Upharsin (vs. 25) is a participle of the same word from which Peres is derived. It means *and they divided it.* The Persians were known to the Chaldeans as *Paros* therefore is a play upon the words. Peres indicated not only the dividing that would take place but also hinted it would be given to the Persians.] **Thy kingdom is divided, and given to the Medes and Persians.** [With the armies of the Medes and the Persians at the gates this was not a risky interpretation. Isaiah had already told them who would take the city. <Isa 45:1Thus saith the LORD to his anointed, to Cyrus, whose right hand I have holden, to subdue nations before him; and I will loose the loins of kings, to open before him the two leaved gates; and the gates shall not be shut;> Daniel had been waiting for this to happen because he looked to the restoration of the people to the land by Cyrus. He had watched as Cyrus seemed to ignore Babylon by attacking Nineveh, Asia Minor and other nations before turning his attention to Babylon. He must have felt the same impatience as the saints do today as they wait for the coming of the Kingdom.]

VS30 In that night was Belshazzar the king of the Chaldeans slain. [Cyrus knew of the festival, and that the men in the city would be drunk and unaware, and he used that to his advantage. Herodotus (Book 1:19) quotes Cyrus. "Now let us go up against them. Many are asleep; many are intoxicated and all of them unfit for battle. It was a day of festivity among them; and whilst the citizens were engaged in dance and merriment, Babylon was taken for the first time." So he opened the dykes made by Semiramis and her successors to confine the Euphrates to a single channel, and flooded the country so he could enter Babylon beneath its walls in the original channel of the river. Isaiah predicted the brass gates and iron bars would be no help in the defense of the city. <Isa 45:2 I will go before thee, and make the crooked places straight: I will break in pieces the gates of brass, and cut in sunder the bars of iron:> Herodotus states these brazen gates were along the river banks but at the time of the attack they were left open.]

VS31 And Darius the Median took the kingdom, [Twenty years before the fall of Babylon, Cyrus had risen to power as a 12 year old. At a tender age he dethroned Astyages, the last king of Media and absorbed that country into the empire. The wealthy Croesus of Lydia who then dominated most of Asia Minor was next and he became master of the Lydian Empire. Next he swept over Babylon defeating Nabonidus at Borsippa.

When he came to Babylon, he found a city with massive double walls some of them hundreds of feet high and eighty—five feet thick. Some 250 towers strengthened the walls. The Euphrates cut the city in two and the river was enclosed on both banks by quays which were protected by walls with brass gates. In the attack on the city, Belshazzar was slain, Nabonidus had already surrendered and been given a principality in Carmania and Babylon became part of Cyrus' Persian Empire.] **being about threescore and two years old.** [Who was Darius? Darius is not a name, but a title that means The Subduer. Some feel he was Cyaxeres II son of Astyages and the uncle or father in law of Cyrus. It would have been a smart move to place a relative on the Median throne.

Whitcomb in *Darius the Mede* feels it was a title given to Gubaru the Governor of Babylon who is referred to in various 6th century cuneiform texts. He claims that Cyrus left Babylon after its fall departing for Ecbatana and appointed Gubaru as subordinate ruler.

In the prophecy relating to the Medo-Persian, the bear is shown as lop-sided, suggesting to John Thomas that it represented the dominance of the Persians over the Medes. But, the Medes only ruled 2 years and the Persians ruled for 200. This claim that Gabaru was the Mede does not fit in view of the great authority exercised by this Cyrus.

Rollin's *Ancient History* claims that Cyrus as a diplomatic move elevated a Median relative to power in Babylon who ruled there a short time. This conforms to the character of Cyrus and answers the requirements of Daniel's prophecy. In Daniel 9:1, Darius is said to be made king of the Chaldeans which describes an appointment but not a conquest. <Dan 9:1 In the first year of Darius the son of Ahasuerus, of the seed of the Medes, which was made king over the realm of the Chaldeans;> Made is from *gebel* which signifes to acquire a thing. The RV translates received it.

If Cyrus left and appointed a ruler over the Chaldeans it fits. R. Collins in *The Medes and the Persians, states,* "Contrary to custom, Astyages wasn't slain. Cyrus-great-great-Grandson of Achaegmenes and soon to be the noblest Persian of all took the old man into the court and dealt sympathetically with him. It was an unusual touch of humanity for a savage time.

The reference to the age of Astyages by R. Collins confirms this statement. As with Darius, Astyages is a title meaning The Mighty and as such was used by a number of Persian monarchs. It therefore could be related to the father of Astyages who was a relative of Cyrus. To give it to a relative like this rather than a stranger like Gubaru makes more sense. It is more likely that this man was a relative of Cyrus. With Daniel the appointed ruler of Belshazzar, Darius as representative of Cyrus negotiated the peace with the prophet and brought the two men into contact.]

Chapter six of Daniel describes the famous story of the lion's den. It makes interesting reading, and shows how God protects his servants'. The rest of the chapters in Daniel are remarkable historic prophecies that have been proven true by the passage of time. In the next chapter, Daniel has a dream of his own and an angelic interpretation.

CHAPTER 11

Daniel's Vision

The first portion of Daniel 7 is history that can be proven; the second describes the universal kingdom that will one day govern the world. The chapter divides naturally into these parts: The Dream vv. 1-14; Daniel's concern and first question vv.15-16; The angel's explanation vv. 17-18; Daniel's further enquiry relating to the fourth beast vv. 19-22; the second angelic explanation vv. 23-27 and a final summary of Daniel's concern vs. 28.

Vs7:1 In the first year of Belshazzar king of Babylon Daniel had a dream and visions of his head upon his bed: [The elevation of Belshazzar to power marked a decline in the morality of Babylon. It terminated the dynasty of Nebuchadnezzar and the 70 year period allocated to it by Jeremiah. <Jer 25:11 And this whole land shall be a desolation, and an astonishment; and these nations shall serve the king of Babylon seventy years. And it shall come to pass, when seventy years are accomplished, that I will punish the king of Babylon, and that nation, saith the LORD, for their iniquity, and the land of the Chaldeans, and will make it perpetual desolations.> <Jer 29:10 For thus saith the LORD, That after seventy years be accomplished at Babylon I will visit you, and perform my good word toward you, in causing you to return to this place.> Daniel wrote down the dream and related it to his friends]

VS2 Daniel spake and said, I saw in my vision by night, and, behold, [Night prophetically refers to the Gentile night as used by the Lord Jesus. <John 9:4 I must work the works of him that sent me, while it is day: the night cometh, when no man can work. 5 As long as I am in the world, I am the light of the world.>] **the four winds of the**

heaven strove upon the great sea. [Prophetically a wind is an army on the march. <Jer 4:13 Behold, he shall come up as clouds, and his chariots shall be as a whirlwind: his horses are swifter than eagles. Woe unto us! for we are spoiled.> The four winds thus represent the four world powers that successively struggled for the mastery of Babylon.]

VS3 And four great beasts came up from the sea, diverse one from another. [Gentile nations are elsewhere symbolized as beasts. <Prov 28:15 As a roaring lion, and a ranging bear; so is a wicked ruler over the poor people.> Daniel is later told the beasts represent four kingdoms in vs. 17. Like the metals of the Image they emerge as 4 world powers. Each is absorbed and built on by the succeeding power until the 4th; unnamed power is a combination of all that went before it. There was a common element of ruthlessness anti-Semitism in all of them. <Rev 13:2 And the beast which I saw was like unto a leopard, and his feet were as the feet of a bear, and his mouth as the mouth of a lion: and the dragon gave him his power, and his seat, and great authority.>]

VS4 The first was like a lion, [This was the symbol Chaldean and Assyrian empires the powers responsible for the scattering of the divided kingdom of Israel and Judah. <Jer 50:17 Israel is a scattered sheep; the lions have driven him away: first the king of Assyria hath devoured him; and last this Nebuchadrezzar king of Babylon hath broken his bones.> Archaeologists have unearthed many huge images of lions in both Nineveh and Babylon. This answers to the golden portion of the Image.] **and had eagle's wings:** [The out-stretched wings of the eagle symbolized the widespread extensive territory of Assyria which incorporated most of the then known world. Many statues of winged lions have been unearthed.] **I beheld till the wings thereof were plucked,** [As the central administration weakened, the provinces of the real represented by the wings, revolted against the central domination of Nineveh. This was caused by the violent invasions of Scythians and revolts on the part of Media and Babylonia. In Babylon Nabopolassar took power and not only asserted his independence but ultimately dominated Nineveh so as to replace its power and influence. The plucking of the wings suggest the revolution by which this was brought about.] **and it was lifted up from the earth,** [It is transported from one place to another, Nineveh to Babylon.] **and made stand upon the feet**

as a man, [Chaldean influence rose again to power but form a different center, Babylon instead of Nineveh. Statues of standing lions have been uncovered.] **and a man's heart was given to it.** [Nebuchadnezzar's rule was more susceptible to human considerations than the brutal Assyrians. Influenced by the prophet, he ruled humanly.]

VS5 And behold another beast, a second, like to a bear, [The second shows this beast came after the first and that the four beasts didn't come at the same time. The bear was Medo Persia which overthrew Babylon in 536 BC. The bear was feared only slightly less that the lion in the Promised Land. Strong, cruel, cunning and greedy, the bear is not as powerful or as courageous as the lion but still and animal to be avoided. The bear is omnivorous eating both vegetables and meat. The lion is more predictable while the bear is more cunning. Medo-Persian rulers were more cunning and diplomatic than the Babylonians. They were also greedy for prey and extended their borders beyond those of the Babylonian Empire.] **and it raised up itself on one side,** [Cyaxares the Mede perfected his army and waged war on Nineveh. They were noted for their ruthless efficiency in war. Median rulers dominated until Cyrus revolted against the Median tyrant Astyages.

As Daniel shows, even after the fall of Babylon, Cyrus diplomatically used the authority of the Medes to consolidate his power, but it was not long before Persians controlled the government and continued to do so for the long period of Medo-Persian rule.] **and it had three ribs in the mouth of it between the teeth of it:** [When Cyrus rose to power, there were three powerful rivals contesting for dominion. They were Babylonia, noted for its strength, Lydian noted for its wealth and Egypt noted for its antiquity and culture. One by one Cyrus conquered each of them and dominated the civilized world. Until Persian soldiers faces the Greek armies they never lost a battle.] **and they said thus unto it,** [Who are they? Obviously they are the angelic watchers through whom Yahweh dictates the course of history. While he consolidated his power, he appointed three presidents, one over each "rib", and one of them was Daniel.] **Arise, devour much flesh.** [The rulers after Cyrus extended the Empire by more conquests. They became the best trained fighting force in history. Men sought to serve in the army due to the special privileges the soldiers received. The core of the arm was the 10,000 immortals. They were equivalent to the Praetorian Guard or Napoleon's old guard. When one fell in battle he was immediately replaced so the number was always 10,000 thus the term immortal.]

VS6 After this I beheld, and lo another, like a leopard, [The next beast was a leopard with four heads and a pair of birds wings on the side. The leopard is a handsome cat and Greece is considered by many the most cultured of nations. As an animal, it is more adaptable, and has a greater range of habitats than other predators. It is noted for its speed and the unexpected nature of its attacks. It is also strong and versatile and all these characteristics make it the ideal symbol for Greece.] **which had upon the back of it four wings of a fowl;** [Wings add speed to the leopard. The leopard represents Macedonia's Alexander the great and the four principal successors who divided his Empire among themselves. The body of the beast represents the nation before it was divided and the four heads the divisions. Alexander's life and conquests were as rapid as the animal described here.] **the beast had also four heads;** [At age 33, Alexander died in Babylon and his empire was divided. First Head: Kingdom of the south comprising Egypt Libya Arabia, Coele-Syria and Palestine under the Ptolemies.

Second Head: The Kingdom of the North-West including Thrace, Bithynia or the Thraco-Macedonian established by Lysimachus. Third Head: The Kingdom of the North East that included the rest of Asia, inclusive of Babylon and its provinces and extending beyond the Euphrates to the Indus. India beyond that river though allotted to this head revolted so that the Indus became its boundary.

This was the Macedo-Babylonian Kingdom of the Seleucidae. This is the king of the north in Daniel 11. Though suppressed during the Middle Ages, prophecy requires it to re-emerge at the time of the end. <Dan 11:40 And at the time of the end shall the king of the south push at him: and the king of the north shall come against him like a whirlwind, with chariots, and with horsemen, and with many ships; and he shall enter into the countries, and shall overflow and pass over.>

Fourth Head: Kingdom of the West embracing Greece and Macedonia.] **and dominion was given to it.** [This links Greece and the leopard to the brass portion of the Image. <Dan 2:39 And after thee shall arise another kingdom inferior to thee, and another third kingdom of brass, which shall bear rule over all the earth.>

However, this kingdom didn't outlast his death. With cold hearted brutality they murdered his mother, brother, wife and young son. The heads of the army divided the spoils. They were Cassander, West; Seleucus, North-West; Lysimachus, North-East and Ptolemey the south.]

VS7 After this I saw in the night visions, [Gentile times.] **and behold a fourth beast,** [There is nothing in nature as cruel and ruthless and deadly as this fourth beast, so it has no name. It represents Rome. It combined and added to the fearsome characteristics of all the beasts before it. It is the legs of iron and the feed ant toes of iron and clay of the Image.] **dreadful** [The Chaldean word is *dechal* meaning to slink in fear or to crawl. It is not described as an upright noble animal as those who preceded it. The crocodile, called a dragon, became the fitting symbol of Rome.] **and terrible,** [which describes Rome] **and strong exceedingly;** [This was the iron portion of the image, and iron breaks apart all the other metals of the Image. At the height of its power, Rome occupied the known world and broke into part all the nations before it.] **and it had great iron teeth:** [Later on, when Daniel looks closer, he sees this beast has nails of brass, linking it with Nebuchadnezzar's dream in Ch. 4:5] **it devoured and brake in pieces,** [Daniel saw this fearful beast on a rampage extending its conquests swallowing up territory after territory reducing all victims to impotence. In BC 168 Macedonia was swallowed up. In 133 Pergamum was bequeathed to Rome. In BC 65 it was Syrian and in BC 30 Egypt. **and stamped the residue with the feet of it:** [They ground to powder the residue of all the other kingdoms before it.] **and it was diverse from all the beasts that were before it;** [In fact, all the beasts were diverse from each other, but this one defied description.] **and it had ten horns.** [The ten horns link this with the toes of the Image seen by Nebuchadnezzar.]

VS8 I considered the horns, and, behold, there came up among them another little horn, [As Daniel watched, a little 11ᵗʰ horn sprouted from the midst of the ten horns and was personalized with a mouth eyes and nose. It represented the religious system of Rome (Roman Catholicism) that grew slowly over the centuries.

The Roman Empire was divided into two parts answering to the legs of Nebuchadnezzar's image. Constantine did this in 330 AD when he moved the political capitol to Constantinople and left the religious center in Rome. Theodosius I consolidated this East West division in 395 AD.

In the 11th century the ecclesiastical split occurred when the Greek Orthodox Catholic Church was formed, the brass and iron of Daniel 4. Barbarian hoards gradually overran Rome and split into ten ethnic groups in the areas that they conquered the ten horns or kingdoms of Western Europe. Gradually they embraced an apostate form of Christianity based on the Arian unity of God principal and were bitterly opposed to the Trinitarians and Catholics.

The Goths, Ostergoths and Heruil occupied Italy and embracing this theory challenged the authority of the Bishop of Rome whose influence was greatly reduced as a result. In AD 476 through the conquering sword of Odoacer the Goth, Rome fell and the Empire in the west ended.

Opposed by the Arian Goths the Pope appealed to the Emperor in Constantinople for assistance. Justinian came to his aid and defeated the Italian Goths in 527 AD. Justinian was proclaimed sole Emperor and supported the pretension of the Pope and his false doctrines. In 533 the Pope was proclaimed Universal Bishop. From 549-554, Justinian published his list of pragmatic sanctions that became the foundation of European Law, giving the Pope control of the Municipal and Provincial governments and the little horn began to grow.

Between 590 and 600 AD the ambitious Pope Gregory I gave the horn eyes and a mouth and by his death in 604 the Pope was recognized as head of the entire church.

In 608 Emperor Phocas of Constantinople confirmed the decree of Justinian and proclaimed that the Pope was head of all the churches. We must recognize that the little horn does not represent Roman Catholicism as a church for the horns are described as kingdoms not churches. This little horn was an ecclesiastical kingdom that history calls the Holy Roman Empire.

From 622 on, Islam began to challenge the Easter Empire until Constantinople fell in 1493, stripping the pope of his military support. He found it in the Franks of Charlemagne who conquered Islamas described in Revelation 9.

But, the Arabs quickly overran the Eastern Empire and North Africa and in 700 Tarik crossed the Gates of Hercules and occupied Gibraltar.

Eleven years later in the battle of Xerxes de la Frontera he defeated the king of the Visigoths and crossed the Pyreness. The Moslems defeated the Duke of Aqutania who tried to stop them at Bordeaux but they marched on Paris.

Thus in a great pincer movement, the Moslems forces challenged Constantinople in the East and Europe through Spain and the West. Their credo was the Koran or the sword. The time was ripe for the complete manifestation of the little horn and the development of the Holy Roman Empire.

In 732 the Moslems were beaten in a battle fought between Tours and Poitiers in Western Europe. On that day, Charles Martel, (Charles the Hammer) saved Europe from Moslem domination and drove them out of France into Spain where they remained until 1492 where they were called the Kindgom of the Moors.

By now the Pope was weakened politically and militarily. Pepin the Short, son of Charles Martel was a clever diplomat. Intriguing to be proclaimed king by the other Germanic chieftains, Pepin staged an elaborate coronation for himself where the great Catholic missionary, Boniface anointed him "King by the grace of God."

Adding *Dia gratiat* to the coronation service linked state and church. It was claimed anyone opposing the king opposed God. The little horn now had a new military champion to replace Constantinople and was fully endowed with human features.] **before whom there were three of the first horns plucked up by the roots:** [In Pepin the Pope had a powerful new friend but Italy itself was dominated by Arians who showed little respect for "His Holiness" as the Pope now liked to be called. Pepin invaded Italy in 758 and conquered the Arians giving the Pope what became known as the states of the church,

The Exarchate of Ravenna, the Kingdom of the Lombards, and the State of Rome. Charlemagne, Pepin's son, confirmed this and they Pope now wore the crown of the "three horns," plucked up by the roots to establish Papal political and temporal power.

These States of the Church remained until 1870 when they were taken from the Pope's temporal power. A millennium of wickedness was terminated. In the Conquests of Charlemagne, through which the Pope's temporal power increased, three of the major horns or kingdoms of the Heruli, Ostergoths and Vandals were uprooted.

In 789, Pope Leo III was attacked in the street in Rome and left for dead. He was rescued and made his way to the camp of Charles here he asked for help. A Frank army restored authority and conveyed Leo to the Lateran Palace which ever since the days of Constantine had been the home of the Pope.

That was in December 799. Christmas day, Charlemagne who was in Rome attended the service in St. Peters. When he arose from prayer, the Pope placed a crown on his head and called him Emperor of the Holy Roman Empire and hailed him with the title "Augustus," which had not been heard for hundreds of years. Charlemagne supported the Pope vigorously and conquered the Saxons in Germany and built towns and monasteries all over Europe. Under the rule of this Germanic chieftain, the Holy Roma Empire was firmly established and given the title, The Holy Roman Empire of the German Nation. From then on the German rulers were given this title at their coronation.] **and, behold, in this horn were eyes like the eyes of man,** [It is interesting that the office of a Roman Catholic Bishop is a See, and the Pope itself, The Holy See relating to the supervision he exercises over the church. The eyes of the church extend to the ends of the earth. They claim to do the will of God. <Zech 4:10 For who hath despised the day of small things? for they shall rejoice, and shall see the plummet in the hand of Zerubbabel with those seven; they are the eyes of the LORD, which run to and fro through the whole earth.>

The eyes of the beast can be linked with the number of the best which is the number of man. <Rev 13:18 Here is wisdom. Let him that hath understanding count the number of the beast: for it is the number of a man; and his number is Six hundred threescore and six.> Zechariah predicted the downfall of this power. <Zech 11:17 Woe to the idol shepherd that leaveth the flock! the sword shall be upon his arm, and upon his right eye: his arm shall be clean dried up, and his right eye shall be utterly darkened.>] **and a mouth speaking great things.** [The great things are the Papal Bulls and decrees that issue forth from Rome. There was a great voice that sounded forth decrees from historic Babylon as well and it was stilled by the conquest of Cyrus, just as the antitypical Cyrus, the Lord Jesus Christ, will destroy modern Babylon. <Jer 51:55 Because the LORD hath spoiled Babylon, and destroyed out of her the great voice; when her waves do roar like great waters, a noise of their voice is uttered:> Then will the word of the Psalm be fulfilled. <Ps 12:3 The LORD shall cut off all flattering lips, and the tongue that speaketh proud things:>]

The Ancient of Days and The Judgment

VS9 I beheld till [This suggests the 4th beast and its horn will be in power till the judgment.] **the thrones were cast down,** [The judgment described here is not of individuals but nations. Christ's victory over the Northern Confederacy at Armageddon will be followed by a lull during which an ultimatum will be sent to all nations demanding their subjugation to the king in Jerusalem. <Ps 2:8 Ask of me, and I shall give thee the heathen for thine inheritance, and the uttermost parts of the earth for thy possession. 9 Thou shalt break them with a rod of iron; thou shalt dash them in pieces like a potter's vessel. 10 Be wise now therefore, O ye kings: be instructed, ye judges of the earth. 11 Serve the LORD with fear, and rejoice with trembling. 12 Kiss the Son, lest he be angry, and ye perish from the way, when his wrath is kindled but a little. Blessed are all they that put their trust in him.> <Isa 15:32 What shall one then answer the messengers of the nation? That the LORD hath founded Zion, and the poor of his people shall trust in it.> <Rev 14:6 And I saw another angel fly in the midst of heaven, having the everlasting gospel to preach unto them that dwell on the earth, and to every nation, and kindred, and tongue, and people, Saying with a loud voice, Fear God, and give glory to him; for the hour of his judgment is come: and worship him that made heaven, and earth, and the sea, and the fountains of waters. And there followed another angel, saying, Babylon is fallen, is fallen, that great city, because she made all nations drink of the wine of the wrath of her fornication. 9 And the third angel followed them, saying with a loud voice, If any man worship the beast and his image, and receive his mark in his forehead, or in his hand, 10 The same shall drink of the wine of the wrath of God, which is poured out without mixture into the cup of his indignation; and he shall be tormented with fire and brimstone in the presence of the holy angels, and in the presence of the Lamb:> Acceptance or rejection of this ultimatum will determine the fate of nations. <Isa 60:12 For the nation and kingdom that will not serve thee shall perish; yea, those nations shall be utterly wasted.> Various judgments are mentioned in the verses that follow.] **and the Ancient of days did sit,** [As the divine judge, he takes the seat of honor. Who is the Ancient of Days? In vs. 13 it is the Deity, and in vs. 22 it is Christ. How can it be both? It is through the terms of God-manifestation. As a trusted son may represent his father and indeed speak with the authority of his father, so the Son in heaven and on earth in the future represent the Father. He is already granted all the power in heaven and earth. <Matt 28:18 And Jesus came and spake unto them, saying, All power is given unto me in heaven and in earth.> So, he acts with the full authority and in the name of the Father. That exalted status in the Age to come is offered to the saints under Christ. <Rom 5:2 By whom also we have access by faith into this grace wherein we stand, and rejoice in hope of the glory of God.> <Rev 3:12 Him that overcometh will I make a pillar in the temple of my God, and he shall go no more out: and I will write upon him the name of my God, and the name of the city of my God, which is new Jerusalem, which cometh down out of heaven from my God: and I will write upon him my new name.>

What does the title Ancient of Days mean? <Job 36:26 Behold, God is great, and we know him not, neither can the number of his years be searched out.> <Ps 41:13 Blessed be the LORD God of Israel from everlasting, and to everlasting. Amen, and Amen.> <Ps 90:2 Before the mountains were brought forth, or ever thou hadst formed the earth and the world, even from everlasting to everlasting, thou art God.> <Ps 102:24 I said, O my God, take me not away in the midst of my days: thy years are throughout all generations.> <Ps 102:24 I said, O my God, take me not away in the midst of my days: thy years are throughout all generations. 25 Of old hast thou laid the foundation of the earth: and the heavens are the work of thy hands. 26 They shall perish, but thou shalt endure: yea, all of them shall wax old like a garment; as a vesture shalt thou change them, and they shall be changed: 27 But thou art the same, and thy years shall have no end.>

God is above and beyond all measurement of time and is unchangeable. Divine, indestructible and is manifest to us by Christ and the Angels. He is from everlasting to everlasting, the beginning and the end. As son of God, The Lord can trace his ancestry back to the beginning of time. <Mic 5:2 But thou, Bethlehem Ephratah, though thou be little among the thousands of Judah, yet out of thee shall he come forth unto me that is to be ruler in Israel; whose goings forth have been from of old, from everlasting.> So the Ancient of Days is Christ, the manifestation of his divine Father.] **whose garment was white as snow,** [The robe represents both nature and status. <Gal 3:26 For ye are all the children of God by faith in Christ Jesus.> At Baptism we put on the divine nature and it is our duty to keep it clean and pure. <Jude 21-23 Keep yourselves in the love of God, looking for the mercy of our Lord Jesus Christ unto eternal life. 22 And of some have compassion, making a difference: 23 And others save with fear, pulling them out of the fire; hating even the garment spotted by the flesh.> Ultimately, the righteous will be offered to complete the change of nature the white robe signifies. <Rev 19:8 And to her was granted that she should be arrayed in fine linen, clean and white: for the fine linen is the righteousness of saints.>] **and the hair of his head like the pure wool:** [The pure white hair is symbolic of the white miter of the High Priest. On the forehead of the priest was a gold band inscribed, Holiness to Yahweh. They wore the band because through weakness of the flesh, they did not consistently manifest the holiness to which they were called. Such artificial appendage was not needed for the Lord. His sinless life was a constant dedication to Yahweh. This holiness and perfection of character came from his mind. His flesh was like all other but his mind was unique. His Divine Conception made it possible for him to develop a mind like Yahweh's and thus allowed him to conquer the flesh. This was what the gold band signified.] **his throne was like the fiery flame,** [Fire is used as the symbol for the consuming powr of the Spirit as manifested through the Elohim. <Gen 3:24 So he drove out the man; and he placed at the east of the garden of Eden Cherubims, and a flaming sword which turned every way, to keep the way of the tree of life.> <Ps 104:4 Who maketh his angels spirits; his ministers a flaming fire:>

Flame is from a Chaldean root that means to divide up. As a flame split into tongues as on the Day of Pentecost (from Strong) the spirit-flame will divide and go into all the world to preach and later to judge for Yahweh. The cherubic throne seen by Ezekiel was similarly encased in fire. <Ezek 1:26 And above the firmament that was over their heads was the likeness of a throne, as the appearance of a sapphire stone: and upon the likeness of the throne was the likeness as the appearance of a man above upon it. 27 And I saw as the colour of amber, as the appearance of fire round about within it, from the appearance of his loins even upward, and from the appearance of his

loins even downward, I saw as it were the appearance of fire, and it had brightness round about.>

This throne was a likeness of the Davidic throne: <Rev 4:3 And he that sat was to look upon like a jasper and a sardine stone: and there was a rainbow round about the throne, in sight like unto an emerald. 4 And round about the throne were four and twenty seats: and upon the seats I saw four and twenty elders sitting, clothed in white raiment; and they had on their heads crowns of gold. 5 And out of the throne proceeded lightnings and thunderings and voices: and there were seven lamps of fire burning before the throne, which are the seven Spirits of God.>

The fire associated with this throne, indicates the consuming and purging anger of Yahweh manifested through the Spirit. By this the nations will be subdued and purged and made fit as mortal participants in the Kingdom of God Isaiah saw this fiery flame proceeding through the earth. <Isa 30:27 Behold, the name of the LORD cometh from far, burning with his anger, and the burden thereof is heavy: his lips are full of indignation, and his tongue as a devouring fire: 28. And his breath, as an overflowing stream, shall reach to the midst of the neck, to sift the nations with the sieve of vanity: and there shall be a bridle in the jaws of the people, causing them to err.> **and his wheels as burning fire.**[Wheels of fire give it mobility to go to the ends of the earth and also identifies it with Ezekiel's vision. <Ezek 1:12 And they went every one straight forward: whither the spirit was to go, they went; and they turned not when they went.> They went straight, undeterred from their singular mission to accomplish Yahweh's will.

Ezekiel described the wheels as linking the chariot of Yahweh on earth with heaven itself in an awe-inspiring manner. <Ezek 1:15 Now as I beheld the living creatures, behold one wheel upon the earth by the living creatures, with his four faces. 16 The appearance of the wheels and their work was like unto the colour of a beryl: and they four had one likeness: and their appearance and their work was as it were a wheel in the middle of a wheel. 17 When they went, they went upon their four sides: and they turned not when they went. 18 As for their rings, they were so high that they were dreadful; and their rings were full of eyes round about them four. 19 And when the living creatures went, the wheels went by them: and when the living creatures were lifted up from the earth, the wheels were lifted up. 20 Whithersoever the spirit

was to go, they went, thither was their spirit to go; and the wheels were lifted up over against them: for the spirit of the living creature was in the wheels. 21 When those went, these went; and when those stood, these stood; and when those were lifted up from the earth, the wheels were lifted up over against them: for the spirit of the living creature was in the wheels. 22 And the likeness of the firmament upon the heads of the living creature was as the colour of the terrible crystal, stretched forth over their heads above. 23. And under the firmament were their wings straight, the one toward the other: every one had two, which covered on this side, and every one had two, which covered on that side, their bodies. 24 And when they went, I heard the noise of their wings, like the noise of great waters, as the voice of the Almighty, the voice of speech, as the noise of an host: when they stood, they let down their wings.>

Who are the cherubim? In *Phanerosis* John Thomas notes the relationship of the word to chariots and aligns the charioteers with the Spirit. <Ps 18:10 And he rode upon a cherub, and did fly: yea, he did fly upon the wings of the wind.> <1 Chron 28:18 And for the altar of incense refined gold by weight; and gold for the pattern of the chariot of the cherubims, that spread out their wings, and covered the ark of the covenant of the LORD.>

The wheels on the throne illustrate its unlimited influence throughout the earth. <Isa 9:7 Of the increase of his government and peace there shall be no end, upon the throne of David, and upon his kingdom, to order it, and to establish it with judgment and with justice from henceforth even for ever. The zeal of the LORD of hosts will perform this.>]

VS10 A fiery stream issued and came forth from before him:

[Reminiscent of the flaming sword in Eden, a river of fire flowed from the throne. See prior references to fire. <Ps 50:3 Our God shall come, and shall not keep silence: a fire shall devour before him, and it shall be very tempestuous round about him. 4 He shall call to the heavens from above, and to the earth, that he may judge his people.> <1 Cor 3:13 Every man's work shall be made manifest: for the day shall declare it, because it shall be revealed by fire; and the fire shall try every man's work of what sort it is.> <Matt 13:40 As therefore the tares are gathered and burned in the fire; so shall it be in the end of

this world. 41 The Son of man shall send forth his angels, and they shall gather out of his kingdom all things that offend, and them which do iniquity; 42 And shall cast them into a furnace of fire: there shall be wailing and gnashing of teeth.>] **thousand thousands ministered unto him, and ten thousand times ten thousand stood before him:** [In the courtroom scene before us, these represent the witnesses for the prosecution competent to testify against the nations to be judged so as to determine the extent of national judgment to be administered. The numerals are not exact numbers, but represent large unspecified multitudes. In Biblical numbers 10 is for completeness. <1 Sam 29:5 Is not this David, of whom they sang one to another in dances, saying, Saul slew his thousands, and David his ten thousands?> <Ps 3:6 I will not be afraid of ten thousands of people, that have set themselves against me round about.> <1 Cor 4:15 For though ye have ten thousand instructors in Christ, yet have ye not many fathers: for in Christ Jesus I have begotten you through the gospel.>

These witnesses testify as outlined by John. <Rev 18:24 And in her was found the blood of prophets, and of saints, and of all that were slain upon the earth.>] **the judgment was set,** [This does not mean the judgment was already made or set. It refers to the act of setting down. As in a courtroom, those who are connected with the case rise when the judge enters, then take their seats to hear the evidence. That's the case here.] **and the books were opened.** [Remember, this is describing the judgment of the nations and not individuals, so there is a national record book as well as the Lamb's Book of Life. <Dan 12:1 And at that time shall Michael stand up, the great prince which standeth for the children of thy people: and there shall be a time of trouble, such as never was since there was a nation even to that same time: and at that time thy people shall be delivered, every one that shall be found written in the book.> From this and from the parable of judgment in Matthew, <Matt 25:32 And before him shall be gathered all nations: and he shall separate them one from another, as a shepherd divideth his sheep from the goats: 33 And he shall set the sheep on his right hand, but the goats on the left.> there appears no doubt that nations shall be judges as well as people.]

VS11 I beheld then because of the voice of the great words which the horn spake: [The evidence of the arrogance, haughtiness, pride, blasphemy and violent suppression of saints by the papal system, the atrocities of the inquisition and cruel brutality of the system will be recalled for all in the court to hear. Because the ten horns identified with the little horn, they are guilty by association.] **I beheld even till the beast was slain, and his body destroyed, and given to the burning flame.** [The fourth beast is judged guilty and sentenced to be consumed by the fiery judgment of Yahweh. The city of Rome with its ecclesiastical organization will be destroyed. <Rev 18:21 And a mighty angel took up a stone like a great millstone, and cast it into the sea, saying, Thus with violence shall that great city Babylon be thrown down, and shall be found no more at all. 22 And the voice of harpers, and musicians, and of pipers, and trumpeters, shall be heard no more at all in thee; and no craftsman, of whatsoever craft he be, shall be found any more in thee; and the sound of a millstone shall be heard no more at all in thee; 23 And the light of a candle shall shine no more at all in thee; and the voice of the bridegroom and of the bride shall be heard no more at all in thee: for thy merchants were the great men of the earth; for by thy sorceries were all nations deceived.>

But, the fourth beast must rise in power for this to happen as Daniel will learn subsequently. The Concordat signed by Mussolini and the Pope restored in some measure the power lost by the Papacy in 1870. The Treaty of Rome in 1957 that established the common market is establishing in Western Europe a confederation of nations in the very area of Charlemagne's Empire. It is forming the western foot of the Image. The eastern foot, the old Warsaw Pact nations will be gradually drawn into the alliance as it strengthens.]

VS12 As concerning the rest of the beasts, they had their dominion taken away: [This suggests that the other beasts were not completely destroyed but only absorbed by the fourth beast. After that fourth beast is destroyed, the other nations will have an opportunity to rescue their national identity. <Rev 14:8 And there followed another angel, saying, Babylon is fallen, is fallen, that great city, because she made all nations drink of the wine of the wrath of her fornication. 9 And the third angel followed them, saying with a loud voice, If any man worship the beast and his image, and receive his mark in his forehead, or in his hand, 10 The same shall drink of the wine of the wrath of God, which is poured out without mixture into the cup of his indignation; and he shall be

tormented with fire and brimstone in the presence of the holy angels, and in the presence of the Lamb:>] **yet their lives were prolonged** [The destruction of the fourth beast will be followed by the extension of Christ's rule through the earth. This was symbolized by the Image being broken into pieces by the Divine stone and later ground into powder and carried away as the stone grew into a mountain. As Christ's kingdom spreads throughout the earth, cities and nations will be placed in the care of his immortal associates. <Matt 19:28 And Jesus said unto them, Verily I say unto you, That ye which have followed me, in the regeneration when the Son of man shall sit in the throne of his glory, ye also shall sit upon twelve thrones, judging the twelve tribes of Israel.> <Luke 19:17 And he said unto him, Well, thou good servant: because thou hast been faithful in a very little, have thou authority over ten cities.> <Rev 2:26 And he that overcometh, and keepeth my works unto the end, to him will I give power over the nations: 27 And he shall rule them with a rod of iron; as the vessels of a potter shall they be broken to shivers: even as I received of my Father.> <Rev 5:9 And they sung a new song, saying, Thou art worthy to take the book, and to open the seals thereof: for thou wast slain, and hast redeemed us to God by thy blood out of every kindred, and tongue, and people, and nation; 10 And hast made us unto our God kings and priests: and we shall reign on the earth.>] **for a season and a time.** [The season and the time is considered by most to be the millennium. Thomas suggests the season is two lunar cycles or years of 360 days each or 720 years. The time is likely the 280 day gestational period of a human infant. This is hinted at in Genesis. <Gen 21:2 For Sarah conceived, and bare Abraham a son in his old age, at the <u>set time</u> of which God had spoken to him.>]

VS13 I saw in the night visions, [The expression night vision relates to Gentile times. <John 9:4 I must work the works of him that sent me, while it is day: the night cometh, when no man can work.> This vision takes us to that time. Christ has ascended to heaven and a shroud of gloom encompasses the earth.] **and, behold, one like the Son of man** [This is a title of the Lord Jesus Christ as Judge. <John 5:25 Verily, verily, I say unto you, The hour is coming, and now is, when the dead shall hear the voice of the Son of God: and they that hear shall live. 26 For as the Father hath life in himself; so hath he given

to the Son to have life in himself; 27 And hath given him authority to execute judgment also, because he is the Son of man.> Christ was the son of Adam and inherited those weaknesses, but overcame them triumphantly.] **came with the clouds of heaven,** [These clouds are the "heavens" that rule,<Dan 4:26 And whereas they commanded to leave the stump of the tree roots; thy kingdom shall be sure unto thee, after that thou shalt have known that the heavens do rule.> the angelic hosts that minister for the benefit of the saints. <Heb 1:14 Are they not all ministering spirits, sent forth to minister for them who shall be heirs of salvation?>

When Christ left the earth the Apostles saw a cloud, "receive him out of their sight." He did not disappear into a cloud, it received him. That cloud is identical with this one that now conducts the son of man into the presence of the Ancient of Days. This cloud doubtless contained Gabriel, Michael and others including the one who was sent to strengthen the Lord in Gethsemane. Reference to this joyous company of rejoicing angels is made in Hebrews. <Heb 12:22 But ye are come unto mount Sion, and unto the city of the living God, the heavenly Jerusalem, and to an innumerable company of angels,> Now, they triumphantly convey the resurrected and glorified Son into the presence of the great Increate the Father in heaven.] **and came to the Ancient of days,** [A title of Yahweh relating to His purpose with the earth, as noted in verse 9. Can the father and the Son have the same Title? Yes n terms of God manifestation. It is Yahweh who will reign on earth. <Zech 14:9 And the LORD shall be king over all the earth: in that day shall there be one LORD, and his name one.>

But not Yahweh personally whom no man hath seen or can see, but Yahweh in manifestation in both Christ and the Glorified saints. <Rom 5:2 By whom also we have access by faith into this grace wherein we stand, and rejoice in hope of the glory of God.> <2 Peter 1:4 Whereby are given unto us exceeding great and precious promises: that by these ye might be partakers of the divine nature, having escaped the corruption that is in the world through lust.> <Rev 3:12 Him that overcometh will I make a pillar in the temple of my God, and he shall go no more out: and I will write upon him the name of my God, and the name of the city of my God, which is new Jerusalem, which cometh down out of heaven from my God: and I will write upon him my new name.>

Here Ancient of Days is revealed in three particulars. First as Judge of the earth (vs.9). Second as Yahweh enthroned in heaven (vs. 13). Third as Christ returned to the earth. (vs. 22). In order of events they should be second, third first reference. Divine method is to reveal the final picture first.

Accordingly Isaiah first describes the Kingdom and then the events leading to its consummation. <Isa 2:2 And it shall come to pass in the last days, that the mountain of the LORD's house shall be established in the top of the mountains, and shall be exalted above the hills; and all nations shall flow unto it. 3 And many people shall go and say, Come ye, and let us go up to the mountain of the LORD, to the house of the God of Jacob; and he will teach us of his ways, and we will walk in his paths: for out of Zion shall go forth the law, and the word of the LORD from Jerusalem. 4 And he shall judge among the nations, and shall rebuke many people: and they shall beat their swords into plowshares, and their spears into pruninghooks: nation shall not lift up sword against nation, neither shall they learn war any more.>

In Rev. 11:15 the coming dominion of Christ is set forth and then in vs. 18 the manner in which it is to be brought about. This is a principle of prophetic revelation teaching an important fact: that to please God and successfully overcome the flesh, the saints must keep their eyes on the ultimate result. So heaven is taken to the presence of the Father. Yahweh's throne is set above the heavens in glory so grand and dazzling to be beyond the ability of human eyes to behold or the mind of man to comprehend. Into this august presence, the Son of Man is conveyed.] **and they brought him near before Him.** [The beloved son in whom He is well pleased is brought before his Father.]

VS14 And there was given him dominion, [Before ascending into heaven the Lord explained to the Apostles that all power is given to him in heaven in earth and Peter later confirmed it. <Matt 28:18 And Jesus came and spake unto them, saying, All power is given unto me in heaven and in earth.> <1 Peter 3:22 Who is gone into heaven, and is on the right hand of God; angels and authorities and powers being made subject unto him.>

A complete Revelation was given him on his ascension into heaven. <Rev 1:1 The Revelation of Jesus Christ, which God gave unto him, to

shew unto his servants things which must shortly come to pass; and he sent and signified it by his angel unto his servant John:> The destiny of the nations is now under his control. In the Apocalypse, some of the angels are depicted as performing the bidding of the Lord. Some were sent to John in Patmos to supervise the giving of the Apocalypse as seen in the reference above, and others under the direction of the Son have played a part in the development of the Divine purpose through Gentile times. For example: <Rev 7:1 And after these things I saw four angels standing on the four corners of the earth, holding the four winds of the earth, that the wind should not blow on the earth, nor on the sea, nor on any tree.> When the Lord returns the saints will be made equal to angels not merely in status but nature as well. <Luke 20:36 Neither can they die any more: for they are equal unto the angels; and are the children of God, being the children of the resurrection.> This new race of angelic being will take over the supervision of the nations during the Millennium. <Heb 2:5 For unto the angels hath he not put in subjection the world to come, whereof we speak.>

And, they will constitute the cloud of witnesses who accompany the Son of Man as he takes over his great power and reigns. <Rev 1:7 Behold, he cometh with clouds; and every eye shall see him, and they also which pierced him: and all kindreds of the earth shall wail because of him. Even so, Amen.>

The world will see Matthew's words confirmed. <Matt 24:30 And then shall appear the sign of the Son of man in heaven: and then shall all the tribes of the earth mourn, and they shall see the Son of man coming in the clouds of heaven with power and great glory.> These clouds of heaven will be the saints for with the return of the Lord to the earth, Heaven's rule will be extended to earth that Yahweh's will may be done on earth as it is in heaven.] **and glory, and a kingdom, that all people, nations, and languages, should serve him:** [The word people should be peoples, for it relates to the ethnic groups of humanity. The expressions uses are frequently found in The Apocalypse. Saints are taken out of such and ultimately will be sent back to rule and educate them. <Rev 5:9 And they sung a new song, saying, Thou art worthy to take the book, and to open the seals thereof: for thou wast slain, and hast redeemed us to God by thy blood out of every kindred, and tongue, and people, and nation; 10 And hast made us unto our God kings and priests: and we shall reign on the earth.> <Rev 10:11 And

he said unto me, Thou must prophesy again before many peoples, and nations, and tongues, and kings.>] **his dominion is an everlasting dominion, which shall not pass away, and his kingdom that which shall not be destroyed.** [This is indeed a kingdom without end, but it will undergo evolutionary changes. For a millennium the saints will rule the mortals of the earth. At the end of that epoch, when every enemy has been destroyed including isn and death, the perfected kingdom will be delivered up to the father with "the Son also himself subject unto Him that put all things under him that God may be all in all. <1 Cor 15:28 And when all things shall be subdued unto him, then shall the Son also himself be subject unto him that put all things under him, that God may be all in all.>]

VS15 I Daniel was grieved in my spirit in the midst of my body, [The body is the house for the spirit. Daniel was grieved by his inability to understand.] **and the visions of my head troubled me.** [The head is the seat of intelligence. Daniel's eyes had seen the vision, and conveyed them to the brain, but though he had pondered over them he had failed to ascertain their significance. This deeply concerned and troubled him.]

VS16 I came near unto one of them that stood by, [Angels were present to supervise the vision, as other prophets have experienced. <Zech 4:3 And two olive trees by it, one upon the right side of the bowl, and the other upon the left side thereof. 4 So I answered and spake to the angel that talked with me, saying, What are these, my lord? 5 Then the angel that talked with me answered and said unto me, Knowest thou not what these be? And I said, No, my lord.> <Rev 7:13 And one of the elders answered, saying unto me, What are these which are arrayed in white robes? and whence came they?> Daniel approached one of them for assistance.] **and asked him the truth of all this.** [James 1:5 If any of you lack wisdom, let him ask of God, that giveth to all men liberally, and upbraideth not; and it shall be given him. 6 But let him ask in faith, nothing wavering. For he that wavereth is like a wave of the sea driven with the wind and tossed.>

Merely to read the word is not enough. Understanding is also needed. <Rev 1:3 Blessed is he that readeth, and they that hear the words of this prophecy, and keep those things which are written therein: for

the time is at hand.> <Col 1:10 That ye might walk worthy of the Lord unto all pleasing, being fruitful in every good work, and increasing in the knowledge of God;>] **So he told me, and made me know the interpretation of the things.** [The angel explained the meaning of the symbols. It is hardly likely that the exposition was limited to the brief outline of the following verses, but enough is found there to excite the mind to search the Scriptures" to obtain a better understand of a vision so important to Daniel until the key was granted him.]

VS17 These great beasts, which are four, are four kings, [This reference is to the four dynasties or dominions that would succeed one another.] **which shall arise out of the earth.** [In vs. 3 they arise from the "sea" a reference to the Mediterranean, and a symbol of turbulent nations. <Isa 57:20 But, the wicked are like the troubled sea, when it cannot rest, whose waters cast up mire and dirt.> Here they arise out of the earth to signify the earthly nature of their rule and the extension of their influence. Arising out of the sea, they laid claim to the whole earth and particularly that portion of the globe around the Mediterranean Sea.]

VS18 But the saints of the most High shall take the kingdom, [The singular noun indicates the four kingdoms of the beast are now one. They are all part of the kingdom of flesh and it matters not who controls it. The most High usually refers to Yahweh the possessor of heaven and earth <Gen 14:18 And Melchizedek king of Salem brought forth bread and wine: and he was the priest of the most high God. 19 And he blessed him, and said, Blessed be Abram of the most high God, possessor of heaven and earth:> and therefore the great Disposer of nations. <Acts 17:26 And hath made of one blood all nations of men for to dwell on all the face of the earth, and hath determined the times before appointed, and the bounds of their habitation;> The term most High in this verse and in vv. 22 and 25 is in the pleural, High Ones. In the 7th of Daniel there are three parties associated together in executing judgment upon the Beasts-the High Ones, the holy ones and the people of the holy ones.

The holy ones are the saints, and the High Ones are termed Most High in the singular. The word saint signifies a holy one but it has been misapplied by the Gentiles. In the original Chaldee, the word is elyonin and is not accidental. It occurs 4 times in the same chapter which supply the reason of the expression in the introduction of the Ancient of Days and the High Ones to whom the holy ones belong.

The saints of the most high can be rendered the holy ones of the High Ones, those High Ones being the Ancient of Days and one like unto the Son of Man. Associate with them though in a subordinate position in relation to the dominion granted are the angles of heaven over whom Yahweh has set his throne.

They all comprise the portion of the "heavens that rule." The drama of history since the days of Babylon can be summarized in this brief statement of the angel. The saints shall take the Kingdom. Time may appear long to mortals but not to Ancient of Days. When the saints are clothed upon with immortality the 6000 years of human rule will appear as but a brief moment of time in comparison with eternity.

The term saint however is not limited to those who are called to immortality. In this chapter the term issued for various groups both mortal vs. 21 and immortal vs. 27. Israel the holy nation will comprise the first dominion of the universal real of Christ. <Mic 4:8 And thou, O tower of the flock, the strong hold of the daughter of Zion, unto thee shall it come, even the first dominion; the kingdom shall come to the daughter of Jerusalem> and as such will occupy a dominant position among the nations while the glorified saints are the King-priests of the age to come. <Rev 2:26 And he that overcometh, and keepeth my works unto the end, to him will I give power over the nations: 27 And he shall rule them with a rod of iron; as the vessels of a potter shall they be broken to shivers: even as I received of my Father.> <Rev 5:9And they sung a new song, saying, Thou art worthy to take the book, and to open the seals thereof: for thou wast slain, and hast redeemed us to God by thy blood out of every kindred, and tongue, and people, and nation; 10 And hast made us unto our God kings and priests: and we shall reign on the earth.>] **and possess the kingdom for ever,** [The Chaldean word for possess is *chasan* and means not only to occupy but to control the wealth and power of the subject as well. Ever is Chaldean *olam* meaning hidden period. That is the millennium. The saints will possess the kingdom for 1000 years, after which the priesthood will no longer be necessary.] **even for ever and ever.** [This is translated by Rotherham age for age of ages. The Millennium, though an age in itself will be divided into epochs even as the Mosaic age. It will in its completeness comprise the age of the ages since creation after which it shall merge into Ad or eternity.]

VS19 Then I would know the truth of the fourth beast, which was diverse from all the others, exceeding dreadful, [The beast was so hideous in appearance so frightening in its brutality as to cause him to shrink back in fear to be so affected as to almost immobilize him, causing him to crawl away. This doubtless was due to its hideous appearance and its violent persecution of the saints, as subsequent verses describe.] **whose teeth were of iron, and his nails of brass;** [The Roman and Greek elements of iron and brass from Nebuchadnezzar's image are here. This shows that though they claim to be Christian they remain Babylonian in character. Here the fourth beast is linked to this same symbolism. It describes the divided state of the 4th beast militarily and ecclesiastically.

Militarily the division between West and East was initially established in Rome by Constantine who subsequently centered it in Constantinople while Rome remained the religious headquarters. This led to the West and East division of the empire.

The former was overthrown by the Goths in AD 476 and the latter by the Ottoman power in 1453. The Empire was also divided Ecclesiastically between Rome and Constantinople.

From the establishment of so-called Christianity as a State religion for many years there was great rivalry between the bishops of Rome and Constantinople. This was ultimately decided in favor of Rome by the decree of Justinian and later confirmed by Phocas. A semblance of unity then existed in the church which acknowledged the supremacy of the Pope. However, controversy developed over the use of images, Rome endorsing them and Constantinople opposing the practice. In 869 following the 8th Ecumenical Council the great Schism took place.

Constantinople and its supporters served connection with Rome and established the Greek Orthodox Church. Now there were two churches in apostasy, Roman Catholicism and Greek Orthodoxy. The former continued in Rome and the latter in Constantinople.

When the Moslems offered them the Koran or the sword the Patriarch of Constantinople fled to Moscow where the church had significant influence. Moscow was called the third Rome. The religion of both remained forms of Babylonian idolatry formed in the pagan roots of that city.

What is particularly significant about the next vision shown to Daniel is that the Fourth Beast, as Daniel beheld it, represents its state on the eve of the judgment to be administered to it by the Burning Flame. In other words there must be a revival of that beast as it existed in the past a union of the military religious and political powers.]

which devoured, brake in pieces, and stamped the residue with his feet; [Three times similar statements are made in this chapter vv.7, 23. Moreover the attention of Daniel was drawn to this aspect of the Beast before he directed his attention to the horns, suggesting that the treading down was a dominant aspect of the latter-day prophecy.

The significance of this action is emphasized by the nature of the feet of the Beast for they are the feat of a bear. <Rev 13:2 And the beast which I saw was like unto a leopard, and his feet were as the feet of a bear, and his mouth as the mouth of a lion: and the dragon gave him his power, and his seat, and great authority.> the latter day symbol of Russia.

However as Daniel was shown, it will accomplish its purpose not only by ruthless aggression but also by peace. <Dan 8:25 And through his policy also he shall cause craft to prosper in his hand; and he shall magnify himself in his heart, and by peace shall destroy many: he shall also stand up against the Prince of princes; but he shall be broken without hand.> As yet the brass and iron are not part of the Beast, but they will be.]

VS20 And of the ten horns that were in his head, and of the other which came up, and before whom three fell; [See notes v. 8] **even of that horn that had eyes, and a mouth that spake very great things,** [It was speaking wicked words with great authority.] **whose look was more stout than his fellows.** [This horn commenced as a little horn but grew to exceed it fellows in arrogance and power. <2 Thess 2:4 Who opposeth and exalteth himself above all that is called God, or that is worshipped; so that he as God sitteth in the temple of God, shewing himself that he is God.> The pretensions of the Pope, the title claimed by him as Vicar of God on Earth, and the absolute power granted him over the worship of millions are illustrations of this.]

VS21 I beheld, and the same horn made war with the saints, and prevailed against them; [John describes a similar vision in Revelation. <Rev 13:4 And they worshipped the dragon which gave power unto the beast: and they worshipped the beast, saying, Who is like unto the beast? who is able to make war with him? 5 And there was given unto him a mouth speaking great things and blasphemies; and power was given unto him to continue forty and two months. 6 And he opened his mouth in blasphemy against God, to blaspheme his name, and his tabernacle, and them that dwell in heaven. 7 And it was given unto him to make war with the saints, and to overcome them: and power was given him over all kindreds, and tongues, and nations. 8 And all that dwell upon the earth shall worship him, whose names are not written in the book of life of the Lamb slain from the foundation of the world.>

The 11th chapter describes this warfare in greater detail with the saints represented as two olive trees and two lamp stands. <Rev 11:4 These are the two olive trees, and the two candlesticks standing before the God of the earth.> The god of the earth denoting the Papacy against whom the two witnesses stand and oppose is contrasted with the God of heaven. These witnesses are not the saints but those who stand before or oppose the god of the earth, as shown by their readiness to go to war with the Papacy. <Rev 11:5 And if any man will hurt them, fire proceedeth out of their mouth, and devoureth their enemies: and if any man will hurt them, he must in this manner be killed.>

According to John Thomas, there are three groups embodied in the witness symbol, the protestants or religious opposition to tyranny, Communism or political opposition to tyranny and a third class so small as to be ignored by the prophecy of Revelation 11. These are the remnant, the true brethren of Christ.

Apocalyptically these are represented as "the earth" politically, "the woman" ecclesiastically, "the remnant" or true brethren of Christ. <Rev 12:16 And the earth helped the woman, and the earth opened her mouth, and swallowed up the flood which the dragon cast out of his mouth. 17 And the dragon was wroth with the woman, and went to make war with the remnant of her seed, which keep the commandments of God, and have the testimony of Jesus Christ.>

Because the two witnesses, though not of the remnant, allowed the true remnant to survive by their actions, they can be called "saints" in the same terminology as the bloodthirsty Medes were God's "sanctified ones or saints" as they poured out Divine judgment on Babylon. Isaiah speaking of the Medes states: <Isa 13:3 I have commanded my sanctified ones, I have also called my mighty ones for mine anger, even them that rejoice in my highness.>

Thus the saints in this verse are the two witnesses who vigorously and militarily opposed the Papacy. The word prevailed suggests mutual warfare, likewise described in Revelation 11 in which success attended the arms of the Catholics. But the time came when as the prophecy states when their testimony would be finished. <Rev 11:7 And when they shall have finished their testimony, the beast that ascendeth out of the bottomless pit shall make war against them, and shall overcome them, and kill them.>

When the doctrine of the remnant became compromised, and they compromised with the world in teaching and in practice, the beast was allowed to overcome and destroy them. Yet, within that remnant was a small kernel of those with the truth.>]

VS22 Until the Ancient of days came, [The Ancient of Days is God manifestation of the Father and the son, but not in the Trinitarian sense. Yahweh's purpose is to manifest Himself in a multitude upon whom he will bestow His name. <Rom 5:2 By whom also we have access by faith into this grace wherein we stand, and rejoice in hope of the glory of God.> <2 Peter 1:4 Whereby are given unto us exceeding great and precious promises: that by these ye might be partakers of the divine nature, having escaped the corruption that is in the world through lust.> <Rev 3:12 Him that overcometh will I make a pillar in the temple of my God, and he shall go no more out: and I will write upon him the name of my God, and the name of the city of my God, which is new Jerusalem, which cometh down out of heaven from my God: and I will write upon him my new name.>

Now consider Zechariah's words.< Zech 14:9 And the LORD shall be king over all the earth: in that day shall there be one LORD, and his name one.> In this verse one is from *echad* which Strong states is one in a multitude, or to be at one, or united. Yahweh will be manifest in a large community of immortals who will be one with Him and with each other and who will rule on His behalf on the earth. All titles and terms of Christ being form old, from everlasting such as Micah states for example <Mic 5:2 But thou, Bethlehem Ephratah, though thou be little among the thousands of Judah, yet out of thee shall he come forth unto me that is to be ruler in Israel; whose goings forth have been from of old, from everlasting.> is a symbol of God manifestation and not Trinitarianism.

Christ himself told us the truth of this. <Matt 16:27 For the Son of man shall come in the glory of his Father with his angels; and then he shall reward every man according to his works.> <1 Tim 6:15 Which in his times he shall shew, who is the blessed and only Potentate, the King of kings, and Lord of lords; 16 Who only hath immortality, dwelling in the light which no man can approach unto; whom no man hath seen, nor can see: to whom be honour and power everlasting. Amen.>] **and judgment was given to the saints of the most High;** [A repeat of the title used in verse 18-see notes. After being judged,< 1 Peter 4:17 For the time is come that judgment must begin at the house of God: and if it first begin at us, what shall the end be of them that obey not the gospel of God?> the immortal saints will execute God's judgment on the world.] **and the time came that the saints possessed the kingdom.** [The Lord will come at the appointed time. Subsequently, Daniel was given time periods to mark of the chronologically the epochs of the Time of the End.]

VS23 Thus he said, The fourth beast shall be the fourth kingdom upon earth, [From the explanation it surely is obvious that the four beats represent four kingdoms or empires and thus match the four metals of the Image seen by Nebuchadnezzar in chapter 2.] **which shall be diverse from all kingdoms,** [The Fourth Beast in its final or latter-day manifestation is said to be diverse or different form the others being a confederacy of nations represented by ten horns.] **and shall devour the whole earth, and shall tread it down, and break it in pieces.** [The Roman Empire developed into a world-power far more extensive than those of earlier history. It was far more ruthless, brutal and tyrannical than those that went before it. Concerning the iron power of Rome, Daniel told Nebuchadnezzar, <Dan 2:40 And the fourth kingdom shall be strong as iron: forasmuch as iron breaketh in picces and subdueth all things: and as iron that breaketh all these, shall it break in pieces and bruise.>]

VS24 And the ten horns out of this kingdom are ten kings that shall arise: [These are the kingdoms that rose on the ashes of Rome and there was no time in history when they were all there at the same time. The prophecy does not require that, merely that it be divided up by ten nations. Ten has the spiritual significance of completeness and as such can apply to the complete division of the Roman Empire. Political Rome was completely overthrown as to leave no part of it remaining.] **and another shall rise after them;** [This is identified as the Holy Roman Empire that is after the manifestation of the 10 horns. In Revelation, the horns are identified in two states. First as dominated by crowned heads, and second as ruling in their own right and so depicted as crowned. <Rev 12:3 And there appeared another wonder in heaven; and behold a great red dragon, having seven heads and ten horns, and seven crowns upon his heads.> <Rev 13:1 And I stood upon the sand of the sea, and saw a beast rise up out of the sea, having seven heads and ten horns, and upon his horns ten crowns, and upon his heads the name of blasphemy.>

The first symbol represents the united Empire extended over Europe having subject nations in complete domination. The second symbol is Europe divided into several nations having thrown off the political domination of Rome, but linked with it by religion. Out of that state arose Germanic power known to history as the Holy Roman Empire.] **and he shall be diverse from the first,** [This repeats vs. 23 suggesting that the horn power is Roman in character but different from the first pagan manifestation of the Four Beast. And different it was.] **and he shall subdue three kings.** [See notes vs. 8. This horn was little at first, vs. 8, but assumed great power after the ten horns obtained their independence answering exactly to the rise of the Holy Roman Empire.]

VS25 And he shall speak great words against the most High, [Against here is from the Chaldean *letsad* from a root meaning to sidle off, diverge or at the side of. The idea is that he would speak words concerning the most High, which would be a divergence form the Truth, but would be designed to place the speaker deceptively alongside the most High.

This is exactly what the Papacy does. Papal Rome does not openly oppose God as Pagan Rome did. And, in that regard it is diverse from

Paganism. But, it does claim to be in place of God, by His side, though its divergence from the truth is only apparent to "saints of the most High." <2 Thess 2:3 Let no man deceive you by any means: for that day shall not come, except there come a falling away first, and that man of sin be revealed, the son of perdition; 4 Who opposeth and exalteth himself above all that is called God, or that is worshipped; so that he as God sitteth in the temple of God, shewing himself that he is God.>

The titles that Catholicism heaps on the Pope, his claims though his Priests to forgive sins, the so-called infallibility of his utterances, are some of the "great words" spoken in the name of God, but which, while seeming to place the Pope at the side of God are destructive to His truth.

The Title Most High in this verse is different from v. 18. Here it is in the singular, *Illay,* the Lofty One from *alah* to ascend, be high, supreme. The reference is to Yahweh Himself: the Pope being elevated on behalf of the Supreme Deity.]

and shall wear out the saints of the most High, [The original for wear out carries the connotation of mental stress or wearing out. The true saints were more affected by the teaching and pressure of Rome than actual persecution. The constant witnessing wore out the true saints. They became tired of the unpleasant separation the truth demanded of them, and the stigma attached to the peculiar restraint they had to observe and the doctrines they had to maintain. Slowly, their Christian virtue became too easy and tolerant of the traditions apostasy, until at length their individuality converged toward and was finally lost in the indefiniteness and confusion of the Lutheran and Calvin movements of the 16th century.

This fatal termination of their labors is in the prophecy of Revelation. <Rev 11:7 And when they shall have finished their testimony, the beast that ascendeth out of the bottomless pit shall make war against them, and shall overcome them, and kill them.>

The opposition of Rome gradually silenced the voice of Truth and the Dark Ages settled over Europe. This continued until the French Revolution snapped the shackles of Rome and the witnesses arose again to the power. With the revival of political agitation and of Protestantism there was manifested an increasing interest in the Bible, which ultimately led the way to the restoration of the Truth.]

and think to change times and laws: [Yahweh alone does this.

2:21And he changeth the times and the seasons: he removeth kings, and setteth up kings: he giveth wisdom unto the wise, and knowledge to them that know understanding: <Acts 17:26 And hath made of one blood all nations of men for to dwell on all the face of the earth, and hath determined the times before appointed, and the bounds of their habitation; > But Catholicism has arrogated to itself the Divine right to change the course of history. The Pope has the power to change the laws of the church at his discretion.] **and they shall be given into his hand** [The Catholic little horn had temporary success against the saints of the Most High. This came to a head with the massacre of St Bartholomew in 1572, 1260 years after the triumph of Constantine in 312, when every brutal attempt by Rome to silence all opposition to Catholicism. The forces of the state were used to kill their adversaries and this they did by the thousands. Every form of cruel and vicious torture was used to force the Jews and Protestants to recant.

Why did Yahweh allow this? Because, the Truth had been polluted, as described earlier. The prophecy give to Daniel as well as that revealed to John in Patmos placed a time limit on the triumph of the western horn of the beast.] **until a time and times and the dividing of time.** [The word time denotes a set time technically a year which is the obvious appointed division of time whether it be lunar and solar. The phrase, therefore, represents 3.5 years which according to a Jewish year of 360 days representing 1260 days and on the day for a year principle outlined before, 11260 years. This is the period allocated by the little horn of the west to wear out the saints.

How does it conform with history? Exactly. There are several important key-years in which vital decrees gradually increased Papal power, but which exactly 1260 years later introduced events that dramatically contributed to its decline.

For example:**AD 529-533** Justinian, Emperor of Constantinople proclaimed legislation which supported building up and strengthening the Catholic Church. In it he proclaimed the Bishop of Rome the Universal Bishop. 1260 years later, 1789-93 the National Assembly of Revolutionary France passed legislation directed to the destruction of Catholic power. Note the following all 1260 years apart. **539** Ravenna, Italy is conquered by Justinian and Papal authority installed there, increasing its power considerably. In 1799 the wars of Napoleon against the Papal countries of Europe reduced the Church's influence.

549-554 Justinian's Progmatic Sanction (a Byzantinc term signifying a public decree) decreed that Rome which had been freed by his forces from Anti-Papal Gothic domination was to be placed under the authority of the Pope. The Pope was granted control of the Municipal and Provincial government which greatly enhanced Papal influence and power throughout Italy.

In 1809, Napoleon amended the Papal status and continued to devastate Catholic Europe until 1814 when he was finally defeated.
590 Gregory 1ˢᵗ is elected Pope and his political skill opened a new era of grater influence for the Papacy.

In 1850 under Pope Pius IX the authority of the Papacy came under threat. In 1846 four years earlier, with revolution fermenting in Europe, Cardinal Mastai became Pius IX. In spite of his liberal policy he was opposed by the revolutionaries of Italy. He sought for the Church the official endorsement of the papal claim of infallibility of the Pope. This was refused and instead a Committee of Public Safety in Italy demanded among other things the abolition of Papal temporal power the appointment of Rome as the capital of an all-Italian republic instead of the centre of Papal power and the convocation there of an all-Italian Constituent Assembly.

This the Pope rejected out of hand in consequence of which he was besieged in Quirinal (his palace in Rome) by menacing crowds of armed men. Firing broke out and a bishop in his entourage was killed. Only the presence of a few members of the diplomatic corps saved the Pope himself from physical violence. (see *The Keeper of The Keys* p. 260).

In 1850, 1260 years from the accession of Gregory, church influence was weakened by a devastating challenge form the civil government of Italy. In the midst of this political upheaval and the French Revolution, (the resurrected witness mentioned earlier and the "unclean spirits as of frogs" <Rev 16:13 And I saw three unclean spirits like frogs come out of the mouth of the dragon, and out of the mouth of the beast, and out of the mouth of the false prophet. 14 For they are the spirits of devils, working miracles, which go forth unto the kings of the earth and of the whole world, to gather them to the battle of that great day of God Almighty.> the Pope made strenuous efforts to preserve the ecclesiastical influence of the Papacy as well as the temporal power. In regard to the first, he prepared *A Syllabus of modern Errors and False*

Doctrines to be condemned and refuted as well as a request for church endorsement of Papal infallibility.

In regard to the second, he ordered military intervention to enforce his temporal power over those portions of Italy remaining under political power. Napoleon III put his army at the service of the Pope in support of his temporal power. Prior to 1870 the Pope exercised temporal power that is in addition to his ecclesiastical power he possessed civil authority as a secular king does over the Papal States of Italy. As a token of this, the Popes wore a three-tiered crown or miter which indicated their regal authority over the three Papal States of Italy. He maintained an army that fought at his bidding.

This allowed the Pope to have diplomatic relations on equal terms with other nations. This power had been granted to the Pope by Pepin and Charlemagne when the three horns had been broken off as predicted by Daniel. This allowed the little horn of the Papacy to grow to a powerful horn dominating the beast and exercising international representation.

In the days of Pius, Rome was the capital of Papacy but not Italy, then divided into several different nationalities. The wars of Napoleon had weakened the Pope's influence in that regard and even after he had been deposed the spirit of revolution swept Italy as it had Europe, eroded Papal influence further. The chief revolutionary was Garibaldi and he agitated for a united Italy which was only possible by the overthrow of the Pope's sovereignty in the Papal States and the establishment of Rome as the national capital.

Garibaldi and his associates gradually eroded papal sovereignty in those States until the Pope's control was limited to Rome and its immediate surroundings. Garibaldi was determined to wrest Rome from the Pope and ordered an attack on the city. It was repulsed with the help of French troops. But the decline was well on the way after the 1260 years predicted in the prophecy.

600 Gregory the Great was at his zenith. He overthrew the influence of Arianism in Lombardy and insisted the Apostolic See was head of all the churches. He never lost sight of the aim of establishing the papacy as the head of the universal church. The Emperor in Constantinople and Justinian in particular had decreed that "nothing shall be done in the church against the command and will of the Empror." Gregory tried to set that aside and almost succeeded before his death in 604.

1260 years later, Garibaldi wrested 2/3 of the Papal states from Papal control.

608-610 Gregory's successors Sabinian (604-606) and Boniface III (607) were so able to manipulate Phocas, then ruling in Constantinople, that he issued a decree proclaiming the Pope, Head of all the Churches. Boniface IV was on the Papal throne then. Shortly thereafter, Phocas was overthrown and put to death by Heraclius who reigned in his stead in 610. In 1868-70 Garibaldi finally occupied Rome making it capitol of united Italy. With the aid of French troops the Pope opposed this but the French troops were withdrawn when the war of 1870 between France and Prussia began. Now lacking any political power, the Pope withdrew into the Vatican where he became, as he called himself, "the prisoner of the Vatican." Though a prisoner in the Vatican, Pius was able to secure the claim of Papal infallibility by a vote of 533 to 2 by the Cardinals.

The vote declared that the Roman Pontiff was infallible when he spoke *ex cathedra* when in exercise of his official duties as pastor and teacher of all Christians he defines by virtue of his supreme apostolic authority doctrines concerniting faith or morals to be held by the universal church.

The overthrow of the Pope's temporal power brought an end to the ability of the church to enforce the Inquisition that began in 1227 and ended with the last known execution of a Cyetano Ripoll who was hanged as an unrepentant diest. It must be pointed out that in South America the tactics of the Inquisition continued for many years. But as far as Europe and the prophecy of Daniel was concerned, the "time, times and dividing of time," terminated with the French Revolution and loss of the temporal power of the Pope in 1970.]

VS26 But the judgment shall sit, [The angelic judges of Daniel 4:17 reconvene but this time with Christ as presiding judge. The decision is reached that it is time for the power of the Pope to end, and it will suffer at the hands of those it previously tormented. The balance of the verse gives the consequences.] **and they shall take away his dominion,** [Who are the they of this verse? In *Elpis Israel*, Thomas identifies them with the saints of this chapter or the two witnesses of Rev. 11. They are the earth and woman of the Apocalypse.] **to consume and to destroy**

it unto the end. [That is from the French Revolution until the time of Christ's return.]

VS27 And the kingdom and dominion, and the greatness of the kingdom under the whole heaven, [This expression denotes world domination and strikes a blow at the heaven-going theory of some religions. Under the whole heavens is where the true saints will spend eternity. < Rev 20:6 Blessed and holy is he that hath part in the first resurrection: on such the second death hath no power, but they shall be priests of God and of Christ, and shall reign with him a thousand years.>] **shall be given to the people of the saints of the most High,** [The people of the saints must be distinguished from the saints. As explained, the saints are those used to oppose the power of the Papacy, just as the Medes and Persians were used against Babylon by Yahweh. The people of the saints are those individuals who are true believers who will inherit the kingdom and are a small portion of the two witnesses. This is the Israel of God. < Gal 6:16 And as many as walk according to this rule, peace be on them, and mercy, and upon the Israel of God.>] **whose kingdom is an everlasting kingdom,** [This again is the Chaldean *alam* which means hidden period. This is the millennium, at the end of which the kingdom will be Yahweh's and He will be All in All.] **and all dominions shall serve and obey him.** [This has not yet happened, but it will at Christ's return. < Ps 102:22 When the people are gathered together, and the kingdoms, to serve the LORD.> Those who refuse will be cut off. < Isa 60:12 For the nation and kingdom that will not serve thee shall perish; yea, those nations shall be utterly wasted.>]

28 Hitherto is the end of the matter. [The angel's statement in the previous verse had ended the vision and its interpretation.] **As for me Daniel, my cogitations much troubled me,** [Daniel thought that the establishment of the Kingdom of God was at hand. < Dan 9:2 In the first year of his reign I Daniel understood by books the number of the years, whereof the word of the LORD came to Jeremiah the prophet, that he would accomplish seventy years in the desolations of Jerusalem.>

This vision described long epochs of suffering and persecution for Yahweh's people. He found that difficult to reconcile with

111

Jeremiah's prophecy. He was saddened and perplexed by it all.] **and my countenance changed in me:** [So deeply did he feel for his people that it mad a physical change in his appearance.]

but I kept the matter in my heart.: [As did Mary at the birth of our Lord.]

CHAPTER 12

Alexander The Goat

Reference to the 4 divisions of Alexander's empire is frequent in Daniel. The Greek leopard is shown having four wings of a fowl. < Dan 7:6 After this I beheld, and lo another, like a leopard, which had upon the back of it four wings of a fowl; the beast had also four heads; and dominion was given to it.>

In the he goat manifestation, the goats main horn is broken and in its place are found, < Dan 8:8 Therefore the he goat waxed very great: and when he was strong, the great horn was broken; and for it came up four notable ones toward the four winds of heaven.>

On the death of the mighty King, four King's appear on the stage of history. < Dan 11:3 And a mighty king shall stand up, that shall rule with great dominion, and do according to his will. 4 And when he shall stand up, his kingdom shall be broken, and shall be divided toward the four winds of heaven; and not to his posterity, nor according to his dominion which he ruled: for his kingdom shall be plucked up, even for others beside those.>

The four-fold division plays a profound part in history and the fulfillment of prophecy. Two are titled the Kings of North and South in Daniel 11. Though suppressed by the ruler of Constantinople, < Dan 11:36 And the king shall do according to his will; and he shall exalt himself, and magnify himself above every god, and shall speak marvelous things against the God of gods, and shall prosper till the indignation be accomplished: for that that is determined shall be done.> they will arise at the time of the end. < Dan 11:40 And at the time of the end shall the king of the south push at him: and the king of the north shall come against him like a whirlwind, with chariots, and with horsemen, and with many ships; and he shall enter into the countries, and shall overflow and pass over.> In this chapter, Daniel predicts a little horn that will absorb all others into its empire. In a latter day manifestation it will stand up against the Prince of princes and ultimately be broken without hands of human agency, and its territory incorporated into the Kingdom of God The historical facts are important and are outlined below.

1. When Alexander the Great died in BC 323, his widow Rosanne was pregnant and the son she bore was named Alexander. Pending the growth of the boy to manhood, an organization of the Empire was agreed upon along the following lines.
2. Philip Aridaeus was titular king, but was murdered a few years later on the order of Olympia Alexander the Great's mother.
3. Perdiccas based in Greece was regent and authorized to manage home affairs. He died a natural death a few years later.
4. Five (and later 6) main "satrapys" under the trusted generals of Alexander's army with full military power governed different sections of the empire.
   a. Ptolemy-Egypt
   b. Antipater-Macedonia and was followed by his son Cassander
   c. Lysimachus-Thrace
   d. Antigonus-Phrygia, later joined by his son Demetrius
   e. Eumenes-Paphlagonia
   f. Seleuchus-Babylonia. He was younger than the others and the last appointed.

Some of the boundaries of influence were ill-defined. To that end, despite trading wives in arranged marriages, border clashes broke out into warfare. Antigonus coveted the whole of Egypt while Ptolemy was reasonably satisfied but kept an eye on Palestine and Syria with a desire to move in that direction.

Antipater, Lysimachus and Eumenes were to close to each other for mutual comfort while Seluchus was isolated far to the east in Babylon and unsure of his position with the others. In BC 315 Antigonus killed Eumenes in battle and assumed his control of all the northeast save Babylon. In 311, Cassander was confirmed in Greece and Macedonia and Roxanne and her son placed in his care. Instead, Cassander killed

Roxanne and her 14 year old son. Now there were five satraps and no overall control

1. Ptolomy-Egypt
2. Cassander-Macedonia and Greece
3. Lysimachus-Thrace
4. Antigonus and Demetrius—Asia Minor, Phrygia, Syria
5. Seleuchus-Babylonia and east to the river Indus.

In 301 BC a great battle was fought at Ipsus in Phrygia between Antigonius and Demetrius on one side and Cassander, Lysimachus and Seleuchus on the other. Ptolomy gave material aid to these three but failed to join the battle physically. Antigonius was killed in battle and Demetrius fled. Now there were four Satraps.

1. Ptolomy-Egypt. He gained control over Palesine but mist out on Syria which went to Secleuchus. He died in peace in 285 BC and his successors styled Kings of the South by Daniel ruled until BC 30 when Rome conquered Egypt.
2. Cassander-a tenuous hold on Macedonia and Greece. He died in 297 BC and the Romans took control in 168 BC
3. Lysimachus-Thrace, Asia Minor, Pergamum. He died in battle in 281 BC. Pergamum was bequeathed to Rome in 133 BC and from it came the little horn of Daniel 8:9
4. Seleuchus-Phoenicia, Syria, Babylon to the Indus. The Western Section fell to Rome in 65 BC. The title given to him and his successors is King of the North by Daniel.

The prophecy of Daniel 11 relates principally to the struggles and intrigues between the Ptolemaic and Seleucidae dynasties as they concern the Eastern Mediterranean counties of Palestine and Syria. The time of the end section of that chapter, vv. 40-45, requires the reemergence of a king of north and south in the latter days. The political divisions of the Middle East during recent times have vindicated Daniel's prophecy and continue to do so.

VS1 In the third year of the reign of king Belshazzar [Belshazzar was appointed co-regent in the 3rd year of the reign of Nabonidus about 533 BC and continued in some capacity till the fall of Babylon in 539. Nabonidus was away a great deal of his reign and Belshazzar had sole control. The city and Empire was overwhelmed by the Medes, the ram of this chapter. This prophecy was issued in the time of rapid Babylonian decline.] **a vision appeared unto me, even unto me Daniel, after that which appeared unto me at the first.** [Daniel links the vision of chapters 7 & 8 by his reference to "the first." The second vision of this chapter foreshadows the rise of the eastern Roman Empire just as 7 did for the western section. Both describe the rise of the little horn, Chapter 7 as ecclesiastical and 8 as military. The former was in Rome, the latter in Constantinople.]

VS2 And I saw in a vision; and it came to pass, when I saw, that I was at Shushan [Although still in Babylon, in the vision he saw himself in Shushan, the palace of the Medo-Persians. This signifies the defeat of Babylon by the Medeo-Persians and that they would honor Daniel after the conquest. Shushan means lily for the abundance of them that grown there. It was the seat of Persian rule. <Neh 1:1 The words of Nehemiah the son of Hachaliah. And it came to pass in the month Chisleu, in the twentieth year, as I was in Shushan the palace,> <Est 1:2 That in those days, when the king Ahasuerus sat on the throne of his kingdom, which was in Shushan the palace,>

The mound there was excavated and the famous Code of Hammurabi, identified by some experts as the Amraphel of Genesis. <Gen 14:1 And it came to pass in the days of Amraphel king of Shinar, Arioch king of Ellasar, Chedorlaomer king of Elam, and Tidal king of nations;> and if so was a contemporary of Abraham. His Code is the earliest known record of a set of coded laws and the similarity of it in some respects to Mosaic Law that it has caused some scholars to suggest the Mosaic Law was based on it. But, Divine law existed well before this. <Gen 26:5 Because that Abraham obeyed my voice, and kept my charge, my commandments, my statutes, and my laws.> More than likely, Hammurabi borrowed these laws from Abraham. The Palace of Shushan was a winter residence of Persian kings. It was a large, beautiful structure. Susa became a part of the Achaemenid (Persian) Empire when Cyrus took Babylon and its Provinces.] **in the palace, which is in the**

province of Elam; [Palace is *biyrah* or fortress or fortified castle. Elam was the name of region in East Babylon extending to the mountains of Media in the north-east and along the Persian Gulf to the porders of ancient Persis in the south. Persian annexed it in about 600 BC.

The Elamites were the Semites, a name signifying hidden, distant or highland.<Gen 10:22 The children of Shem; Elam, and Asshur, and Arphaxad, and Lud, and Aram.> <1 Chron 1:17 The sons of Shem; Elam, and Asshur, and Arphaxad, and Lud, and Aram, and Uz, and Hul, and Gether, and Meshech.>] **and I saw in a vision,** [This is to emphasize he was still in Babylon and had been transported to these places in the vision.] **and I was by the river of Ulai.** [This comparatively small river divided Shushan into two parts. It is suggested that the current upper Khekhah and low Karum Rivers may have been one stream in ancient time before the dealt at the head of the Persian Gulf was formed. The river appears in reliefs of Ashurbanipal's assult on Susa. It's ancient name was Eulaeus. (Zonderheim's Pictorial Encyclopedia.) The Eulaeus or Ulai was a large artificial canal that connected two rivers known as the Choaspes and Coprates that flowed on the south and east of Susa. Daniel stood by this canal in the spirit when he had this vision.]

VS3 Then I lifted up mine eyes, and saw, and, behold, [Daniel's attention was suddenly drawn to the Ram he proceeds to describe.] **there stood before the river a ram which had two horns:** [There is no doubting the significance of the ram. Daniel was told that it represented the dual power of Medo-Persia (vs.20). It was a very appropriate symbol for it is said that Persian Kings wore crowns shaped like ram's heads, and Persian coins bearing the stamp of a ram have been found. The two horns represent the dual power of the Medes and the Persians.] **and the two horns were high;** [An uplifted horn represents power. <Ps 75:5 Lift not up your horn on high: speak not with a stiff neck. 6 For promotion cometh neither from the east, nor from the west, nor from the south.> The two high horns of the ram represent to the extensive power of the Persian Empire that far exceeded that of Babylon. See Dan. 7:5] **but one was higher than the other,** [At first the Medes were stronger, but in the end the Persians became the longer horn so it became the Persian Empire.] **and the higher came up last.** [From this, Daniel apparently watched the horns grow, and the larger representing the extensive conquests of Cyrus of Persian.] **I saw the ram pushing westward, and northward, and southward;** [The Persians under Cyrus came from the east, the direction predicted by the prophet. In the west, he conquered Babylon, Mesopotamia, Syria and Asia Minor; in the north Colchis, Armenia, Iberia and the region around the Caspians; in the south, his conquests took in Palestine, Egypt, Ethiopia and Libya.] **so that no beasts might stand before him, neither was there any that could deliver out of his hand; but he did according to his will, and became great.** [Cyrus, son of Cambyses founded this empire. By his mother Mandane, he was the grandson of Astyages, king of Media and he married the only child of his uncle Cyaxetes uniting both crowns and kingdoms. Media was the most famous of the two in history at that point. In his conquests, Cyrus extended his empire eastward as well, as far as India, but since that had no effect on the prophecy it is ignored.]

VS5 And as I was considering, [Daniel pondered the meaning of what he saw.] **behold,** [His attention is drawn from the ram to this new figure bursting on the scene representing the suddenness with which Alexander the Great rose to menace the Persians.] **an he goat came from the west** [The goat is an appropriate symbol for Greece and Alexander. Legend has it that Caremus their first king was seeking new habitation in Macedonia when he was directed to follow a herd of goats fleeing a storm and followed them to Edessa and established his city and called it Aegeoe (The Goat's City). The people were called Aegeadoe or Goat's People and the same name the Aiegos (modernized to the Agean sea) was given to the ocean surrounding it. Alexander's son was named Alexander Aegus, Son of the Goat. As Macedonia and Greece are west of Persia and Susa the vision moved the Greeks properly.] **on the face of the whole earth,** [Alexander set his sights on world domination, developing novel military tactics to accomplish that goal.] **and touched not the ground:** [The goat with the notable horn in front moved so swiftly it did not appear to touch the ground.] **and the goat had a notable horn between his eyes.** [Margin renders this horn of sight. It was so prominent it dominated the vision. It represents the first king, (vs.21) Alexander the Great. The swiftness of his conquest is an historic fact. In twelve years he overran the civilized world. It is described in the 1ˢᵗ Book of the Maccabees. (\1 Maccabees\ 1\2 And made many wars, and won many strong holds, and slew the kings of the earth, 3 And went through to the ends of the earth, and took spoils of many nations, insomuch that the earth was quiet before him; whereupon he was exalted and his heart was lifted up. 4 And he gathered a mighty strong host and ruled over countries, and nations, and kings, who became tributaries unto him.) With continuous victories at Granicus 334 BC, Issus 333 BC, Arbela 331 BC and so on, he crushed the mighty Persian Empire. In that short space of time he conquered Syria, Phoenicia, Cyprus, Tyre, Gaza, Egypt, Babylonia, Media, Persia Hyracania and moved into India.]

VS6 And he came to the ram that had two horns, [In 336 BC Alexander was chosen at Corinth to lead the united Greek States against their Persian over-lords. He accepted the challenge with enthusiasm declared war on Persia determined to avenge the suffering of his countrymen by the enemy, and to destroy its power.] **which I had there seen standing before the river,** [The Persians had ruthlessly invaded Greece and enslaved it. Athens was treated particularly cruelly. In 334, Alexander lusted for revenge and brought his army to the Granicus behind which the Persian general waited with an army five times the size of Alexander's.] **and ran unto him in the fury of his power.** [Alexander introduced the phalanx to warfare. A phalanx could be any size and the infantry comprising it were armed with spears 20 feet long. When advancing they moved in a solid mass 8 ranks deep. The front rank held their spears near the point, the second rank somewhat further down the shaft and so on to the last rank so the spear tips of the entire phalanx were in front of the first rank.

If attacked they shifted immediately to a square bristling with spears on all sides. On each side of the phalanx were detachments of archers, infantry with swords and cavalry. Those troops were able to move very fast and it was their duty to flank the enemy army or even attack it from the rear as the phalanx advanced. Alexander crossed the Hellespont (Dardanelles) and confronted the Persians at the Granicus.

The Greeks swam the river, defeated the Persians and drove them back in disarray. This Greek victory in Phrygia in BC 344 was the beginning of the end for Persia]

VS7 And I saw him come close unto the ram, [At Issus on the borders of Asia minor and Syria, Darius III (Commodius) awaited with a huge army. So sure was he of victory he brought his wife and children to watch. He was soundly defeated and members of his family captured. Ignoring favorable peace offerings and reluctant to march on Darius personally, Alexander turned south, thus coming close to the ram. He then turned south, capturing the great Phoenician city of Tyre after a long siege in 322 BC. Then, he invaded Philistia and occupied Egypt, a Persian province since 525 BC where he founded Alexandria in 331.

Then turning north and moving into the heart of Persian Empire. Alexander overran Mesopotamia crossed the Tigrus and outmaneuvered and over-whelmed Darius at Gaugemela (Arbela). The victory allowed him to capture the Persian centers of Babylon, Susa and Persepolis which went down in flames. Darius fled to Media south of the Caspian sea where he was murdered. Alexander assumed the dead man's royal title. Still in his twenties, it was obvious his military skill was unmatchable.] **and he was moved with choler against him,** [Darius tried to bribe Alexander's generals to betray him. This further infuriated Alexander, causing him to refuse all attempts a peace with Darius as Alexander drove relentlessly to destroy him.] **and smote the ram, and brake his two horns:** [Their military power broken by Alexander.] **and there was no power in the ram to stand before him, but he cast him down to the ground, and stamped upon him: and there was none that could deliver the ram out of his hand.** [Persia's power was completely and absolutely broken.]

VS8 Therefore the he goat waxed very great: [He had conquered the known world in only 13 years. Alexander's conquests are the subject of other prophecies. Ezekiel 26 refers not to Nebuchadnezzar personally (v. 7) but to his successors also, including Alexander who set up his headquarters in Babylon, called "they" in vs. 12.

In Zechariah 9 Alexander's attack on Palestine and Gaza is foretold in v. 5. The prophet contrasts Alexander with the lowly King of Israel. <Zech 9:9 Rejoice greatly, O daughter of Zion; shout, O daughter of Jerusalem: behold, thy King cometh unto thee: he is just, and having salvation; lowly, and riding upon an ass, and upon a colt the foal of an ass.> where Alexander is always pictured riding a war horse.

Alexander was capricious and unjust toward anyone who challenged his monumental ego. He executed 10,000 citizens of Gaza and dragged the defeated King behind a chariot to his death to show his contempt for Israel's Messiah King. Indeed, Alexander's temporal power waxed very great.] **and when he was strong, the great horn was broken;** [At the height of his power, Alexander died of a fever seven days after a drunken orgy at age 33.] **and for it came up four notable ones** [His empire was divided among his generals, Lysimachus, Cassander, Ptolemy and Seleuchus. (See discussion at the beginning of the chapter.) The horns of the powers controlling Syria and Egypt that directly affect the Holy Land are the subject of the prophecy in Chapter 11. The future of the Macedonian horn is all but ignored.] **toward the four winds of heaven.** [This figurative expression denotes the civilized world. <Deut 30:4 If any of thine be driven out unto the outmost parts of heaven, from thence will the LORD thy God gather thee, and from thence will he fetch thee:>]

VS9 And out of one of them [The little horn of the goat grew out of one of the four horns that had appeared following the breaking of the notable horn of the previous verses, for it had risen out of the ten horns.] **came forth a little horn,** [The horn is described like that of 7:8 but lacked eyes and a mouth. That denoted the Ecclesiastical. Here it has none because it is military. The two little horns of Daniel's prophecy are thus different aspects of the same power, the east-west divisions of the Roman Empire. This little horn developed out of the principality of Pergamos. Attalus I of Pergamum, BC 241-197, together with Thrace and Byzantium become allied to Rome which drew the growing Empire of that city more directly to the east.

Attalus III bequeathed his Kingdom to Rome which subsequently annexed it. Thus it can be properly claimed therefore that the power of Rome in the east grew out of the little horn of the goat.]

which waxed exceeding great, [Like the other horn, it started small and grew in power, as the Roman Legions gradually became the match for the Greek phalanx.] **toward the south, and toward the east, and toward the pleasant land.** [The south is Egypt and the east is Asia and Persia, while the pleasant land it the land promised to Abraham by Yahweh. Rome's political influence moved into Palestine by invitation, not conquest, but remained there to dominate and govern. Macedonia fell to Rome in BC 148, Achaia (southern Greece) in 146. The last ruler of the Attalid dynasty of Pergamum which had broken from the Seleucids of Syria bequeathed the heavily populated province to Rome.

Pompey's conquests in the east in the 60's BC abolished the Seleucid (Syrian) monarchy. Judea was annexed to heavily populated Syria which Rome used as a buffer against the Parthians across the Euphrates. The lands in this part of Asia looked to Rome for military assistance.

In 40 BC Herod was made king of the Jews but the throne was occupied by Antigonus II last of the Hasmonean (Maccabean) rulers, newly placed there by Rome's enemies, the Parthians. Assisted by his friend Mark Anthony, Herod took Jerusalem in 37 BC and Antigonus was executed by the Romans.

Till his death in AD 4 Herod held the throne by switching allegiance from Anthony to Octavia, later Agustus after the Battle of Actium in BC 31. His authority was always subject to Rome. With Rome in the pleasant land, in the days of the Messiah, Daniel's prophecy was vindicated.]

VS10 And it waxed great, [The military power of Rome took its turn on the world stage.] **even to the host of heaven;** [The host of heaven denotes Israel. <Ex 12:41 And it came to pass at the end of the four hundred and thirty years, even the selfsame day it came to pass, that all the hosts of the LORD went out from the land of Egypt.> <Isa 24:21 And it shall come to pass in that day, that the LORD shall punish the host of the high ones that are on high, and the kings of the earth upon the earth.>

Because of the disobedience of the people, Rome was allowed to triumph over this "host." Rome's attack in AD 70 is described as punishment from Yahweh. <Deut 28:49 The LORD shall bring a nation against thee from far, from the end of the earth, as swift as the eagle flieth; a nation whose tongue thou shalt not understand;>

The Legions are described as His armies sent to administer punishment for transgression. <Matt 22:7 But when the king heard thereof, he was wroth: and he sent forth his armies, and destroyed those murderers, and burned up their city.> Herod, an Idumean and a gentile tool of Rome partly fulfilled the prophetic warning in

Deuteronomy. <Deut 28:43 The stranger that is within thee shall get up above thee very high; and thou shalt come down very low.>] **and it cast down some of the host** [The Jewish Army was no math for the well-trained, Legions of Rome.] **and of the stars to the ground,** [Stars represent the leaders and statesmen of the Jews. <Luke 21:25 And there shall be signs in the sun, and in the moon, and in the stars; and upon the earth distress of nations, with perplexity; the sea and the waves roaring;>Many Jewish leaders were deported to Rome. Even the High Priest appointment was subject to approval from Rome. This grated on the people until they revolted and the temple destroyed in AD 70.] **and stamped upon them.** [The little horn of the goat treated the Jewish authority with utmost contempt.]

VS11 Yea, he magnified himself [This Rome did in its arrogance.] **even to the prince of the host,** [This is the Lord Jesus Christ as King and commander of Israel. <Isa 55:4 Behold, I have given him for a witness to the people, a leader and commander to the people.> <Ezek 21:22 At his right hand was the divination for Jerusalem, to appoint captains, to open the mouth in the slaughter, to lift up the voice with shouting, to appoint battering rams against the gates, to cast a mount, and to build a fort. 23 And it shall be unto them as a false divination in their sight, to them that have sworn oaths: but he will call to remembrance the iniquity, that they may be taken. 24 Therefore thus saith the Lord GOD; Because ye have made your iniquity to be remembered, in that your transgressions are discovered, so that in all your doings your sins do appear; because, I say, that ye are come to remembrance, ye shall be taken with the hand. 25 And thou, profane wicked prince of Israel, whose day is come, when iniquity shall have an end, 26 Thus saith the Lord GOD; Remove the diadem, and take off the crown: this shall not be the same: exalt him that is low, and abase him that is high. 27 I will overturn, overturn, overturn, it: and it shall be no more, until he come whose right it is; and I will give it him.> This title should be compared with vs. 25 where it is changed to Prince of princes (general of generals). Pilate, as Rome's representative did not recognize the Lord's credentials nor his claim as earth's future monarch.] **and by him the daily sacrifice was taken away,** [<Ex 29:38 Now this is that which thou shalt offer upon the altar; two lambs of the first year day by day continually. 39 The one lamb thou shalt offer in the morning; and the

other lamb thou shalt offer at even:> How did Rome take this away? In AD 70 the Roman Legions destroyed the Temple. In this act of Divine Judgment they were acting as the Legions of Yahweh.] **and the place of his sanctuary was cast down.** [Sanctuary is *miqdash*=Holy place or the Temple. The prophecy required the Temple to be destroyed and Jerusalem to be overthrown]

VS12 And an host was given him against the daily sacrifice [Host, *tsaba*, denotes not only an army but a period of warfare or an appointed time. It is rendered war and warfare in Job 10:17 and Isa. 40:2. Gesenius comments that in such a context as this verse it almost always is used figuratively of the wretched and miserable condition of the one referred to. This became the state of Israel after AD 70 when so many were sold into slavery that they became a drug on the market.

The power of the little horn to persecute was limited to an appointed time not then revealed to Daniel, but later made know to him in 12:7. So long as this period contained the daily sacrifice ceased. Nevertheless, it is destined to be restored at the conclusion of Israel's warfare at the appointed time. <Ezek 46:13 Thou shalt daily prepare a burnt offering unto the LORD of a lamb of the first year without blemish: thou shalt prepare it every morning.>] **by reason of transgression,** [The transgression of the Jews was the cause of Rome's triumph. <John 19:15 But they cried out, Away with him, away with him, crucify him. Pilate saith unto them, Shall I crucify your King? The chief priest answered, We have no king but Caesar.> So to the brutal hand of Caesar they were delivered in AD 70.] **and it cast down the truth to the ground;** [Pagan Rome exerted itself against the Christian religion as well as the Jewish people. The little horn of the Goat in Daniel's prophecy is the great red dragon of Revelation. <Rev 12:3 And there appeared another wonder in heaven; and behold a great red dragon, having seven heads and ten horns, and seven crowns upon his heads.> It is shown opposition to the Christian religion both true and false in the Apocalyptic prophecy. <Rev 12:7 And there was war in heaven: Michael and his angels fought against the dragon; and the dragon fought and his angels, 8 And prevailed not; neither was their place found any more in heaven. 9 And the great dragon was cast out, that old serpent, called the Devil, and Satan, which deceiveth the whole world: he was cast out into the earth, and his angels were cast out with him. 10 And I heard a

loud voice saying in heaven, Now is come salvation, and strength, and the kingdom of our God, and the power of his Christ: for the accuser of our brethren is cast down, which accused them before our God day and night. 11 And they overcame him by the blood of the Lamb, and by the word of their testimony; and they loved not their lives unto the death. 12 Therefore rejoice, ye heavens, and ye that dwell in them. Woe to the inhabiters of the earth and of the sea! for the devil is come down unto you, having great wrath, because he knoweth that he hath but a short time. 13 And when the dragon saw that he was cast unto the earth, he persecuted the woman which brought forth the man child. 14 And to the woman were given two wings of a great eagle, that she might fly into the wilderness, into her place, where she is nourished for a time, and times, and half a time, from the face of the serpent. 15 And the serpent cast out of his mouth water as a flood after the woman, that he might cause her to be carried away of the flood. 16 And the earth helped the woman, and the earth opened her mouth, and swallowed up the flood which the dragon cast out of his mouth. 17 And the dragon was wroth with the woman, and went to make war with the remnant of her seed, which keep the commandments of God, and have the testimony of Jesus Christ.>] **and it practised, and prospered.** [The word practiced denotes to accomplish what is set out to be done. Pagan Rome opposed the Truth in the days of Christ and Papal Rome has done similarly since that time. The Great Red Dragon symbolizing Papal Rome for it superimposed upon the name of Christ. After paganism had been overthrown militarily by Constantine its superstitions, festivals and teaching were adopted by Papal Rome and in that for it prospered. Daniel's prophecy takes in the whole course of Roman power and influence, first as a pagan military power in opposition to Christianity and later as a paganised "Christian" military power in opposition to the Truth.]

VS13 Then I heard one saint speaking, [Saint here is Chaldean for Holy One and denotes an angel. This is evidently the angel supervising the vision.] **and another saint said unto that certain saint which spake,** [The word translated certain saint is Palmoni which is a name meaning wonderful numberer. Palmoni evidently was the speaking angel. Gabriel was the name of the interpreting angel on another occasion <Dan 9:21 Yea, whiles I was speaking in prayer, even the man Gabriel, whom I

had seen in the vision at the beginning, being caused to fly swiftly, touched me about the time of the evening oblation.> and Michael the name of the angelic Prince of Princes. <Dan 12:1And at that time shall Michael stand up, the great prince which standeth for the children of thy people: and there shall be a time of trouble, such as never was since there was a nation even to that same time: and at that time thy people shall be delivered, every one that shall be found written in the book.> Pamoni, as his name implies, was evidently the chronologer of events, and thus best able to answer Daniel's question as to how long it would be before Jerusalem and the Temple were destroyed. It is evident from a number of references in Daniel that various angels had various jobs.]

How long shall be the vision concerning the daily sacrifice, and the transgression of desolation [The vision of this chapter predicted the victory of Alexander over the Persians. This paved the way for the manifestation of the Little Horn of the goat that overthrew the Temple, terminating the daily sacrifice. The transgression of the desolation is seen again in chapter 9:27 and will be considered there. Just remember, Jesus quoted this verse and added whoso readeth let him understand. < Matt 24:15 When ye therefore shall see the abomination of desolation, spoken of by Daniel the prophet, stand in the holy place, (whoso readeth, let him understand:)] **to give both the sanctuary and the host to be trodden under foot?** [Sanctuary in this verse is *qodesh* and means holy people, ground city or thing, as it is translated elsewhere. The sanctuary of verse 11 is *miqdash* and means temple. The Lord cited a section of this verse and applied it to the destruction of the holy city Jerusalem, in AD 70. < Luke 21:24 And they shall fall by the edge of the sword, and shall be led away captive into all nations: and Jerusalem shall be trodden down of the Gentiles, until the times of the Gentiles be fulfilled.>]

VS14 And he said unto me, [Palmoni did not answer the other angel, but addressed Daniel directly so there would be no misunderstanding.] **Unto two thousand and three hundred days;**[The literal Hebrew for days is evening and morning and requires some explanation. < Gen 1:5 And God called the light Day, and the darkness he called Night. And the evening and the morning were the first day.>

Apparently the Greeks adopted the same peculiar way to describe a day as reflected in the writings of the Apostle in the letter to Corinth.

< 2 Cor 11:25 Thrice was I beaten with rods, once was I stoned, thrice I suffered shipwreck, a night and a day I have been in the deep;> Palmoni's reason for describing it this way instead of Daniel's use of the word, < Dan 9:7 O Lord, righteousness belongeth unto thee, but unto us confusion of faces, as at this day; to the men of Judah, and to the inhabitants of Jerusalem, and unto all Israel, that are near, and that are far off, through all the countries whither thou hast driven them, because of their trespass that they have trespassed against thee.> <Dan 9:15 And now, O Lord our God, that hast brought thy people forth out of the land of Egypt with a mighty hand, and hast gotten thee renown, as at this day; we have sinned, we have done wickedly.> was to emphasize that this prophecy was related to the Greeks and would commence at the time of Alexander's conquest of Medo-Persia. The evening morning expression, besides a day, is used to describe an epoch of time. < Ps 30:5 For his anger endureth but a moment; in his favour is life: weeping may endure for a night, but joy cometh in the morning.>

The expression here reads 2300 evening mornings and expresses a period of suffering for Judah that lasts through the long day of 2300 years. The period began after the battles of Granicus 334 and Issus 333 BC and thus would end in 1967.

The Six Days War gave an overwhelming and unexpected victory for the reborn Jewish state. In a lightning move reminiscent of Alexander's swift victories, the Jordanians were swept from Jerusalem and it became a Jewish controlled city for the first time in more than 2000 years. Christ words, till the time of the Gentiles is fulfilled was vindicated.] **then shall the sanctuary be cleansed.** [Sanctuary here is *quodesh* signifying the holy place and not the temple. Cleansed is from *nitzadaq* meaning to make or render just or vindicated from violence and injury. This does not mean the process of cleansing is over, but Israel is rapidly moving toward the condition outlined in Ezekiel when he saw the beginning of the resurrection of the dry bones. < Ezek 37:88 And when I beheld, lo, the sinews and the flesh came up upon them, and the skin covered them above: but there was no breath in them.>]

VS15 And it came to pass, when I, even I Daniel, had seen the vision, and sought for the meaning, [It came to pass suggests Daniel had studied the vision and prayed for enlightenment as to its meaning.

A good example for all Christians. < Matt 7:7 Ask, and it shall be given you; seek, and ye shall find; knock, and it shall be opened unto you:> <Col 1:10 That ye might walk worthy of the Lord unto all pleasing, being fruitful in every good work, and increasing in the knowledge of God;> <2 Tim 2:7 Consider what I say; and the Lord give thee understanding in all things.> <James 1:5 If any of you lack wisdom, let him ask of God, that giveth to all men liberally, and upbraideth not; and it shall be given him.>] **then, behold,** [The sudden appearance of the angel evoked an exclamation from Daniel.] **there stood before me as the appearance of a man.** [The Hebrew word for man here is *geber* meaning strength and actually forms part of Gabrial's name. The man who appeared was viral and strong and his message was equally strong.]

VS16 And I heard a man's voice [Here the word for man is *Adam* as the angel spoke on behalf of man calling upon Gabriel to minister for such by explaining in simple terms the meaning of the vision] **between the banks of Ulai,** [Ulai has been said to mean peradventure, suggesting the fulfillment of the vision is in the future. The Ulai River was where the prophet stood in vs. 2. The speaker of this verse is apparently not seen by the prophet but he could clearly here the angelic voice speaking on behalf of man and directing Daniel as to what he should do.] **which called, and said, Gabriel, make this man to understand the vision.** [Gariel is compounded of El Gibbor from geber as noted, and means Mighty Warrior or Warrior of God. It is a title of Christ in Isaiah but is translated Mighty God in that instance. < Isa 9:6 For unto us a child is born, unto us a son is given: and the government shall be upon his shoulder: and his name shall be called Wonderful, Counsellor, The mighty God, The everlasting Father, The Prince of Peace.>

Once again, an angelic name or title is appropriate for Christ who had been given power over all the angels. This is the first time we meet Gabriel who is obviously under the direction of the Spirit who gives him the command in this verse. Elsewhere he describes himself as being in the presence of God. < Luke 1:19 And the angel answering said unto him, I am Gabriel, that stand in the presence of God; and am sent to speak unto thee, and to shew thee these glad tidings.> It was appropriate that Gabriel spoke to Daniel in instructing the prophet in visions of the coming Messiah, just as he did to Zacharias about the birth of John the Baptist, < Luke 1:13 But the angel said unto him, Fear not, Zacharias: for thy prayer is heard; and thy wife Elisabeth shall bear thee a son, and thou shalt call his name John.> In vs. 19 above he tells Zacharias his name. He was also the angel who brought the news of Jesus birth to Mary.< Luke 1:26 And in the sixth month the angel Gabriel was sent from God unto a city of Galilee, named Nazareth, 27 To a virgin espoused to a man whose name was Joseph, of the house of David; and the virgin's name was Mary.>]

The Angels of Daniel

Daniel 8:13-20 describes a most remarkable and dramatic incident in which Daniel is privileged to overhear a conversation between two angels and then is drawn into the discuss of the vision as other angelic beings join in. Four angels are mentioned n the discourse. Palmoni v. 13, an unnamed holy one v. 13, Gabriel, vs. 15-16 and "the voice of a man," possibly Michael v. 16.

(1) In verse 13, the "one who is speaking" is equal to "that certain saint" referred to later in the verse whose Hebrew name is Palmoni.

(2) There is one styled "another saint" who can most likely be identified as the "watcher" or "holy one" of 4:13

(3) In v. 15, as Daniel sought the meaning of the vision he was confronted by the "appearance of a man," (Gibbor) who is later identified as Gabriel.

(4) In v. 16 Gabriel is instructed to explain the vision to Daniel by "the voice of a man," (Adam). Though not named here, further evidence in the book suggests it may be Michael. This is supported by the fact that in 10:21, the only angel named in the Book of Daniel with that kind of authority is Michael < Dan 10:21 But I will shew thee that which is noted in the scripture of truth: and there is none that holdeth with me in these things, but Michael your prince.> If he was Israel's prince, he was Daniel's prince. Since the prophecy had relation to the treading down of the Holy Land and the Jews, then Michael had authority over such affairs and was in a position to instruct Gabriel. <Jude 9 Yet Michael the archangel, when contending

with the devil he disputed about the body of Moses, durst not bring against him a railing accusation, but said, The Lord rebuke thee.>

This discussion is helpful not only in understanding the narrative but to make real the presence of the Divine influence in our lives today.

VS17 So he came near where I stood: [<Heb 1:14 Are they not all ministering spirits, sent forth to minister for them who shall be heirs of salvation?] **and when he came, I was afraid, and fell upon my face:** [Symbolically Daniel enacted his own death and resurrection which was appropriate. The prophecy would begin after his death and culminate at his resurrection.] **but he said unto me, Understand, O son of man:** [Ezekiel uses son of man over 100 times as a type of Christ. In Dan. 7:13 it was used that was as discussed. Daniel foreshadowed Christ in a number of ways. It is the title of Christ as judge, see notes on 7:13] **for at the time of the end shall be the vision.** [Here again time means set time or a terminal date in the development of the Divine purpose. There is frequent reference to such periods in Daniel and they will be dealt with as they occur. There is a time of the end at the termination of the Mosaic era. < Heb 9:26 For then must he often have suffered since the foundation of the world: but now once in the end of the world hath he appeared to put away sin by the sacrifice of himself.> One at the end of Gentile times < Luke 21:24 And they shall fall by the edge of the sword, and shall be led away captive into all nations: and Jerusalem shall be trodden down of the Gentiles, until the times of the Gentiles be fulfilled.> Both relate to the resurrection; the first being Christ's as the firstfruit and the second or afterwards they that are Christ's at his coming.]

VS18 Now as he was speaking with me, I was in a deep sleep on my face toward the ground: [The symbolic death mentioned earlier] **but he touched me, and set me upright.** [The symbolic resurrection]

VS19 And he said, Behold, I will make thee know what shall be in the last end of the indignation: [This is the time of the final stages of judgment or the outpouring of Yahweh's wrath.] **for at the time**

appointed the end shall be. [Nothing is left to chance. All is on God's timetable.]

VS20 The ram which thou sawest having two horns are the kings of Media and Persia. [Gabriel's explanation of the vision already seen by Daniel is introductory to the time of the end]

VS21 And the rough goat is the king of Grecia: [Or Greece.] **and the great horn that is between his eyes is the first king.** [None but Alexander the Great and this epoch began with his conquests.]

VS22 Now that being broken, whereas four stood up for it, four kingdoms shall stand up out of the nation, but not in his power. [See vs. 8-9 for details]

VS23 And in the latter time of their kingdom, [After the death of Antigonus when the Greek Empire was divided into four parts as described in vs. 8-9] **when the transgressors are come to the full,** [After the conquest of Greece by Rome, wickedness and irreligion flourished in Judea, leading the Lord to remark, < Matt 23:31 Wherefore ye be witnesses unto yourselves, that ye are the children of them which killed the prophets. 32 Fill ye up then the measure of your fathers. 33 Ye serpents, ye generation of vipers, how can ye escape the damnation of hell?>] **a king of fierce countenance,** [This describes the warlike countenance of Rome in almost the same terms as Moses who prophesied Rome's coming. < Deut 28:49 The LORD shall bring a nation against thee from far, from the end of the earth, (Rome was located at the western end of the know world as far as Jerusalem was concerned) as swift as the eagle flieth; (The Roman standard was a flying eagle.) a nation whose tongue thou shalt not understand; (Latin is far removed in idiomatic structure from Hebrew and is truly a foreign language.) 50 A nation of fierce countenance, (The same words used by Daniel) which shall not regard the person of the old, nor shew favour to the young: 51 And he shall eat the fruit of thy cattle, and the fruit of thy land, until thou be destroyed: which also shall not leave thee either corn, wine, or oil, or the increase of thy kine, or flocks of thy sheep, until he have destroyed thee. 52 And he shall besiege thee in all thy gates, until thy high and fenced walls come down, wherein thou trustedst, throughout all thy land: and he shall besiege thee in all thy gates throughout all thy land, which the LORD thy God hath given thee.>] **and understanding dark sentences,** [A master of cunning. Augustus used Herod to his own ends, undermining and dividing Jewry. Using that tactic, he won Palestine by diplomacy and not by war, fulfilling this prophecy.] **shall stand up.** [Suggesting the supreme control Rome eventually had of the known world.]

VS24 And his power shall be mighty, [As prophesied in the image-vision, this kingdom is as strong as iron.] **but not by his own power:** [The other power was that of Yahweh, who allowed Rome's world conquest as a punishment of His people for rejecting their Messiah. <Deut 28:49 The LORD shall bring a nation against thee from far, from the end of the earth, as swift as the eagle flieth; a nation whose tongue thou shalt not understand;>

In the parable, Christ calls the Roman army, his army. <Luke 20:16 He shall come and destroy these husbandmen, and shall give the vineyard to others. And when they heard it, they said, God forbid.> Jesus told Pilot he was only allowed by Yahweh to do what he was doing. <John 19:11 Jesus answered, Thou couldest have no power at all against me, except it were given thee from above: therefore he that delivered me unto thee hath the greater sin.> The motive of Rome was not please God, but for their self-glorification.]

and he shall destroy wonderfully, [The destruction wrought on Jerusalem by Rome is unparalleled in Jewish history, and not even Gog's invasion will do as much damage. <Matt 24:21 For then shall be great tribulation, such as was not since the beginning of the world to this time, no, nor ever shall be. 22 And except those days should be shortened, there should no flesh be saved: but for the elect's sake those days shall be shortened.> And the end of Gog's invasion will be the opposite for Jerusalem will be restored, and the Temple rebuilt as a House of Prayer for All People.] **and shall prosper, and practise,** [Practice means accomplish what they set out to accomplish.] **and shall destroy the mighty and the holy people.** [In AD 70 the first revolt was crushed and in 135 during the second revolt of Bar-Kochba. The Jews were ruthlessly crushed. Hadrian changed the name of the city, built a temple to Pagan gods and had the temple site plowed as a field to show his contempt to Israel and its God.]

VS25 And through his policy also [Constantine, in 324 AD transferred the civil and military administration to Constantinople, now Istanbul, on the Bosporus. This became the headquarters of the little horn of the goat, while Rome remained the home of the horn of the 4th beast. Justinian and Phocas followed on the throne of the united empire and conform to the his of this chapter. Though his is singular, it is not to one individual but a succession of individuals who held the throne, and it is an outgrowth of one of the four previous divisions and as noted in v. 23, it too must reach forward to a latter time. The secular power of the Roman rulers is touched on here and the spiritual in the 11th chapter.] **he shall cause craft to prosper in his hand;** [Craft is *mirmah* or fraud or deceit. In Jeremiah the word is used to in relation to false religious teaching and is appropriate here for the power referred to is described as casting down the truth to the ground in vs. 12 of this chapter of Daniel. <Jer 9:6 Thine habitation is in the midst of deceit; through deceit they refuse to know me, saith the LORD.>

This characterized those reigning in Constantinople form that time forward. The development of the Roman Catholic Church is directly tied to the actions of Constantine, Justinian and Phocas. Their support gave the Pope power and authority well before Charlemagne established the Holy Roman Empire in 800 AD. Their policies caused the craft to prosper.

In a letter dated March 533 from Justinian to the Pope, the king recognizes the Pope as the legal had of all churches in the Empire. Phocas in 604 wrote to the Bishop of Rome, as the Pope was called then, and acknowledged his spiritual supremacy. In return, the Pope acknowledged the bloodthirsty Phocas as the pious avenger of the church.

By this mutual admiration society, Boniface III in 606 received the title Universal Bishop. A gold statue of Phocas was erected in Rome, to honor this event and the Little horn of the goat, "in his kingdom do honor to a god of guardian saints" was fulfilled. When the Bishop of Rome was honored by the little horn of the Goat the little horn that arose from the ten-fold kingdom had not yet arisen. 226 years after Justinian's decree and 193 after Phocas letter, that came to pass in 800 with the coronation of Charlemagne who at that time also honored the Pope.

This continued until controversy arose and the Great Schism of 1054 led to the founding of Greek Orthodoxy. Simultaneously war weakened the eastern kingdom and the Pope had to look elsewhere for support.

Turkish pressure in the east collapsed Constantinople in 1453. Churches were turned to mosques and the people given the choice of the Koran or the sword. Church headquarters were transferred to Moscow, and the Third Rome was founded. This prophecy requires a resurgence of that power. This means that eventually, a power occupying Constantinople, and supporting the Papacy will come down against the Prince of Peace and be destroyed.] **and he shall magnify himself in his heart,** [This policy does not stem from love of the Papacy but as a means of gaining more prestige.] **and by peace shall destroy many:**[Today, Russia is torn by internal strife, and cries "Peace" to the world, but prophecy declares that Russia will once again rise to an aggressive power. <1 Thess 5:3 For when they shall say, Peace and safety; then sudden destruction cometh upon them, as travail upon a woman with child; and they shall not escape.> For this manifestation to appear, the Ottoman dynasty must of course be driven out of Europe.

The occupation of the Dragon's throne by a non-catholic royalty is clearly exceptional. The Ottoman Empire has not magnified himself above all, nor honored the Pope as a god or shown himself at all a gracious patron of his saints or their temples. Still this is necessary. Perhaps the modern increase in strife between the Arab and Western worlds is preparation to that event.] **he shall also stand up** [The addition of "also" presumes a pause and further action on the pat of the latter day little horn of the goat. It suggests a lapse of time between the occupation of Constantinople by Russia to constitute in the latter-day little horn of the goat, and his descent south against Egypt and Israel. The order of events thus indicated is occupation of Constantinople by Russia, its growth of power by which its leader is magnified; the alignment between Rome and Russia forming the confederacy of Ezekiel 38 cemented by promises of peace and finally when he is ready, the sweeping aside of the protests of the West. <Ezek 38:13 Sheba, and Dedan, and the merchants of Tarshish, with all the young lions thereof, shall say unto thee, Art thou come to take a spoil? hast thou gathered thy company to take a prey? to carry away silver and gold, to take away cattle and goods, to take a great spoil?> and the invasion of the south. <Dan 11:40 And at the time of the end shall the king of the south push at him: and the king of the north shall come against

him like a whirlwind, with chariots, and with horsemen, and with many ships; and he shall enter into the countries, and shall overflow and pass over. 41 He shall enter also into the glorious land, and many countries shall be overthrown: but these shall escape out of his hand, even Edom, and Moab, and the chief of the children of Ammon. 42 He shall stretch forth his hand also upon the countries: and the land of Egypt shall not escape. 43 But he shall have power over the treasures of gold and of silver, and over all the precious things of Egypt: and the Libyans and the Ethiopians shall be at his steps. 44 But tidings out of the east and out of the north shall trouble him: therefore he shall go forth with great fury to destroy, and utterly to make away many. 45 And he shall plant the tabernacles of his palace between the seas in the glorious holy mountain; yet he shall come to his end, and none shall help him.> This will ultimately bring the king of the North or Gog against Jerusalem and the Prince of princes.] **against the Prince of princes;** [This is Jesus. When he was crucified 2000 years ago, Jesus held the title of Prince v. 11. At this future epoch he will have greatly increased in number by the resurrection and glorification of the saints to earn the title Prince of princes. In v. 11 his title is *Sar* but here it is *Sar-sarim* for other princes are with him.] **but he shall be broken without hand.** [A similar expression is uses for cutting the stone that broke the image in Dan. 2:34. <Dan 2:34 Thou sawest till that a stone was cut out without hands, which smote the image upon his feet that were of iron and clay, and brake them to pieces.>

In Daniel 11:45 the coming to an end of the King of the North is consequent on the standing up of Michael the prince. The power that will destroy the horn of the goat in its latter-day manifestation will be no human agency, But Divine. <Matt 21:43 Therefore say I unto you, The kingdom of God shall be taken from you, and given to a nation bringing forth the fruits thereof. 44 And whosoever shall fall on this stone shall be broken: but on whomsoever it shall fall, it will grind him to powder.>]

VS26 And the vision of the evening and the morning which was told is true: [Some have claimed that the prophet lived in the epoch of Antiochus Epiphanes some 300 years later and that he fraudulently set forth in his book that he was contemporary with the fall of Babylon. By such interpretation of his prophecies and accusations of falsehood against the prophet do not dispose of other prophecies tht were fulfilled long after his time, such as the succession of the Empires of Daniel 2. Past an present history are enough to vindicate that the prophets words are true.] **wherefore shut thou up the vision;** [The vision was closed awaiting its confirmation. <Dan 12:4 But thou, O Daniel, shut up the words, and seal the book, even to the time of the end: many shall run to and fro, and knowledge shall be increased.>] **for it shall be for many days.** [The vision extended until the time of the end, far beyond the time of Antiochus in which some would place it.]

VS27 And I Daniel fainted, and was sick certain days; [Daniel had been allowed to peer into the future and the destruction of Jerusalem, the death of its princes, the slaughter of the Messiah, depressed him so much that he became physically ill.] **afterward I rose up, and did the king's business;** [He was apparently sent to Sushan on the King's business and we are not told what it was. The important reason was the vision, but he still faithfully attended to the temporal business assigned to him. **and I was astonished at the vision,** [He was astonished because as the next chapter reveals, he had been expecting the imminent restoration of the nation of Israel and the rebuilding of the Temple in its full glory. That was not to be and this prophecy revealed it.] **stood it.** [This suggests he discussed it with others, perhaps Hananiah, Mishael and Azariah, but a true and satisfying solution of it was not found. God's truth and purpose gradually unfold and are not absorbed or revealed immediately. Time is required to understand the Divine revelation in its fullness. To that end, further visions were later granted to the prophet.]

What marvelous insight into the character of the man, Daniel. Hopefully, by now, the reader will be enticed to look into the rest of the prophecies of Daniel. A complete, verse by verse study is available from www.logos.org.au. In the next chapter we shall look at the last chapter of Daniel in detail. But, first the subject of Michael the archangel must be addressed, since many who read the Bible casually are often confused by who he is. We first contact Michael in Daniel 10:13 : But the prince of the kingdom of Persia withstood me one and twenty days: but, lo, Michael, one of the chief princes, came to help me; and I remained there with the kings of Persia. It is dangerous to take any single passage of scripture out of context.

When examined in detail it reveals the nature of Michael. Remember, angels are the agents of God who make sure conditions exist for Yahweh's will to be accomplished.

VS13 But the prince of the kingdom of Persia withstood me one and twenty days: [It had taken the angel 21 days to bring the policy of Persia into conformity with Yahweh's purpose for which Daniel had been praying. At the beginning of this period Daniel had turned to God, mourning, fasting and praying for the restoration of his people. His prayers were heard and acted on though he was unaware of the angelic works during the period. The angle had to re-arrange so the prince of Persia would voluntarily act in a certain way. This was the year the decree of Cyrus took place. We cannot always see the manipulation of God's angels on our behalf but they are there.

As Ezra describes it, < Ezra 1:1 Now in the first year of Cyrus king of Persia, that the word of the LORD by the mouth of Jeremiah might be fulfilled, the LORD stirred up the spirit of Cyrus king of Persia, that he made a proclamation throughout all his kingdom, and put it also in writing, saying,> Although Cyrus didn't know he was doing God's will. The unseen angle stood in Balaam's way to prevent him from frustrating the Divine will. < Num 22:32 And the angel of the LORD said unto him, Wherefore hast thou smitten thine ass these three times? behold, I went out to withstand thee, because thy way is perverse before me:> In this manner, the Elohim work to dictate personal and national events.] **but, lo, Michael** [The archangel in charge of Israel's affairs. < Ex 23:20 Behold, I send an Angel before thee, to keep thee in the way, and to bring thee into the place which I have prepared.

21 Beware of him, and obey his voice, provoke him not; for he will not pardon your transgressions: for my name is in him.

22 But if thou shalt indeed obey his voice, and do all that I speak; then I will be an enemy unto thine enemies, and an adversary unto thine adversaries.

23 For mine Angel shall go before thee, and bring thee in unto the Amorites, and the Hittites, and the Perizzites, and the Canaanites, and the Hivites, and the Jebusites: and I will cut them off.> <Josh 5:13 And it came to pass, when Joshua was by Jericho, that he lifted up his eyes and looked, and, behold, there stood a man over against him with his sword drawn in his hand: and Joshua went unto him, and said unto

him, Art thou for us, or for our adversaries? 14 And he said, Nay; but as captain of the host of the LORD am I now come. And Joshua fell on his face to the earth, and did worship, and said unto him, What saith my lord unto his servant? 15 And the captain of the LORD's host said unto Joshua, Loose thy shoe from off thy foot; for the place whereon thou standest is holy. And Joshua did so.> <Jude 9 Yet Michael the archangel, when contending with the devil he disputed about the body of Moses, durst not bring against him a railing accusation, but said, The Lord rebuke thee.> Michael's work as your prince < Dan 10:21 But I will shew thee that which is noted in the scripture of truth: and there is none that holdeth with me in these things, but Michael your prince.> will be taken over by Jesus himself when he appears for the salvation of Israel. < Dan 12:1 And at that time shall Michael stand up, the great prince which standeth for the children of thy people: and there shall be a time of trouble, such as never was since there was a nation even to that same time: and at that time thy people shall be delivered, every one that shall be found written in the book.>] **one of the chief princes,** [The angels have a hierarchy, just as the saints will have in the age to come. < Matt 19:27 Then answered Peter and said unto him, Behold, we have forsaken all, and followed thee; what shall we have therefore?

28 And Jesus said unto them, Verily I say unto you, That ye which have followed me, in the regeneration when the Son of man shall sit in the throne of his glory, ye also shall sit upon twelve thrones, judging the twelve tribes of Israel.> <1 Cor 15:40 There are also celestial bodies, and bodies terrestrial: but the glory of the celestial is one, and the glory of the terrestrial is another. 41 There is one glory of the sun, and another glory of the moon, and another glory of the stars: for one star differeth from another star in glory.>] **came to help me;** [That the angels work in harmony to accomplish God's will is evident from the very first acts of creation. < Gen 1:26 And God said, Let us make man in our image, after our likeness: and let them have dominion over the fish of the sea, and over the fowl of the air, and over the cattle, and over all the earth, and over every creeping thing that creepeth upon the earth.> Exactly how Michael helped Gabriel we are not informed but it seems likely that the situation in Persia with Cyrus was involved.] **and I remained**

there with the kings of Persia. [There was only one king of Persia but there were a number of sub rulers as discussed earlier.]

In summary, Michael is the Archangel or Commander in Chief of Angels. He is not Christ, but a type of Christ. He will continue in that post until a new Commander in Chief is appointed (that will be Jesus Christ) when he returns to earth.

CHAPTER 13

Come and Get It: Daniel 11:40 to 12:13

Hopefully, by now, a convincing argument for the accuracy of Biblical prophecy as actual history has been presented. Before a discussion of the end time prophecies that follow, some facts whose proof lies in the Bible, must be kept in mind. These facts fly in the face of some modern religious teaching, but are undeniably scriptural. They are as follows:

1. Christ left the earth with a promise to return. Acts 1:10-11
2. He will return at a time known only to God himself. Math. 23:9
3. He shall return to judge the world. Math. 16:27
4. Resurrection and judgment will occur 1 Tim. 4:13
5. Christ will announce his return to the world and demand surrender to his will. The battle of Armegeddon will ensue and the forces opposing Christ will be destroyed. An appeal will go forth to the remaining nations of the world to accept the messiah. If any nation refuses, they will be destroyed by his immortal army of resurrected saints and angels. Isa. 60:12 (A hard thing for traditional Christians to accept). At this juncture, the world will consist of both mortal survivors of the world wars and the immortal saints and angels.
6. A thousand years of peace and unopposed teaching of the Word will follow.
7. At the end of that time, free will once again will be allowed free reign.
8. A revolt against the rule of Christ will be harshly dealt with.
9. A final judgment will occur and sin will be abolished forever. The kingdom will be returned to God, leaving a vast future for the glorified to contemplate.

What will trigger the return of Christ? Quite simply, the world situation will be the trigger. When mankind backs himself into a corner where world destruction is imminent, Christ will return. Although we are not able to know exactly when that is, the Bible leaves broad clues as to the circumstances. These are given in the last chapter of Daniel and in a section of Ezekiel that will be subsequently presented. Now, let us examine Daniel.

VS40 And at the time of the end [This is the time mentioned in Dan. 7:26, see notes on that verse. This time includes the return of Christ (12:1) personal judgment (11:34) resurrection and deliverance (12:2) and complete explanation of the Divine secret (12:4,6,9) This time concludes with Christ as victor over a world at peace and commenced with the re-appearance of the "kings of the north and south" and a third party termed "him."]

shall the king of the south [This power was last heard of in verse 29 when the force of the Ptolemys in Egypt was overthrown by Antiochus (Dan 11:26). Since then, the king of the south, (the power occupying Egypt) disappeared from prophecy to allow events in Palestine and Europe to take precedence.

Now the scene turns to Egypt. This time Britain was to become king of the south and in 1882 circumstances forced Britain to intervene in Egyptian affairs. Against severe opposition, Disraeli, Prime Minister of Britain, bought control of the Suez Canal leading to sole domination of Egypt by Britain. For 72 years Britain remained in Egypt until an agreement was signed in 1954 relinquishing British influence in the area. By 1956 the last British troops were gone, but for a time Britain was king of the south.] **push at him:** [The him here refers to the king of verse 36, the power in Constantinople. From the days of Constantine (BC 324) this city became the capital of the Roman Empire. In 1453 it fell to the Turks who made it their capital and destroyed the remnants of the Roman Empire, to become "the him" of this verse. The prophecy thus requires that at the time of the end the power in occupation of Egypt (Britain) should push at him (the Turks.)

The first movement from Egypt against the Turks was 1832 when the army of Muhammad Ali under the direction of his son Ibrahim was sent against the Turks in Syria. He did not succeed because the Angelic Controllers recognized that the full time was not yet, but it was the beginning of a situation that would lead ultimately to the time of the end.

Britain and France were forced into the arena and were to ultimately provide the needed "push". This occurred in 1917 when Turkey controlled most of the Middle East including Palestine and Jerusalem. But, supporting Germany against Britain in WWI she attracted the opposition of the king of the south and British forces under the direction of General Allenby attacked and defeated the Turkish forces in Palestine.] **and the king of the north shall come against him** [Subsequent to the attack of the king of the south, the fulfillment must await the final forming of the ancient Seleucidean Kingdom of Syria, which the northern Russian power is poised to accomplish. She is spreading her net of control over the territory of the ancient king of the north and only requires a controlling influence in Iran, Iraq and Syria to qualify for the title. Then, she will be ready to come against, "him." (Turkey) Significantly the same year that saw the push of the king of the south (Britain) against Turkey (1917) also witnessed the Russian Revolution when Lenin overthrew the Tzarist capitalist regime and introduced a movement that would ultimately become king of the north. In her final onslaught, Russia will first attack Constantinople (Istambul) to control the seaways into the Mediterranean, then proceed against Egypt(v.42) and the Holy Land (v. 45)] **like a whirlwind,** [A sudden unexpected attack that will take the world off guard.] **with chariots, and with horsemen, and with many ships;** [A vast array of military equipment.] **and he shall enter into the countries,** [The area occupied by the king of Constantinople. Russia's desire to dominate Turkey will provide a spring-board for her design on the Middle East] **and shall overflow and pass over.** [Once Russia possesses Constantinople they will flow on and pass over into the Middle East.]

VS41 He shall enter also into the glorious land, [Having absorbed the little horn, Russia will act the part required by the prophecy and invade the areas of Lebanon and Israel, driving along the coastal plains intent on securing a foothold in the south.] **and many countries shall be overthrown:** [Many cities and states will be overthrown. This will be the beginning of the time of Jacob's trouble. <Jer 30:7 Alas! for that day is great, so that none is like it: it is even the time of Jacob's trouble;

142

but he shall be saved out of it.> <Isa 8:22 And they shall look unto the earth; and behold trouble and darkness, dimness of anguish; and they shall be driven to darkness.>] **but these shall escape out of his hand, even Edom, and Moab, and the chief of the children of Ammon.** [Edom Moab and Ammon describe the modern kingdom of Jordan and the Arabian Peninsula. This area subject or allied to Antiochus (and Turkey) in the past so this prophecy relates to the future. It is to this territory that many of the distressed in Israel will flee from the Russian onslaught through the Holy Land as the ultimate fulfillment of Isaiah. <Isa 16:3 Take counsel, execute judgment; make thy shadow as the night in the midst of the noonday; hide the outcasts; bewray not him that wandereth. 4. Let mine outcasts dwell with thee, Moab; be thou a covert to them from the face of the spoiler: for the extortioner is at an end, the spoiler ceaseth, the oppressors are consumed out of the land.>The angels will provide for the protection of threatened Jews while the final destiny is played out on the mountains of Israel.]

VS42 He shall stretch forth his hand also upon the countries: [Repeating the exploits of the Assyrian oppressors who destroyed the nations of Palestine and took away many captives. Whereas verse 41 reported that many shall be overthrown thus describing the devastation of cities and peoples this verse shows that various countries will come under Russian control. His southward thrust for world control will see the overthrow of Turkey, Asia, Greece, Syria and costal Israel.] **and the land of Egypt shall not escape.** [Notice the King of the South is not mentioned. This role was assumed by Britain, who was required to push at Turkey. Britain was forced to relinquish control over Egypt and no other power came in to take her place. Today, Egypt exists without direction; she remains a base nation of Ezekiel. <Ezek 29:14 And I will bring again the captivity of Egypt, and will cause them to return into the land of Pathros, into the land of their habitation; and they shall be there a base kingdom. 15 It shall be the basest of the kingdoms; neither shall it exalt itself any more above the nations: for I will diminish them, that they shall no more rule over the nations.> and in that condition will feel the effect of Russia's attack as the northern forces pour down the coast of Israel and across the Mediterranean.

Russia will control Egypt thus domination the southern Mediterranean seaboard. Russia has reason to feel vengeance toward

Egypt. When America pulled out of the projected building of the Aswan Dam in Upper Egypt, Russia stepped in with finances and technical assistance. Then she was unceremoniously ejected from the country leaving behind a tremendous amount of material wealth and expertise. They have not forgotten that. Isaiah speaks of the smiting of Egypt prior to the time when Christ will institute healing policies to restore that base nation to a future glory. Isaiah depicts Egypt under a cruel lord, the Gogian power where it will see civil war that breaks the spirit of Egypt. <Isa 19:2 And I will set the Egyptians against the Egyptians: and they shall fight every one against his brother, and every one against his neighbor; city against city, and kingdom against kingdom. 3 And the spirit of Egypt shall fail in the midst thereof; and I will destroy the counsel thereof: and they shall seek to the idols, and to the charmers, and to them that have familiar spirits, and to the wizards. 4 And the Egyptians will I give over into the hand of a cruel lord; and a fierce king shall rule over them, saith the Lord, the LORD of hosts.>

Economic and political troubles will be felt throughout the land as all industry and farming become subject to Russian claims. <Isa 19:5 And the waters shall fail from the sea, and the river shall be wasted and dried up. 6 And they shall turn the rivers far away; and the brooks of defence shall be emptied and dried up: the reeds and flags shall wither. 7 The paper reeds by the brooks, by the mouth of the brooks, and every thing sown by the brooks, shall wither, be driven away, and be no more. 8 The fishers also shall mourn, and all they that cast angle into the brooks shall lament, and they that spread nets upon the waters shall languish. 9 Moreover they that work in fine flax, and they that weave networks, shall be confounded. 10 And they shall be broken in the purposes thereof, all that make sluices and ponds for fish.> This circumstance will form part of the humbling process by which Yahweh will prepare Egypt for its place in the kingdom under the leadership of Christ. <Isa 19:21 And the LORD shall be known to Egypt, and the Egyptians shall know the LORD in that day, and shall do sacrifice and oblation; yea, they shall vow a vow unto the LORD, and perform it. 22 And the LORD shall smite Egypt: he shall smite and heal it: and they shall return even to the LORD, and he shall be intreated of them, and shall heal them.>]

VS43 But he shall have power over the treasures of gold and of silver, and over all the precious things of Egypt: [Though Egypt is relatively poor, it is rich in the treasures of antiquity and possesses a strategic position in control of the Suez Canal and the gateways to the Mediterranean. **and the Libyans and the Ethiopians shall be at his steps.** [These are Egypt's neighbors to the west and south. Hebrew for Ethiopians is *Cushites* referring to the African Cush which bounded Egypt on the south and included not only Ethiopia above Syene and the Cataracts, but also Thebais or Upper Egypt.

Both are estranged from modern Egypt because of her peace treaty with Israel, and will willingly submit to Gog's control. <Ezek 38:5 Persia, Ethiopia, and Libya with them; all of them with shield and helmet:> becoming part of its confederate forces. Ethiopia is already under Russian influence and virtual control, while Libya has close ties with the Soviets.]

VS44 But tidings out of the east [The direction is to Sinai where the Judgment seat will be established and reports of the unusual circumstances that are there occurring now filter through to the Soviet forces in Egypt. At this point, Christ has already returned and brought the responsible of all ages and generations to judgment. Moses prophesied of this. <Deut 33:2 And he said, The LORD came from Sinai, and rose up from Seir unto them; he shined forth from mount Paran, and he came with ten thousands of saints: from his right hand went a fiery law for them.> The resurrection and gathering of saints takes place before Russia enters Egypt, but the gentile world will be unaware it is happening.] **and out of the north** [Jerusalem is here defined. While the Russian forces consolidate in Egypt and try to strengthen their position in the Holy Land, opposing forces of the western Allies attempting to stop the Russians thrust will come into play.

The Allies will be headquartered in Trans-Jordan where they too will be able to care for the Jews fleeing Russian domination. This is their challenge to the Russians. <Ezek 38:13 Sheba, and Dedan, and the merchants of Tarshish, with all the young lions thereof, shall say unto thee, Art thou come to take a spoil? hast thou gathered thy company

to take a prey? to carry away silver and gold, to take away cattle and goods, to take a great spoil?> Russia's response is to leave a part of his forces to hold Egypt and proceed north to meet the challenge.] **shall trouble him:** [This new challenge and the strange goings on in Sinai will cause the Russian powerhouse to feel the need to destroy all opposition.] **therefore he shall go forth with great fury to destroy, and utterly to make away many.** [Leaving a garrison in Egypt the Russians move north to counter the known and unknown threats. They will not recognize the true nature of immortals who are already emerging from Sinai, likely believing them to be a revolt of local forces. Gogue will consider Western forces the main enemy and go forth as the destroyer.]

VS45 And he shall plant the tabernacles of his palace [When Oriental princes went to war, they marched in great state with a large retinue of court officers and all the luxury they were used to. This describes Gogian leaders.] **between the seas in the glorious holy mountain;** [The Mediterranean and the Dead Seas and the mountain is Zion. Here is the setting for the battle of Armageddon. All nations will be represented in the initial clash, and it will seem that Russia is successful over its enemies for Jerusalem is sacked and her people distressed. <Zech 14:1 Behold, the day of the LORD cometh, and thy spoil shall be divided in the midst of thee. 2 For I will gather all nations against Jerusalem to battle; and the city shall be taken, and the houses rifled, and the women ravished; and half of the city shall go forth into captivity, and the residue of the people shall not be cut off from the city.>

Western forces are humiliated and driven back from Jerusalem and Gogue seems to stand supreme. <Ps 48:7 Thou breakest the ships of Tarshish with an east wind.> <Isa 16:4 Let mine outcasts dwell with thee, Moab; be thou a covert to them from the face of the spoiler: for the extortioner is at an end, the spoiler ceaseth, the oppressors are consumed out of the land. 5 And in mercy shall the throne be established: and he shall sit upon it in truth in the tabernacle of David, judging, and seeking judgment, and hasting righteousness. 6. We have heard of the pride of Moab; he is very proud: even of his haughtiness, and his pride, and his wrath: but his lies shall not be so. 7 Therefore shall Moab howl for Moab, every one shall howl: for the foundations

of Kir-hareseth shall ye mourn; surely they are stricken.>] **Yet he shall come to his end,** [His is destroyed and not by Tarshish, but by the immortalized army of Christ which has moved north in answer to the anguished cry of Israel. <Ezek 37:11 Then he said unto me, Son of man, these bones are the whole house of Israel: behold, they say, Our bones are dried, and our hope is lost: we are cut off for our parts.> Divine vengeance is exacted against Gogue and saviors come to the aid of Zion. <Zech 14:3 Then shall the LORD go forth, and fight against those nations, as when he fought in the day of battle.> <Joel 3:16 The LORD also shall roar out of Zion, and utter his voice from Jerusalem; and the heavens and the earth shall shake: but the LORD will be the hope of his people, and the strength of the children of Israel.> <Obad 21 And saviours shall come up on mount Zion to judge the mount of Esau; and the kingdom shall be the LORD's.> The great fury of Gog will be met with the fierce anger of Yahweh so the political seed of the Serpent will be crushed.] **and none shall help him.** [This is the end of the Gentile dominion, the final answer to the political rebellion of mankind. Christ is supreme and with him are the chosen and faithful.]

CHAPTER 14

Ezekiel and the End

Jeremiah was ministering to the people of Jerusalem during the last years of the declining monarchy while Daniel and Ezekiel were in exile ministering to the captives of Babylon. Daniel was the first to go into exile as a teenager of about 17 years of age. If Ezekiel's reference to the 30th year has relation to his age <Ezek 1:1> it would make him not only a contemporary of Daniel but about the same age.

He would have been born in the significant year when Josiah instituted the nation reform and led the people back to Yahweh in the national covenant that he inaugurated. See 2 Kings 23. In that light, Ezekiel appears in the narrative of his book as typical of the Son of the Covenant, The Lord Jesus Christ. Ezekiel was taken into captivity at the time of king Jehoiachin's captivity. This was the third of the six Jewish deportations in Scripture.

1. In the fourth year of Jehoiakim. Daniel 1:2
2. Six years later when 3023 Jews or families were taken into captivity. Jer. 52:28
3. The next year in Jehoiakim's reign when 10,000 more were taken. 2 Kings 24:12:16
4. Ten years later 832 were led away. Jer. 52:29
5. The next year when the upper classes were deported. 2 Kings 25:11-12
6. Four years later (23 year Nebuchadnezzar 745 exiled to Babylonia Jer. 52:30

The exiles were scattered throughout Babylon where they formed small communities with various amounts of local organization and freedom of worship. This is implied in Ezekiel's experience. He was exiled to the colony at Tel-Abib <Ezek 3:15> about 45 miles northwest of Babylon where he ultimately exhibited a fair amount of influence where he was highly regarded for his wisdom. <Ezek 8:1> and more so later, after some of his prophecies had been fulfilled he was accepted as a prophet.

Daniel had already been prophesying in Babylon for 13 years. But, in Jerusalem, Jeremiah was battling against the deadly message of the false prophets who spread the doctrine that those who remained in the city were Heaven's favorites in contrast to those taken into captivity. They boldly claimed that Jerusalem would not fall and the 70 year captivity predicted by Jeremiah would not take place, but Babylon itself would soon fall. <Jer 27:9>.

In Jer. 28, Hananiah a false prophet in Jerusalem publicly proclaimed that the captives would return in two years. His message greatly influenced the exiles eager to grasp at any straw. When Jeremiah wrote to warn them to take no heed to Hananiah, Jer. 29, his letters were answered by Shemaiah who suggested to the priest Zephaniah of Jerusalem that they imprison Jeremiah as a lunatic for daring to suggest that the Holy City would fall and the captivity would be protracted.

The death of Hananiah as predicted by Jeremiah, the words and enacted prophecies set before the Jews in exile by Ezekiel and Daniel and news of further deportations of Jewish captives revealed that hopes of a speedy return were in vain. When Jerusalem fell, it revealed the truth of Ezekiel's prophecies and resulted in a great change in their attitude toward him.

Ezekiel was a man of indomitable courage who remained undeterred by the fiercest opposition. He was not fluent in speech and words did not come easily to him. <Ezek 3:26> but when he did they were weighty and impressive. He dramatized the prophecies by acting them out for the people.

After the fall of Jerusalem, when his predictions had been vindicated in part, he spoke more fluently, setting before the exiles the thrilling message of coming restoration and glory when the land the people and the Temple will be again brought back from the curse resting on them.

As his character is gradually revealed in his book, he gives the impression that he was an austere man, standing aloof from what took place around him, and from the high plane of divine revelation condemning the apostasy and impiety of the Jews by both word and parabolic action.

Ezekiel means god (El) will strengthen and added to this was the title Son of Man <Ezek 2:1> which is used some 100 times in the book. It links him with the Lord Jesus who had the same title. Thus Ezekiel's name and title proclaim, God will strengthen The Son of Man. Jesus is a priest forever after the order of Melchizedek and is fittingly typified by the priest Ezekiel and they both began their missions at age 30. Unlike Jesus, Ezekiel lived in his own house and was married. Ezekiel's entire life and actions are summarized by this verse <Ezek 12:6 In their sight shalt thou bear it upon thy shoulders, and carry it forth in the twilight: thou shalt cover thy face, that thou see not the ground: for I have set thee for a sign unto the house of Israel.>

Ezekiel's prophecies germane to this discussion covers Chapter 33 through 39 and will be examined in some detail. Chapter 33 could be called a definitions chapter and consists of the following subtitles:

1. Responsibilities of a Watchman vs. 1-6
2. Watchman's duties redefined vs. 7-9
3. A message of hope for Israel vs. 10-11
4. Warnings for the people vs. 12-16
5. Yahweh's judgment is just vs. 17-20
6. Message from Jerusalem vs. 21-22
7. Attitude of the remnant in Jerusalem vs. 23-29
8. Ezekiel is encouraged by Yahweh vs. 30-33

Chapter 34 is the marvelous prophecy of the coming of the Shepherd King who will correct the flaws of Israel's current shepherds. Those flaws are outlined if the first six verses. The rest of the chapter is given to the coming Shepherd King and the glorious, peaceful and fruitful reign that will ensue.

In Chapter 35, the sins of the gentile world are reiterated in prophecies against Mount Seir representing spiritual Edom. Their destruction is outlined, and the terrible consequences of their punishment for the persecution of Jerusalem are detailed. Then in Chapter 36, Israel is promised a return to its former glory as the past gives a clue toward the future. The Old Testament is not just a series of disjointed historic tales. Each one is a schoolmaster to bring us to Christ that we might be justified by faith>, Gal. 3:24.

For example, the story of David and Goliath is not just entertainment for children's Sunday school. It foreshadows an important Biblical premise. In the story, related in 1 Sam. 17: 23-52, the characters, and even the implements mentioned, are symbolic of the work of Messiah.

Goliath, by his arrogance and open defiance of the will of Yahweh represents sinful flesh. David, a slight teenager, with seemingly little power and certainly no match for the likes of the Giant is a type of Christ the Messiah. When David goes out to face certain death, he rejects the armor of King Saul, representing worldly protection, and goes to battle armed only with an unshakable faith in God.

From his time as a shepherd, David had honed his skill with a sling, which when handled properly can have the same end result as a rifle bullet. This types Christ's first thirty years of life when he prepared himself for the task he had accepted from Yahweh. He likewise chose five smooth stone for ammunition. Five is the Biblical number of grace. The use of the stone is also a foreshadowing of future events. In Daniel's prophecy, as foretold by 2:34-35 Nebuchadnezzar in a dream saw an image that was destroyed by a stone formed with hands. The stone ground into powder the sinful image and filled the word with its presence. That stone represents Christ

When the battle is joined, David's stone strikes Goliath in the forehead, not only a killing blow but again a symbolic act. The forehead is the seat of knowledge. Sinful man, with his sinful lusts and appetites is destroyed to be replaced by righteousness. What a wonderful story of the plan of God for mankind.

With that in mind, the Bible also tells of about the future by connecting it to events of the past. Here are but a few of them.

Past: Jerusalem throne of Yahweh: 1 Chron 29:23 Then Solomon sat on the throne of the LORD as king instead of David his father, and prospered; and all Israel obeyed him.

Future: Jer 3:17 At that time they shall call Jerusalem the throne of the LORD; and all the nations shall be gathered unto it, to the name of the LORD, to Jerusalem: neither shall they walk any more after the imagination of their evil heart.

Past: One King United Nation: Future: Ezek 37:22 And I will make them one nation in the land upon the mountains of Israel; and one king shall be king to them all: and they shall be no more two nations, neither shall they be divided into two kingdoms any more at all:

Past: Israel a Powerful Multitudinous Nation 1 Kings 4:20 Judah and Israel were many, as the sand which is by the sea in multitude, eating and drinking, and making merry

Future: Mic 4:77 And I will make her that halted a remnant, and her that was cast far off a strong nation: and the LORD shall reign over them in mount Zion from henceforth, even for ever.

Past: Israel The Chief Among Nations_1 Kings 4:21 And Solomon reigned over all kingdoms from the river unto the land of the Philistines, and unto the border of Egypt: they brought presents, and served Solomon all the days of his life.

Future: Mic 4:8 And thou, O tower of the flock, the strong hold of the daughter of Zion, unto thee shall it come, even the first dominion; the kingdom shall come to the daughter of Jerusalem.

Past: Gentile Wealth Flowing to Jerusalem_2 Chron 9:23 And all the kings of the earth sought the presence of Solomon, to hear his wisdom, that God had put in his heart. 24 And they brought every man his present, vessels of silver, and vessels of gold, and raiment, harness, and spices, horses, and mules, a rate year by year.

Future: Isa 60:11 Therefore thy gates shall be open continually; they shall not be shut day nor night; that men may bring unto thee the forces of the Gentiles, and that their kings may be brought.

Past: A greatly Fertile Land 1 Kings 4:22 And Solomon's provision for one day was thirty measures of fine flour, and threescore measures of meal, 23 Ten fat oxen, and twenty oxen out of the pastures, and an hundred sheep, beside harts, and roebucks, and fallow deer, and fatted fowl. 24 For he had dominion over all the region on this side the river, from Tiphsah even to Azzah, over all the kings on this side the river: and he had peace on all sides round about him. 25 And Judah and Israel dwelt safely, every man under his vine and under his fig tree, from Dan even to Beer-sheba, all the days of Solomon. 26 And Solomon had forty thousand stalls of horses for his chariots, and twelve thousand horsemen. 27 And those officers provided victual for king Solomon, and for all that came unto king Solomon's table, every man in his month: they lacked nothing. 28 Barley also and straw for the horses and dromedaries brought they unto the place where the officers were, every man according to his charge.

Future: Isa 35:1 The wilderness and the solitary place shall be glad for them; and the desert shall rejoice, and blossom as the rose. 2 It shall blossom abundantly, and rejoice even with joy and singing: the glory of Lebanon shall be given unto it, the excellence of Carmel and Sharon, they shall see the glory of the LORD, and the excellence of our God.

Past: Nations Under Submission To Israel:_1 Kings 4:21 And Solomon reigned over all kingdoms from the river unto the land of the Philistines, and unto the border of Egypt: they brought presents, and served Solomon all the days of his life.

Future: Ps 72:8 He shall have dominion also from sea to sea, and from the river unto the ends of the earth.

Past: Israel Secure and At Peace 1 Kings 4:25 And Judah and Israel dwelt safely, every man under his vine and under his fig tree, from Dan even to Beer-sheba, all the days of Solomon.

Future: Ezek 34:28 And they shall no more be a prey to the heathen, neither shall the beast of the land devour them; but they shall dwell safely, and none shall make them afraid.

Past:Jerusalem The Center of Wisdom_1 Kings 4:34 And there came of all people to hear the wisdom of Solomon, from all kings of the earth, which had heard of his wisdom.

Future: Isa 2:2 And it shall come to pass in the last days, that the mountain of the LORD's house shall be established in the top of the mountains, and shall be exalted above the hills; and all nations shall flow unto it. 3 And many people shall go and say, Come ye, and let us go up to the mountain of the LORD, to the house of the God of Jacob; and he will teach us of his ways, and we will walk in his paths: for out of Zion shall go forth the law, and the word of the LORD from Jerusalem. 4 And he shall judge among the nations, and shall rebuke many people: and they shall beat their swords into plowshares, and their spears into pruninghooks: nation shall not lift up sword against nation, neither shall they learn war any more

Past: Jerusalem The Center of Worship 2 Chron 9:23 And all the kings of the earth sought the presence of Solomon, to hear his wisdom, that God had put in his heart.

Future: Zech 14:16 And it shall come to pass, that every one that is left of all the nations which came against Jerusalem shall even go up from year to year to worship the King, the LORD of hosts, and to keep the feast of tabernacles.

Past: A Temple Erected Under Royal Supervision 1 Kings 6:1 And it came to pass in the four hundred and eightieth year after the children of Israel were come out of the land of Egypt, in the fourth year of Solomon's reign over Israel, in the month Zif, which is the second month, that he began to build the house of the LORD.

Future: Ezekiel 40 the entire chapter that outlines structure of The House of Prayer for All People.

Past The Temple Plans Supplied By God 1 Chron 28:12 And the pattern of all that he had by the spirit, of the courts of the house of the LORD, and of all the chambers round about, of the treasuries of the house of God, and of the treasuries of the dedicated things:

Future: Ezekiel 40 the entire chapter that outlines structure of The House of Prayer for All People.

Past: The Work Assisted By Gentile Labor 2 Chron 2:2 And Solomon told out threescore and ten thousand men to bear burdens, and fourscore thousand to hew in the mountain, and three thousand and six hundred to oversee them. 2 Chron 2:17 And Solomon numbered all the strangers that were in the land of Israel, after the numbering wherewith David his father had numbered them; and they were found an hundred and fifty thousand and three thousand and six hundred.

Future Isa 60:10 And the sons of strangers shall build up thy walls, and their kings shall minister unto thee: for in my wrath I smote thee, but in my favour have I had mercy on thee.

Past: Zadok The High Priest Officiates 1 Kings 1:34 And let Zadok the priest and Nathan the prophet anoint him there king over Israel: and blow ye with the trumpet, and say, God save king Solomon.

Future: Heb 7:11 If therefore perfection were by the Levitical priesthood, (for under it the people received the law,) what further need was there that another priest should rise after the order of Melchisedec, and not be called after the order of Aaron? 12 For the priesthood being changed, there is made of necessity a change also of the law.

Past: Tremendous Building Activity 1 Kings 9 the entire chapter

Future: Isa 65:21 And they shall build houses, and inhabit them; and they shall plant vineyards, and eat the fruit of them.

Past: Satan Bound 1 Kings 5:4 But now the LORD my God hath given me rest on every side, so that there is neither adversary nor evil occurrent.

Future: Rev 20:2 And he laid hold on the dragon, that old serpent, which is the Devil, and Satan, and bound him a thousand years,

Past: Israel a Blessing In The Land: 2 Chron 9:26 And he reigned over all the kings from the river even unto the land of the Philistines, and to the border of Egypt.

Future: Isa 19:25 Whom the LORD of hosts shall bless, saying, Blessed be Egypt my people, and Assyria the work of my hands, and Israel mine inheritance.

Past: The King Noted For Piercing Unerring Judgment 1 Kings 4:29 And God gave Solomon wisdom and understanding exceeding much, and largeness of heart, even as the sand that is on the sea shore.

Future: Isa 11:3 And shall make him of quick understanding in the fear of the LORD: and he shall not judge after the sight of his eyes, neither reprove after the hearing of his ears:

Past: Priests Figuratively Immortal Ps 134:1 A Song of degrees. Behold, bless ye the LORD, all ye servants of the LORD, which by night stand in the house of the LORD. 2 Lift up your hands in the sanctuary, and bless the LORD. 3 The LORD that made heaven and earth bless thee out of Zion.

Future: Rev 5:9 And they sung a new song, saying, Thou art worthy to take the book, and to open the seals thereof: for thou wast slain, and hast redeemed us to God by thy blood out of every kindred, and tongue, and people, and nation; 10 And hast made us unto our God kings and priests: and we shall reign on the earth.

Future: Rev 5:9 And they sung a new song, saying, Thou art worthy to take the book, and to open the seals thereof: for thou wast slain, and hast redeemed us to God by thy blood out of every kindred, and tongue, and people, and nation;10 And hast made us unto our God kings and priests: and we shall reign on the earth.]

CHAPTER 15

Dem Dry Bones

Chapter 37 recounts Ezekiel's amazing vision of the valley of dry bones. The dry bones, which represent the dispersed nation of Israel, are resurrected to walk upright once again signifying the restoration of the country. Let's look in detail at this prophecy that was fulfilled in 1948 when the nation of Israel once again appeared on a world map after 2000 years of dispersion.

VS37:1 The hand of the LORD was upon me, [The Spirit took hold of him to show him another prophecy.] **and carried me out in the spirit of the LORD, and set me down in the midst of the valley which was full of bones,** [Valley is literally plain. He is in a large broad valley between two sets of distant mountains and sees the bones of an army that has been ambushed and slain.]

VS2 And caused me to pass by them round about: and, behold, there were very many in the open valley; and, lo, they were very dry. [The prophet was caused to walk silently around viewing the desolation. The bones were very dry and bleached out.]

VS3 And he said unto me, Son of man, [Ezekiel is identified with the Lord Jesus by the title and thus connects Jesus to these prophecies.] **can these bones live?** [The question is put to the prophet who answers cautiously.] **And I answered, O Lord GOD, thou knowest.** [Ezekiel knows that only the power of Yahweh can make this seemingly impossible question receive an affirmative answer so Ezekiel answers hesitantly.]

VS4 Again he said unto me, Prophesy upon these bones, and say unto them, O ye dry bones, hear the word of the LORD. [Christ will cause the bleached bones of Jewry to be formed first into the framework of a skeleton and finally to life. Thus the prophet prophesies as Son of Man.]

VS5 Thus saith the Lord GOD unto these bones; Behold, I will cause breath to enter into you, and ye shall live: [Breath is from *rauch* or spirit. It is the Spirit or the power of Truth believed that alone can bring life to Israel. This is what Ezekiel saw and Hosea predicts a similar national resurrection. <Hos 6:1 Come, and let us return unto the LORD: for he hath torn, and he will heal us; he hath smitten, and he will bind us up. 2 After two days will he revive us: in the third day he will raise us up, and we shall live in his sight. 3 Then shall we know, if we follow on to know the LORD: his going forth is prepared as the morning; and he shall come unto us as the rain, as the latter and former rain unto the earth.>]

VS6 And I will lay sinews upon you, and will bring up flesh upon you, and cover you with skin, and put breath in you, and ye shall live; [This follows the normal anatomic reconstruction of a body, so Ezekiel is seeing the orderly resurrection of the nation.] **and ye shall know that I am the LORD.** [This is a continuing refrain for Ezekiel. When Israel sees the miracle of its resurrection it, and the whole world will know Yahweh is Lord]

VS7 So I prophesied as I was commanded: and as I prophesied, there was a noise, [Noise from *koul* to call aloud. It is used of the trumpet and of the noise of war. <Ex 20:18 And all the people saw the thunderings, and the lightnings, and the <u>noise</u> of the trumpet, and the mountain smoking: and when the people saw it, they removed, and stood afar off.> **and behold a shaking, and the bones came together, bone to his bone.** [A tremendous political earthquake will take place at Christ's return as world leaders, both secular and religious will debate the meaning of his presence. <Rev 16:18 And there were voices, and thunders, and lightnings; and there was a great earthquake, such as was not since men were upon the earth, so mighty an earthquake, and so great.> which will result in the overthrow of the Gentile power and the elevation of Israel to full glory. A literal earthquake will likewise take place. <Ezek 38:19 For in my jealousy and in the fire of my wrath have I spoken, Surely in that day there shall be a great shaking in the land of Israel;> <Zech 14:5 And ye shall flee to the valley of the mountains; for the valley of the mountains shall reach unto Azal: yea, ye shall flee, like as ye fled from before the earthquake in the days of Uzziah king of Judah: and the LORD my God shall come, and all the saints with thee.>]

VS8 And when I beheld, lo, the sinews and the flesh came up upon them, and the skin covered them above: but there was no breath in them. [Like something from a science fiction movie the dry bones revert to a valley full of skin covered dead bodies.]

VS9 Then said he unto me, Prophesy unto the wind, prophesy, son of man, and say to the wind, Thus saith the Lord GOD; [Wind here is *rauch* or spirit. Both in a literal and a spiritual sense man depends on the *rauch*, the breathing forth of the Almighty Who sustains natural man by His spirit and spiritual man by his Spirit Word. <Job 34:14 If he set his heart upon man, if he gather unto himself his spirit and his breath;> <John 6:63 It is the spirit that quickeneth; the flesh profiteth nothing: the words that I speak unto you, they are spirit, and they are life.>] **Come from the four winds, O breath,** [O breath is again spirit. <Zech 6:5 And the angel answered and said unto me, These are the four spirits of the heavens, which go forth from standing before the Lord of all the earth.>] **and breathe upon these slain, that they may live.** [This suggests they have been killed violently as in the destruction in AD 70 and will take place when Gog swoops down on the land.]

VS10 So I prophesied as he commanded me, and the breath came into them, and they lived, and stood up upon their feet, [Ezekiel typed Jesus by doing what God had ordained him to do.] **an exceeding great army.** [Israel will be organized into a powerful fighting force by the Lord Jesus and will be used to subdue the nations. Zechariah makes reference to this army, which staffed by immortal saints will extend the victories of Christ to the ends of the earth. <Zech 9:13 When I have bent Judah for me, filled the bow with Ephraim, and raised up thy sons, O Zion, against thy sons, O Greece, and made thee as the sword

of a mighty man 14 And the LORD shall be seen over them, and his arrow shall go forth as the lightning: and the LORD GOD shall blow the trumpet, and shall go with whirlwinds of the south. 15 The LORD of hosts shall defend them; and they shall devour, and subdue with sling stones; and they shall drink, and make a noise as through wine; and they shall be filled like bowls, and as the corners of the altar.>]

VS11 Then he said unto me, Son of man, these bones are the whole house of Israel: behold, they say, Our bones are dried, [Throughout his prophecies Ezekiel references Israel in addition to Judah which indicates he was in contact with those of the ten tribes. The angel shows him that the prophecies are for the whole house of Israel.] **and our hope is lost:** [They will see what happens and will feel all hope is gone.] **we are cut off for our parts.** [Destruction seems absolute and irreversible.]

VS12 Therefore prophesy and say unto them, Thus saith the Lord GOD; Behold, O my people, I will open your graves, [This verse applies not only to the resurrection of political Israel but the resurrection of the saints who will be part of that Israel. <Hos 13:14 I will ransom them from the power of the grave; I will redeem them from death: O death, I will be thy plagues; O grave, I will be thy destruction: repentance shall be hid from mine eyes.>] **and cause you to come up out of your graves, and bring you into the land of Israel.** [Grave here is the Hebrew *qeber* not *Sheol* as it usually is. A Qeber is a memorial tomb, not a grave, much like Washington Monument or Lincoln Memorial. The use is distinctive here. While many nations will fall into the nameless sheol, Israel will be remembered and the Qeber will be opened and like Lazarus, they will come out to do the bidding of the Lord. Zechariah spoke on the same theme. He declared: <Zech 10:9 And I will sow them among the people: and they shall remember me in far countries; and they shall live with their children, and turn again.> The term sow in this verse implies burial, a similar figure to 1 Cor. Chapter 15. But Zechariah saw the nation living again and restored to their former estate.]

VS13 And ye shall know that I am the LORD, when I have opened your graves, O my people, and brought you up out of your graves,

[Once again, when the world sees the miracle, they will recognize that Yahweh is Lord.]

VS14 And shall put my spirit in you, and ye shall live, [This is the rauch or wind or breath of vs 5 and 9.] **and I shall place you in your own land:** [The complete restoration occurs after Armageddon. The partial restoration in our lifetime is only a token of what will happen] **then shall ye know that I the LORD have spoken it, and performed it, saith the LORD.** [Many today take credit for the partial restoration of Israel. They will be humbled and caused to understand that it is Yahweh who does it and not them. <Ps 127:1 Except the LORD build the house, they labour in vain that build it: except the LORD keep the city, the watchman waketh but in vain.>]

A Transformed Government vs 15-28

VS15 The word of the LORD came again unto me, saying, [A new prophecy announced.]

VS16 Moreover, thou son of man, take thee one stick, and write upon it, [In Numbers Moses was told to take rods for each of the tribes of Israel. <Num 17:2 Speak unto the children of Israel, and take of every one of them a rod according to the house of their fathers, of all their princes according to the house of their fathers twelve rods: write thou every man's name upon his rod.> These were evidently green rods because they budded and blossomed. The word in the current verse is *aits* or a piece of wood. It was doubtless dry and withered as expressed by Jeremiah. <Lam 4:8 Their visage is blacker than a coal; they are not known in the streets: their skin cleaveth to their bones; it is withered, it is become like a stick.>] **For Judah, and for the children of Israel his companions:** [Who were the companions? They were Jacob and Levi that constituted the tribe of Judah after the kingdom divided.] **then take another stick, and write upon it, For Joseph,** [As the birthright was given to Joseph, <1 Chron 5:1 Now the sons of Reuben the firstborn of Israel, (for he was the firstborn; but, forasmuch as he defiled his father's bed, his birthright was given unto the sons of Joseph the son of Israel: and the genealogy is not to be reckoned after the birthright.> Joseph consequently got a double portion in Israel the tribes of Ephraim and

Manasseh. <Deut 21:17 But he shall acknowledge the son of the hated for the firstborn, by giving him a double portion of all that he hath: for he is the beginning of his strength; the right of the firstborn is his.>] **the stick of Ephraim, :** [Epharim the symbol of the northern kingdom was the younger son of Joseph elevated to position of firstborn, <Gen 48:17 And when Joseph saw that his father laid his right hand upon the head of Ephraim, it displeased him: and he held up his father's hand, to remove it from Ephraim's head unto Manasseh's head. 18 And Joseph said unto his father, Not so, my father: for this is the firstborn; put thy right hand upon his head. 19 And his father refused, and said, I know it, my son, I know it: he also shall become a people, and he also shall be great: but truly his younger brother shall be greater than he, and his seed shall become a multitude of nations. 20 And he blessed them that day, saying, In thee shall Israel bless, saying, God make thee as Ephraim and as Manasseh: and he set Ephraim before Manasseh.> Yahweh calls the northern kingdom his firstborn <Jer 31:9 They shall come with weeping, and with supplications will I lead them: I will cause them to walk by the rivers of waters in a straight way, wherein they shall not stumble: for I am a father to Israel, and Ephraim is my firstborn.> and that He loves him with an everlasting love. <Jer 31:3 The LORD hath appeared of old unto me, saying, Yea, I have loved thee with an everlasting love: therefore with loving kindness have I drawn thee.> Because of that love, Ephraim will be restored to the land. The love is not due to the actions of the rebellious people, but rather by God's attitude towards the feelings for the father's of Israel. <Rom 11:28 As concerning the gospel, they are enemies for your sakes: but as touching the election, they are beloved for the fathers' sakes.>

As the principle tribe of the north, Ephraim stands for the Northern Kingdom who separated in the days of Jeroboam while Judah stands for the Southern Kingdom. <1 Kings 11:31 And he said to Jeroboam, Take thee ten pieces: for thus saith the LORD, the God of Israel, Behold, I will rend the kingdom out of the hand of Solomon, and will give ten tribes to thee:>] **and for all the house of Israel his companions** [All the tribes that associated together to revolt against the House of David in the days of Rehoboam, son of Solomon.]

VS17 And join them one to another into one stick; [Reunite and restore Israel.] **and they shall become one in thine hand.** [As he represents the Lord Jesus, the prophet prophetically restores the nation as will Christ acting as a representative of Yahweh.]

VS18 And when the children of thy people shall speak unto thee, saying, Wilt thou not shew us what thou meanest by these? [As always, the people will not understand the signs before them.]

VS19 Say unto them, Thus saith the Lord GOD; Behold, I will take the stick of Joseph, which is in the hand of Ephraim, and the tribes of Israel his fellows, and will put them with him, even with the stick of Judah, and make them one stick, and they shall be one in mine hand. [In his explanation to the people, the prophet was instructed to emphasize that the full restoration of Israel is the work of God. This is important for us to understand now as well in relation to the partial restoration of the land today. Only Yahweh can do the final restoration. Note acting as Son of Man in the previous verse, the statement is that the stick is in "thine hand" or the prophets hand as he represents Jesus. Here it is in "Mine hand" showing that it is Yahweh who accomplishes the resurrection of Israel through Jesus."]

VS20 And the sticks whereon thou writest shall be in thine hand before their eyes. [Ezekiel was told to prominently exhibit the sign before the people of Israel. In like manner the preaching of the hope of Israel should be prominently set before the world as the sign of restored Israel will be also.]

VS21 And say unto them, Thus saith the Lord GOD; Behold, I will take the children of Israel from among the heathen, whither they be gone, The people of Israel will have to fight their way back to the land. < Ezek 20:33 As I live, saith the Lord GOD, surely with a mighty hand, and with a stretched out arm, and with fury poured out, will I rule over you: 34 And I will bring you out from the people, and will gather you out of the countries wherein ye are scattered, with a mighty hand, and with a stretched out arm, and with fury poured out. 35 And I will bring you into the wilderness of the people, and there will I plead with you face to face. 36. Like as I pleaded with your fathers in the wilderness of the land of Egypt, so will I plead with you, saith the Lord GOD. 37 And I will cause you to pass under the rod, and I will bring you into the bond of the covenant: 38 And I will purge out from among you the rebels, and them that transgress against me: I will bring them forth out of the country where they sojourn, and they shall not enter into the land of Israel: and ye shall know that I am the LORD.>] **and will gather them on every side, and bring them into their own land:** [The prophet shows that the Israelites will via two routes, north through the Euphrates or via the south through the Red Sea. < Isa 11:11 And it shall come to pass in that day, that the Lord shall set his hand again the second time to recover the remnant of his people, which shall be left, from Assyria, and from Egypt, and from Pathros, and from Cush, and from Elam, and from Shinar, and from Hamath, and from the islands of the sea. 12 And he shall set up an ensign for the nations, and shall assemble the outcasts of Israel, and gather together the dispersed of Judah from the four corners of the earth.> <Isa 27:12 And it shall come to pass in that day, that the LORD shall beat off from the channel of the river unto the stream of Egypt, and ye shall be gathered one by one, O ye children of Israel. 13 And it shall come to pass in that day, that the great trumpet shall be blown, and they shall come which were ready to perish in the land of Assyria, and the outcasts in the land of Egypt, and shall worship the LORD in the holy mount at Jerusalem.> Either route requires that they pass through water and be nationally baptized as they were when they were first brought out of Egypt with Moses. < 1 Cor 10:2 And were all baptized unto Moses in the cloud and in the sea;> Only this time they will not be baptized to Moses but to the Lord Jesus Christ.]

VS22 And I will make them one nation in the land [Jeremiah likewise refers to this <Jer 50:4 In those days, and in that time, saith the LORD, the children of Israel shall come, they and the children of Judah together, going and weeping: they shall go, and seek the LORD their God. 5 They shall ask the way to Zion with their faces thitherward, saying, Come, and let us join ourselves to the LORD in a perpetual covenant that shall not be forgotten.>] **upon the mountains of Israel;** [Not just the mountains but all of Israel. <Isa 2:2 And it shall come to pass in the last days, that the mountain of the LORD's house shall be established in the top of the mountains, and shall be exalted above the hills; and all nations shall flow unto it. 3 And many people shall go and say, Come ye, and let us go up to the mountain of the LORD, to the house of the

God of Jacob; and he will teach us of his ways, and we will walk in his paths: for out of Zion shall go forth the law, and the word of the LORD from Jerusalem.>] **and one king shall be king to them all:** [This is the prince whose right it is, the Lord Jesus Christ. <Ezek 21:27 I will overturn, overturn, overturn, it: and it shall be no more, until he come whose right it is; and I will give it him.> Some claim this was partly fulfilled during the restoration under Zerubbbel's, but never, since this prophecy was uttered by Ezekiel, has one king ruled over Israel.] **and they shall be no more two nations, neither shall they be divided into two kingdoms any more at all:**[This is the true hope of Israel]

VS23 Neither shall they defile themselves any more with their idols, [The nation will be not only physically, but spiritually rejuvenated.] **nor with their detestable things,** [The grossest of corruptions] **nor with any of their transgressions:** [Transgressions is the Hebrew *pasha* or rebellion, something the Israelites have been noted for in the past, but will not be in the future.] **but I will save them out of all their dwellingplaces, wherein they have sinned, and will cleanse them:** [These dwelling places are the Gentile nations to which they were driven] **so shall they be my people, and I will be their God.** [God considers this His land and His people, even though the Jews don't. When they do, this section of the verse comes to pass.]

VS24 And David my servant shall be king over them; and they all shall have one shepherd: [David whose name means beloved is like Ezekiel a type of Christ. Servant is significant in this sentence because it reminds us of Jesus mission as savior. <Acts 5:31 Him hath God exalted with his right hand to be a Prince and a Saviour, for to give repentance to Israel, and forgiveness of sins.> Ezekiel saw him this way, as both ruler and savior.] **they shall also walk in my judgments, and observe my statutes, and do them.** [Not only will they hear it, but do it thus allowing the outpouring of blessings outlined in Lev. 26.]

VS25 And they shall dwell in the land that I have given unto Jacob my servant, wherein your fathers have dwelt; and they shall dwell therein, even they, and their children, and their children's children for ever: [The land was promised to Jacob when he was in Bethel, fleeing from Esau. <Gen 28:13 And, behold, the LORD stood above it,

and said, I am the LORD God of Abraham thy father, and the God of Isaac: the land whereon thou liest, to thee will I give it, and to thy seed; 14 And thy seed shall be as the dust of the earth, and thou shalt spread abroad to the west, and to the east, and to the north, and to the south: and in thee and in thy seed shall all the families of the earth be blessed. 15 And, behold, I am with thee, and will keep thee in all places whither thou goest, and will bring thee again into this land; for I will not leave thee, until I have done that which I have spoken to thee of.> Verse 15 is the testimonial that the promise is absolute.>] **and my servant David shall be their prince for ever.** [Ever here is *olam* translated, for the age. Christ will reign for 1000 years which constitutes the age, at which time he will deliver a perfect kingdom to Yahweh. <Rev 20:5 But the rest of the dead lived not again until the thousand years were finished. This is the first resurrection.> <1 Cor 15:28 And when all things shall be subdued unto him, then shall the Son also himself be subject unto him that put all things under him, that God may be all in all.>]

VS26 Moreover I will make a covenant of peace with them; [The peace that passes all understanding.] **it shall be an everlasting covenant with them: and I will place them, and multiply them,** [Once again, everlasting is olam suggesting it means the Millennial thousand years.]**and will set my sanctuary in the midst of them** [This will be accomplished when the great temple described beginning in Ezekiel 40 is constructed.] **for evermore.** [Again the word is olam, see above]

VS27 My tabernacle also shall be with them: [The Hebrew word is *Mikshkan* or dwelling place. Yahweh will dwell with his people, but not by personally coming down from heaven, but through the manifestation of His glory in Christ.] **yea, I will be their God, and they shall be my people.** [Moses set this out to Israel as a promise conditioned upon their obedience to Yahweh. <Lev 26:12 And I will walk among you, and will be your God, and ye shall be my people.>Now, when the nation is restored and cleansed and sanctified, they will walk in the land and obey Yahweh's dictates. They will be his people.]

VS28 And the heathen shall know that I the LORD do sanctify Israel, when my sanctuary shall be in the midst of them for evermore. [In the changed regenerated nation, the world will see the hand of Yahweh.]

CHAPTER 16

Ezekiel Chapter 38

The stage is set. Israel is now a nation again. It is time to look at the players. Even though this prophecy speaks of Russia as it was when it was the USSR and threatened to plunge the world into nuclear war during the Cuban missile crisis, it is still a prophecy that will come to pass as all the others of Ezekiel have. The discovery of a large Soviet spy ring in the United States in 2010 is proof positive that Russia's ambitions of world domination have not diminished. This, coupled with the Arab world's vow to wipe the nation of Israel from the face of the earth testifies to the truth of Ezekiel's words.

VS:1 And the word of the LORD came unto me, saying, [A new prophecy that will come true. < Isa 55:11 So shall my word be that goeth forth out of my mouth: it shall not return unto me void, but it shall accomplish that which I please, and it shall prosper in the thing whereto I sent it.>]

Comment on Gog

From *Amplified Old Testament Bible*: "Gog is a symbolic name standing for the leader of the word powers antagonistic to God. Meshech and Tubal are understood to have been the same as the Moschi and Tibareni of the Greeks-tribes that inhabited regions in the Caucasus. Rosh, which would identify with Russia must have been designated a land and people somewhere in the same quarter. And therefore the Gog of Ezekiel must be viewed as in some sense the head of the high regions of northwest of Asia."

Gesenius observes that it can scarcely be doubtful that the first trace of Russia is here. Hengstenberg (1802-1869) could not bear to see "the poor Russians" ranged among the enemies of the kingdom of God. But the One who gave Ezekiel this vision of what was to happen in the latter days made no mistake in such a forecast as all the world would admit today."

VS2 Son of man, [Ezekiel is called by this title since Christ will fulfill this prophecy. < Isa 17:13 The nations shall rush like the rushing of many waters: but God shall rebuke them, and they shall flee far off, and shall be chased as the chaff of the mountains before the wind, and like a rolling thing before the whirlwind.>] **set thy face against** [the Hebrew here for against, means motion against the object, or move against. The multitudinous Son of Man will do this when Gog invades the land. < Isa 30:27 Behold, the name of the LORD cometh from far, burning with his anger, and the burden thereof is heavy: his lips are full of indignation, and his tongue as a devouring fire:>] **Gog,** [Name means a roof and Hamon-Gog the multitude on the roof. This is interesting in view of the destruction of the Philistines, "on the roof" when Samson with renewed strength overthrew it. Samson typed Israel on behalf of whom Gog's hosts will be destroyed.

In numbers Balaam predicted that the future king of Israel < Num 24:7 He shall pour the water out of his buckets, and his seed shall be in many waters, and his king shall be higher than Agag, and his kingdom shall be exalted.>

The *Seputagint* renders Agag as Gog. Thus Balaam prophetically saw the destruction of Gog at the hands of Christ and the exaltation of the Kingdom of God over Edom or the flesh. The Gogian host of the future will be representative of the flesh in political manifestation and as such is doomed for destruction. Thus Gog is represented as the "one on the roof" or the top befits the name.] **the land of Magog,** [Magog is identified by Josephus with the Scythians who according to Herodotus spread from the River Tanais or Don westward along the banks of the Ister or Danube through the area later know as Hungary, Transylvania and Wallachia.

Dion Cassius who lived 150 years after Josephus relates how that Pompey in his return to Europe from Asia, "determined to pass to the Ister or Danube through the Scythae and so to enter Italy" Diodorus Siculus who lived about a century before Josephus traces the Scythians or Magogites much further into Europe than the Danube, even to the shores of the Baltic. The land of Magog therefore comprises central Europe including Germany, but extending to the Baltic. According to the terms of the prophecy, Magog must dominate in that area.

This can only be by conquest or agreement because Gog's title is not Prince of Magag, but Prince of Ros. Gog is three times given this title (but only once is said to be "of the land of Magog." Later the punishment of Magog is shown as being independent of that poured out on Gog's forces showing the two to be different. < Ezek 39:6 And I will send a fire on Magog, and among them that dwell carelessly in the isles: and they shall know that I am the LORD.>] **the chief prince** [This should be treated as a proper noun and not an appellative. Bochart in *Sacred Geography* declares that "Ros is the most ancient form under which history makes mention of the name of Russia."

Stanley in *The Eastern Church*, "the name Russ, Hebrew Roas, LXX, Ros, is unfortunately translated in the English version "the chief" first appears in Ezekiel 38:2 and is the only name of a modern nation to appear in the Old Testament." Gibbon, in *Decline and Fall of the Roman Empire* says, "Among the Greeks the appellation Russians has a single form, Ros."

George Sava in *Russia Triumphant* points out that the earliest name by which the Russians were know by was the title Rus. Ros itself means head or poison and Rosh represents the serpent power politically manifested. The word is translated poison in Job 20:16 and venom in Deut. 32:33 and gal in Deut. 29:18, 32:32. In these places the idea of poison and gall are perhaps derived because of the prominent head (seed-pod) of the poppy-plant from which opium is derived. Moses declared, < Deut 29:18 Lest there should be among you man, or woman, or family, or tribe, whose heart turneth away this day from the LORD our God, to go and serve the gods of these nations; lest there should be among you a root that beareth gall and wormwood;>

He likens gall or rosh to a poisonous philosophy that will turn men from serving Gd, a fit definition of Russian Communism with its Godless philosophy. Thus Rosh fittingly describes the serpent power politically manifested. The venom of the serpent, the dangerous fangs of the head are represented by the dual meanings of Rosh, as both poison and head.] **of Meshech** [The word is identified with Moscovy from where the name Moscow is derived. Bochart writes, "that it is the Rhossi and Moschi of who Ezekiel speaks, descended the Russians

and Moscovites, nations of the greatest celebrity in European Scyhthia"
Thus it appears that the modern names of Russia and Moscow or
Moskwa in the ancient were Ros and Mosc or Musc.] **and Tubal, and
prophesy against him,** [This seems to be Tobolske the metropolis of
Siberia. John Thomas writes," The River Tubal gives name to the city
Tobolium or Tobolksi the metropolis of the extensive region of Siberia
lying immediately eastward of the territories of Moscovy or Mosc.
Tobol and Mosc are mentioned together by Ezekiel who characterizes
them as nations trading in copper a metal plentiful metal in Siberia."]

VS3 And say, Thus saith the Lord GOD; Behold I am against thee,
[The Son of man speaks with authority and in the name of God.] **O
Gog, the chief prince of Meshech and Tubal:**[Note Magog is omitted
as it is in 39:1. From this it is obvious that Gog is of Ros or Russia
and only "of the Land of Magog" or central and western Europe by
extension of his power.]

VS4 And I will turn thee back, [The analogy here is of a fisherman
baiting his prey. Russia will invade Israel due to anti-semitism and due
to Israel's strategic position in the middle-east. Although Russia has
significant oil reserves, if it controls middle east oil, it would be able
to strangle the energy requirements of the rest of the world. **and put
hooks into thy jaws,** [Jaws is the Hebrew *chachiy* or ring for nose or
lip. < Isa 37:29 Because thy rage against me, and thy tumult, is come
up into mine ears, therefore will I put my hook in thy nose, and my
bridle in thy lips, and I will turn thee back by the way by which thou
camest.>

Assyria was a type of Gog and the sudden and unexpected destruction
of his forces outside Jerusalem prophesied by Isaiah foreshadowed the
Gorgion confederacy outside the walls of the same city. Gog will be
controlled by a far greater force than himself and with a hook in his
jaws, he will be controlled by Yahweh.] **and I will bring thee forth,
and all thine army, horses and horsemen, all of them clothed with
all sorts of armour, even a great company with bucklers and shields,**
[Gog gathers a great company under the banner of a holy war against
Yahweh.] **all of them handling swords:**[A great company prepared
for war. Modern weapons will replace the swords, but Gog will be well
armed.]

VS5 Persia, [Now Iran and Iraq, we see them turn against the west, as indeed they have.] **Ethiopia, and Libya with them; all of them with shield and helmet:**[Daniel 11:40-45 describes how the king of the north will drive south along the coastal plains of Palestine to stretch forth his hand on Egypt. His domination of Egypt will bring Libya and Ethiopia at his steps. At this stage, Gog will have bypassed Jerusalem, itself intent on dominating the important and strategic Suez Canal. Then, according to Daniel, < Dan 11:44 But tidings out of the east and out of the north shall trouble him: therefore he shall go forth with great fury to destroy, and utterly to make away many.> The tidings from the east will be the remarkable events of Christ's return. These events demand some alteration in the current co-operation manifested between Russia and the Arabs, since the Arabs are describes as "escaping" or "not escaping" the attack of the king of the north, (vs 41,42) indicating hostility between the two when the king of the north invades. Daniel describes the attack by Russia on Constantinople which will be the event that galvanizes the Arab world against the Russians. < Dan 11:40 And at the time of the end shall the king of the south push at him: and the king of the north shall come against him like a whirlwind, with chariots, and with horsemen, and with many ships; and he shall enter into the countries, and shall overflow and pass over.>]

VS6 Gomer, [Josephus, book 1, ch. 6 sec. 1, identifies these with the Galatians or the Gauls who migrated west to France, Holland, Belgium, etc.] **and all his bands;** [The RV renders this as hordes.] **the house of Togarmah of the north quarters, and all his bands: and many people with thee.** [Most likely Togarmah is Turkey. He was a son of Gomer therefore his posterity would migrate originally from the same locality as Gomer's other descendents-namely from the mountains of Taurus and Armanus; but instead of going west with their brethren, they diffused themselves over the north quarter that is relative to Judah. Ezekiel says < Ezek 27:14 They of the house of Togarmah traded in thy fairs with horses and horsemen and mules.>

This describes a nomadic people, tending flocks and herds in the northern pastures where nature favored their production with little care or expense. Russian and Independent Tatary are the countries of Togmah from which in former times poured the Turcoman cavalry which Gibbon says, "They proudly computed by millions." Georgia and Circassia are probably bands of Togarmah's house. The *Companion Bible* suggests it includes Armenia.]

VS7 Be thou prepared, and prepare for thyself, [Prepared is *kuwh* to be erect, set up or establish. Yahweh challenges Gog to set up his power for the ultimate contest of flesh with Yahweh.] **thou, and all thy company that are assembled unto thee,** [Assembled is *gahal* or ecclesia. They are uniting by invitation for a special purpose.] **and be thou a guard unto them.** [Guard is from *mishmar*, to hedge about as with thorns. This is characteristic of defense. They would defend them. But, Gog's defenses will be futile.]

VS8 After many days [The prophecy would not be fulfilled for a considerable time. In vs. 16 it is said to be the latter days, far into the future from Ezekiel's time.] **thou shalt be visited:** [Rotherham translates, "Thou shall muster they forces."] **in the latter years** [Phrase means at the end of years, or the end of Gentile time.] **thou shalt come into the land,** [Rotherham translates, "into the land of the remnant," a significant statement in view of Israel's partial restoration today.] **that is brought back from the sword** [This points to the people restored from death by the resurrection.] **and is gathered out of many people,** [This speaks to the people not the land itself.] **against the mountains of Israel, which have been always waste:** [Shows the desolation of the land prior to restoration.] **but it is brought forth out of the nations,** [To reinforce it is the people they speak of.] **and they shall dwell safely all of them.** [They will dwell safely on the mountain of Israel where Yahweh will be their refuge.]

VS9 Thou shalt ascend and come like a storm, thou shalt be like a cloud to cover the land, thou, and all thy bands, and many people with thee. [This suggests that Gog shall burst forth on the land like a storm, rage violently, spread quickly, alarm greatly, but cease finally. Storms rage and clash but they do not last indefinitely.]

VS10 Thus saith the Lord GOD; It shall also come to pass, that at the same time shall things come into thy mind, [Rotherham renders things as thoughts. The *Companion Bible* reads matters. Whatever the word, Gog will see an opportunity to achieve his ends.] **and thou shalt**

think an evil thought: [Daniel outlines those evil thoughts and their consequences <Dan 11:40 And at the time of the end shall the king of the south push at him: and the king of the north shall come against him like a whirlwind, with chariots, and with horsemen, and with many ships; and he shall enter into the countries, and shall overflow and pass over. 41 He shall enter also into the glorious land, and many countries shall be overthrown: but these shall escape out of his hand, even Edom, and Moab, and the chief of the children of Ammon. 42 He shall stretch forth his hand also upon the countries: and the land of Egypt shall not escape. 43 But he shall have power over the treasures of gold and of silver, and over all the precious things of Egypt: and the Libyans and the Ethiopians shall be at his steps. 44 But tidings out of the east and out of the north shall trouble him: therefore he shall go forth with great fury to destroy, and utterly to make away many. 45 And he shall plant the tabernacles of his palace between the seas in the glorious holy mountain; yet he shall come to his end, and none shall help him.> The strategic position of Israel in the middle east has been discussed.]

VS11 And thou shalt say, I will go up [To go up, Gog must first go down, if Gog is indeed Russia. As outlined in the above citation, Gog will sweep south with a lightning thrust into Egypt momentarily bypassing Jerusalem. This is reasonable since Egypt and Israel have a peace treaty signed after the Yom Kipper War. Then he will hear tidings from the East and North (Jerusalem). Leaving an occupation force in Egypt, Gog will drive north to the "glorious holy mountain" of verse 45 above. Thus <Zech 14:2 For I will gather all nations against Jerusalem to battle; and the city shall be taken, and the houses rifled, and the women ravished; and half of the city shall go forth into captivity, and the residue of the people shall not be cut off from the city. 3 Then shall the LORD go forth, and fight against those nations, as when he fought in the day of battle.>] **to the land of unwalled villages;** [This is Hebrew for rural or farming communities like the modern day Kibutz of Israel.] **I will go to them that are at rest, that dwell safely, all of them dwelling without walls, and having neither bars nor gates,** [Despite the current middle east turmoil, this is as safe as Jews have been for centuries. Again, the rural hamlets of modern day Israel are described.]

VS12 To take a spoil, and to take a prey; [Israel has been treated such for centuries.] **to turn thine hand upon the desolate places that are now inhabited, and upon the people that are gathered out of the nations, which have gotten cattle and goods,** [The middle east unites three continents, Europe, Asia and Africa. Beneath these desolate places lie the richest of the world's oil deposits. If Gog controls the region, it drives a wedge between eastern and western block nations and constitutes a strangle hold on the west's resources] **that dwell in the midst of the land.** [Margin renders midst, navel. Israel was the center of the ancient world that was limited to Assyria in the north and Egypt in the south. Even today, it remains the strategic center.

The Hebrew *tubbuwr* rendered midst comes from the root meaning that which is elevated. Judges uses it this way. <Judg 9:37 And Gaal spake again and said, See there come people down by the middle of the land, and another company come along by the plain of Meonenim.> Ezekiel points to the mountainous region of Israel, and is validated by Daniel 11:45. This all points to Israel in the land as the are today, occupying the midst, or high ground.]

VS13 Sheba, [Sheba was an Arab kingdom adjacent to modern Aden. To the Tyrian merchants with whom Sheba traded it was known as the spice country. <Ezek 27:22 The merchants of Sheba and Raamah, they were thy merchants: they occupied in thy fairs with chief of all spices, and with all precious stones, and gold.>

Archaeologists have uncovered the glory of this kingdom whose queen visited Solomon. A gigantic dam blocked the river Abhanat in Sheba conserving water for irrigation. Remains of the 60 foot high walls still defy the desert. Marib was the capital, occupying the southern tip of the Arabian Peninsula on the eastern spur of the mountain range that skirts the Red Sea. Inscriptions recording cities of a million inhabitants have been found.

If Sheba (the Arab world) is to protest against In 542 BC the dam broke and the desert claimed the spice nation of Sheba. In the days of Ezekiel it was a powerful kingdom and Isaiah speaks of their worship at the House of Prayer for All People. <Isa 60:6 The multitude of camels shall cover thee, the dromedaries of Midian and Ephah; all they from Sheba shall come: they shall bring gold and incense; and they shall shew forth the praises of the LORD.>

If Sheba (the Arab world) is to protest against Russia or Gog's attack, a change in relations between the two must occurs. As Daniel outlines in 11:41-42 already cited, the Arabs east of the Jordan are said to escape the attack while Egypt doesn't. When Russia moves on Turkey to "dry up the political Euphrates," <Rev 16:12 And the sixth angel poured out his vial upon the great river Euphrates; and the water thereof was dried up, that the way of the kings of the east might be prepared.> any pro Russian sentiment will disappear from the Arab world. They will align with the west, and even their centuries old enemies, the Israelis, against a more formidable enemy, Gog."] **and Dedan,** [Dedan is identified with Muscat on the far eastern tip of Arabia bordering the Arabian Sea. They are listed as traders at the Tyrian fairs of Ezekiel <Ezek 27:15 The men of Dedan were thy merchants; many isles were the merchandise of thine hand: they brought thee for a present horns of ivory and ebony.>

The Sultan of Muscat now rules Dedan. Isaiah 21 identifies Dedan with the Bedouin Arabs. This chapter uses two tribes of Arabs that elsewhere are used for Arabia in general. Why these two? Likely it is because of their geographic position. Sheba is far to the south of Israel and Dedan is to the east and between them they link the borders of Arabia. This in these two titles, the Arabs can be identified. Likewise, the west when it moves to fortify Israel will find it a tactical entry point.] **and the merchants of Tarshish,** [All evidence points to Tarshish as being Britain. Tarshish as a proper name occurs first in Genesis 10:4 and he was the second son of Japeth, who was the fourth son of Japhet, the eldest son of Noah. His descendents settled the Mediterranean and Adriatic and the Atlantic area above Gibraltar. The Mediterranean was called The Sea of Tarshish likely because of the enterprising sons of Tarshish who lived there. The southern coast of Spain abutting both the Atlantic and the Mediterranean, has a settlement named Tartessus believe to be a contraction of Tarsou nasos, or Tarshih's Island. (J. Thomas *Herald of the Coming Age* 1858)

Britain's long term occupation of Gibraltar is significant. < Ezek 27:12 Tarshish was thy merchant by reason of the multitude of all kind of riches; with silver, iron, tin, and lead, they traded in thy fairs. 13 Javan, Tubal, and Meshech, they were thy merchants: they traded the persons of men and vessels of brass in thy market.> These are products of the mines of Spain and Britain which were brought to Tyre in the "ships of Tarshish." *Chamber's Encyclopedia* in an article on Phoenicia declares: "From Tartessus in Spain, outside the Straits, the Atlantic and Bay of Biscay were explored and a trade with Cornwell and the Scily Islands was established and the Baltic Sea possibly entered in search of Amber."

Dickens, in *A Child's History of England* remarks, "It is supposed that the Phoenicians who are ancient people famous for carrying on trade, came in ships to these islands and found that they produced tin and lead both very useful things and produced to this very hour upon the sear coast. The Phoenicians coasting about the islands would come without much difficulty to where the tin and lead were. They traded with the islanders for the metal. It is claimed that a block of tin with Phoenician trade makes was fished up at the mouth of Falmouth Harbor, England and is now in the Royal Institution of Cornwall at Truro. It is further claimed that Britain was once known as the "house of tin."

Encyclopedia Britanica: "There can be no doubt that Cornwall and Devonshire are referred to under the general name of Cassiterides or the "Tin Islands."

Coot's *History of England* states, "Bochart is of the opinion that Phoenicians call the island by the name of Baratanec, that is "The Land of Tin," an appellation which the Greeks called Bretania and from whence comes the name Britanica.

In the remarkable prophecy concerning Tyre (Phoenicia) of Isaiah 23, the decline of Tyre as a mercantile marine power is predicted at which time her maritime dominance would "pass over to Tarshish. <Isa 23:5 As at the report concerning Egypt, so shall they be sorely pained at the report of Tyre. 6 Pass ye over to Tarshish; howl, ye inhabitants of the isle.> Later in the prophecy the ships of Tarshish are made to <Isa 23:14 Howl, ye ships of Tarshish: for your strength is laid waste.> The prophecy predicts the decline of the sea power of both Tyre and Tarshish. The Scriptures indicates two places called Tarshish, both of which have been linked by trade in the past, Britain and India. As noted Ezekiel told us Tarshish was noted for tin and Jonah shows that it lay in a far westerly direction from Palestine. <Jonah 1:3 But Jonah rose up to flee unto Tarshish from the presence of the LORD, and went down to Joppa; and he found a ship going to Tarshish: so he paid the

fare thereof, and went down into it, to go with them unto Tarshish from the presence of the LORD.>

That was a far as Jonah could go to flee the Lord. When he sailed from Joppa, there was only one direction he could sail, a westerly course down the Mediterranean. On the other hand, Solomon built a fleet to sail to Tarshish which sailed from Ebionezer, a port on the red sea. <1 Kings 9:26 And king Solomon made a navy of ships in Ezion-geber, which is beside Eloth, on the shore of the Red sea, in the land of Edom.> <1 Kings 10:22 For the king had at sea a navy of Tharshish with the navy of Hiram: once in three years came the navy of Tharshish, bringing gold, and silver, ivory, and apes, and peacocks.> Those ships could only sail south and east towards the Straits of Babelmandeb from whence they might proceed east or north for India. The goods they brought point to India as the eastern Tarshish. <2 Chron 9:21 For the king's ships went to Tarshish with the servants of Huram: every three years once came the ships of Tarshish bringing gold, and silver, ivory, and apes, and peacocks.> This is a remarkable confirmation of the prophetic picture that British commercial strength developed largely from the Anglo-Indian Company. Any argument against Tarshish as Britain did not examine these facts.] **with all the young lions thereof,** [The Hebrew *kephiyr* with one exception is rendered lions Since Ezekiel uses the name for nations, it is used here despite the fact that the RSV changes the word to villages. <Ezek 32:2 Son of man, take up a lamentation for Pharaoh king of Egypt, and say unto him, Thou art like a young lion of the nations, and thou art as a whale in the seas: and thou camest forth with thy rivers, and troubledst the waters with thy feet, and fouledst their rivers.> <Ezek 19:4 The nations also heard of him; he was taken in their pit, and they brought him with chains unto the land of Egypt.>

Who are the young lions? A young lion is not necessarily a cub, but a strong, viral individual on its own. This aptly describes the nations who have come into being, The United States, Canada, Australia, and South Africa, for example, through the mother country.] **shall say unto thee,** [The prophecy thus demands that each of the nations individually raise a protest. Originally, a British declaration of war would automatically involve the colonies, excluding the USA of course, but since the Statute of Westminster in 1931, the remaining young lions of Britain received the freedom to act independently as required by the prophecy.] **Art thou come to take a spoil? hast thou gathered thy company to take a prey? to carry away silver and gold, to take away cattle and goods, to take a great spoil?** [The threatening voice of protest suggests British and American presence in the middle east, as current news shows in Iraq.]

VS14 Therefore, son of man, prophesy and say unto Gog, Thus saith the Lord GOD; [The usual introduction to a new pronouncement from Yahweh.] **In that day** [The period appointed of Yahweh <Acts 17:31 Because he hath appointed a day, in the which he will judge the world in righteousness by that man whom he hath ordained; whereof he hath given assurance unto all men, in that he hath raised him from the dead.>] **when my people of Israel dwelleth safely,** [Here is remarkable confirmation that the people of Israel are addressed as a people or nation, an event that occurred in 1948. The Jews of today advance Yahweh's purpose, even though they do not realize that fact.] **shalt thou not know it?** [Gog will recognize the vulnerability of the Middle East at the time Israel will be dwelling safely and unsuspectingly. The "peace and safety" cry will resound throughout Europe when sudden destruction overtakes them. <1 Thess 5:3 For when they shall say, Peace and safety; then sudden destruction cometh upon them, as travail upon a woman with child; and they shall not escape.> Since this takes place after Christ's return and while the household is being judged, there is ample time for any further political developments such as required in regard to Israel before Russia's sudden attack.]

VS15 And thou shalt come from thy place out of the north parts, thou, and many people with thee, all of them riding upon horses, a great company, and a mighty army: [The RV renders this "out of the uttermost parts of the north. Draw a line on the map. Moscow is almost directly north of Jerusalem, the uttermost parts of the north.]

VS16 And thou shalt come up against my people of Israel, as a cloud to cover the land; it shall be in the latter days, [There may have been a partial fulfillment of the prophecy of the Scythians in times contemporary with Ezekiel, but here the declaration is clear and certain that it is to be fulfilled and certain that is to be fulfilled at the time of the end, the period that Daniel 11 will also be fulfilled.] **and I will bring thee against my land,** [The land belongs to Yahweh and not Israel after the flesh. Thus Gog is trying to grasp that which is Yahweh's. This is the controversy between Gog and Yahweh. < Joel 3:2 I will also gather all nations, and will bring them down into the valley of Jehoshaphat, and will plead with them there for my people and for my heritage Israel, whom they have scattered among the nations, and parted my land.>] **that the heathen may know me, when I shall be sanctified in thee, O Gog,** [Yahweh's intervention will let the world know He is the God of Israel. It will force the world to recognize Yahweh as God and sanctify the promises of Yahweh.] **before their eyes.** [The amazing overthrow of Gog on the eve of apparent victory will reveal the supernatural means b which it will have been accomplished. This will be displayed before the eyes of all nations and they will learn of it.]

VS17 Thus saith the Lord GOD; Art thou he of whom I have spoken in old time by my servants the prophets of Israel, which prophesied in those days many years that I would bring thee against them? [The theme of Armageddon is found in all the prophets though presented in different ways and diverse manner. The judgment poured out is a bruising on the head (Ros) of the serpent power in political manifestation and as such is a fulfillment of the covenant in Eden. < Gen 3:15 And I will put enmity between thee and the woman, and between thy seed and her seed; it shall bruise thy head, and thou shalt bruise his heel.> The final crush of the serpent power occurs after the Millennium. < Gen 3:15 And I will put enmity between thee and the woman, and between thy seed and her seed; it shall bruise thy head, and thou shalt bruise his heel.>]

VS18 And it shall come to pass at the same time when Gog shall come against the land of Israel, saith the Lord GOD, that my fury shall come up in my face. [The fury of Yahweh's is reflected in the face of Christ and the immortals. This is a common expression though out scripture. For example < Gen 4:14 Behold, thou hast driven me out this day from the face of the earth; and from thy face shall I be hid; and I shall be a fugitive and a vagabond in the earth; and it shall come to pass, that every one that findeth me shall slay me.> From thy face

I hid of course means from the face of the angels who were acting as Yahweh's agents.]

VS19 For in my jealousy [The same word is translated zeal elsewhere. The desecration of His land and people is hateful to Yahweh and his zeal will extend to their cause. It will be manifested in preserving the remnant of Israel. < Isa 37:32 For out of Jerusalem shall go forth a remnant, and they that escape out of mount Zion: the zeal of the LORD of hosts shall do this.>

In arming His warriors < Isa 59:17 For he put on righteousness as a breastplate, and an helmet of salvation upon his head; and he put on the garments of vengeance for clothing, and was clad with zeal as a cloke.> in going forth to war < Isa 42:13 The LORD shall go forth as a mighty man, he shall stir up jealousy like a man of war: he shall cry, yea, roar; he shall prevail against his enemies.> <Zech 8:2 Thus saith the LORD of hosts; I was jealous for Zion with great jealousy, and I was jealous for her with great fury.> in gathering the nations to judgment < Zeph 3:8 Therefore wait ye upon me, saith the LORD, until the day that I rise up to the prey: for my determination is to gather the nations, that I may assemble the kingdoms, to pour upon them mine indignation, even all my fierce anger: for all the earth shall be devoured with the fire of my jealousy.> and finally establishing the throne of David throughout the world. < Isa 9:7 Of the increase of his government and peace there shall be no end, upon the throne of David, and upon his kingdom, to order it, and to establish it with judgment and with justice from henceforth even for ever. The zeal of the LORD of hosts will perform this.>] **and in the fire of my wrath have I spoken,** [Yahweh's fiery wrath is frightening to contemplate.] **Surely in that day there shall be a great shaking in the land of Israel;**[Contrast < Ezek 37:7 So I prophesied as I was commanded: and as I prophesied, there was a noise, and behold a shaking, and the bones came together, bone to his bone.> Israel is shaken together and Gog is shaken apart.> There will great seismographic upheavals and convulsions of nature at Christ's return as there was at his death. In fear and superstition, Gog's forces will destroy themselves.]

VS20 So that the fishes of the sea, and the fowls of the heaven, and the beasts of the field, and all creeping things that creep upon the

earth, and all the men that are upon the face of the earth, [The earthquake will not only disrupt Gog but send fear throughout all creation.] **shall shake at my presence,** [Presence is from *paniym* or faces relating to Christ and the saints in fierce array. The faces here are linked to Ezekiel's view of the Cherubim in chapter one.] **and the mountains shall be thrown down,** [Zechariah shows the Mt. of Olives will be torn asunder. < Zech 14:4 And his feet shall stand in that day upon the mount of Olives, which is before Jerusalem on the east, and the mount of Olives shall cleave in the midst thereof toward the east and toward the west, and there shall be a very great valley; and half of the mountain shall remove toward the north, and half of it toward the south.> That conclusively links Zechariah 14 and Ezekiel 38. This is the tremendous earthquake described by each prophet.] **and the steep places shall fall,** [This agrees with Zechariah who shows that the mountainous regions around Jerusalem will become a plane.] **and every wall shall fall to the ground.** [Reminiscent of the overthrow of Jericho all the natural defenses of man will be destroyed.]

VS21 And I will call for a sword against him throughout all my mountains, saith the Lord GOD: [There is perfect justice in this, because earlier Gog has announced his intention to attack a people, "called back from the sword" vs 8. Now the sword of divine justice and wrath is issued against Gog. In addition to Gog's own mutually antagonistic forces, the remnants of Judah in the land shall also take up weapons and regroup there forces to fight the invader. <Zech 14:14 And Judah also shall fight at Jerusalem; and the wealth of all the heathen round about shall be gathered together, gold, and silver, and apparel, in great abundance.>] **every man's sword shall be against his brother.** [In panic and fear at the unexpected inexplicable antagonist, the confederated forces will turn their weapons on one another. <Hab 3:12 Thou didst march through the land in indignation, thou didst thresh the heathen in anger. 13 Thou wentest forth for the salvation of thy people, even for salvation with thine anointed; thou woundedst the head out of the house of the wicked, by discovering the foundation unto the neck. Selah. 14 Thou didst strike through with his staves the head of his villages: they came out as a whirlwind to scatter me: their rejoicing was as to devour the poor secretly.> And, similar to the host opposed by Gideon they shall largely encompass their own destruction. <Judg 7:21 And they stood every man in his place round about the camp: and all the host ran, and cried, and fled. 22 And the three hundred blew the trumpets, and the LORD set every man's sword against his fellow, even throughout all the host: and the host fled to Beth-shittah in Zererath, and to the border of Abel-meholah, unto Tabbath.>

This victory of the future has thus been typified by the in the past by the courage and faith of Gideon's 300 men, and by the faith of Jehoshaphat at a similar time of crisis. <2 Chron 20:23 For the children of Ammon and Moab stood up against the inhabitants of mount Seir, utterly to slay and destroy them: and when they had made an end of the inhabitants of Seir, every one helped to destroy another. 24 And when Judah came toward the watch tower in the wilderness, they looked unto the multitude, and, behold, they were dead bodies fallen to the earth, and none escaped. 25 And when Jehoshaphat and his people came to take away the spoil of them, they found among them in abundance both riches with the dead bodies, and precious jewels, which they stripped off for themselves, more than they could carry away: and they were three days in gathering of the spoil, it was so much. 26 And on the fourth day they assembled themselves in the valley of Berachah; for there they blessed the LORD: therefore the name of the same place was called, The valley of Berachah, unto this day.>]

VS22 And I will plead against him [Rotherham renders this as contend with certainly expresses the thought better.] **with pestilence and with blood;** [Israel has experienced this in the past. <Ezek 5:17 So will I send upon you famine and evil beasts, and they shall bereave thee; and pestilence and blood shall pass through thee; and I will bring the sword upon thee. I the LORD have spoken it. The form of pestilence is describe by Zechariah <Zech 14:12 And this shall be the plague wherewith the LORD will smite all the people that have fought against Jerusalem; Their flesh shall consume away while they stand upon their feet, and their eyes shall consume away in their holes, and their tongue shall consume away in their mouth.> (Sounds a bit like nuclear injury doesn't it?) and is suggestive of the effect of the belligerent spirit manifestation. This will be used by Christ and the saints as a weapon of aggression against the enemy. Pleading with blood suggests the internecine warfare among the forces of Gog.] **and I will rain upon**

him, and upon his bands, and upon the many people that are with him,[The forces of nature will be used against Gog as Yahweh goes forth to fight as in days of old. <Zech 14:3 Then shall the LORD go forth, and fight against those nations, as when he fought in the day of battle.> <Josh 5:13 And it came to pass, when Joshua was by Jericho, that he lifted up his eyes and looked, and, behold, there stood a man over against him with his sword drawn in his hand: and Joshua went unto him, and said unto him, Art thou for us, or for our adversaries? 14 And he said, Nay; but as captain of the host of the LORD am I now come. And Joshua fell on his face to the earth, and did worship, and said unto him, What saith my lord unto his servant?> <Josh 10:14 And there was no day like that before it or after it, that the LORD hearkened unto the voice of a man: for the LORD fought for Israel.> <Josh 23:3 And ye have seen all that the LORD your God hath done unto all these nations because of you; for the LORD your God is he that hath fought for you.> <Judg 4:15 And the LORD discomfited Sisera, and all his chariots, and all his host, with the edge of the sword before Barak; so that Sisera lighted down off his chariot, and fled away on his feet.>]
an overflowing rain, [This is a rain so intense that it submerges its victims in destructions as it did Sisera in the above reference and in this one <Judg 5:21 The river of Kishon swept them away, that ancient river, the river Kishon. O my soul, thou hast trodden down strength.> and is used in relation to the judgment of Jerusalem. <Ezek 13:11 Say unto them which daub it with untempered morter, that it shall fall: there shall be an overflowing shower; and ye, O great hailstones, shall fall; and a stormy wind shall rend it.> These are typical of the of the coming destructions of Gog.] **and great hailstones,** [Hailstones are literally stones of ice. This suggests a repetition of the victory of Joshua at Bethoron against the confederation of nations. <Josh 10:11 And it came to pass, as they fled from before Israel, and were in the going down to Beth-horon, that the LORD cast down great stones from heaven upon them unto Azekah, and they died: they were more which died with hailstones than they whom the children of Israel slew with the sword.>] **fire, and brimstone.** [This suggests the destruction like that of Sodom and Gomorrah and the warning words of the Lord himself. <Luke 17:28 Likewise also as it was in the days of Lot; they did eat, they drank, they bought, they sold, they planted, they builded; 29 But the same day that Lot went out of Sodom it rained fire and

brimstone from heaven, and destroyed them all 30 Even thus shall it be in the day when the Son of man is revealed.>].

VS23 Thus [This chapter has outlined the great crisis of the last days in which the Lord Jesus with the glorified elect will dramatically introduce himself to a startled world. The last time the world saw him, he hung lifeless from the stake of shame but will return as the Lion of Judah.

The imagery brought together in these verses is borrowed from notable victories of the past when the judgment of Yahweh was poured out upon flesh which are now shown as typical of the coming great judgment of the future. Thus the overthrow of the walls of Jericho foreshadows the coming crisis when all human forms of defense will be overthrown. The destruction of the confederated forces by Gideon and his faithful warriors is seen as a type of the end of the Gogian confederacy the victory of Bark against overwhelming odds anticipates that of the Lord Jesus against the might of the flesh, and the overthrow of Sodom like the overwhelming destruction of the Gentiles who invade and profane the land. In the Great Day of the Lord, flesh will be humbled in the land, and will begin a time of trouble such as never was for the nations.

And though even after this time the Catholic countries of Europe regroup their forces to resist the rising power of Zion, the Lord Jesus through his Israelite army will invade their territories to bring them successively under his power. Thus the Kingdom of Godlike the stone cut out of the mountain without hand will extend its control until all nations are subject to the Lord Jesus. **will I magnify myself,** [Yahweh will be magnified before flesh though the remarkable victory that will be won. It will be apparent to the Jews in the land that it will have been brought about by Divine power. The outpouring of Divine judgment will compel the wicked to acknowledge this.] **and sanctify myself; and I will be known in the eyes of many nations, and they shall know that I am the LORD.** [Yahweh will reveal that He is different from flesh and as this is recognized, mankind will slowly be converted to his cause.]

CHAPTER 17

Ezekiel Chapter 39

The end of the prophecy and the justice of Yahweh conclude in this chapter of Ezekiel. The aftermath of the immortals conquest of the opposition to the returning Christ is described in detail.

VS39:1 Therefore, thou son of man, prophesy against Gog, and say, Thus saith the Lord GOD; Behold, I am against thee, O Gog, the chief prince of Meshech and Tubal: [See notes on 38:2. Again Gog is described as the prince of Meshech and Tubal but Magog is not mentioned and dealt with separately in verse 6.]

VS2 And I will turn thee back, [This is a repetition of 38:4 and not another turning back] **and leave but the sixth part of thee, and will cause thee to come up from the north parts, and will bring thee upon the mountains of Israel:** [RV renders this I will lead you on and the RSV translates I will drive you forward. The Root here is *Shasha*, to lead and not *shech* six. The statement is really explanatory of 38:4 and does not denote that a sixth of Gog will remain, rather nearly all will be destroyed in the Divine holocaust.]

VS3 And I will smite thy bow out of thy left hand, and will cause thine arrows to fall out of thy right hand. [The bow is held in the left hand, the arrows in the right. This signifies that the power of Gog will be destroyed completly but not the nations with him. They will be subject to Divine judgment in their own land if they do not accept Christ's ultimatum which will be issued to all nations commanding them to submit to his rule. <Ps 2:10 Be wise now therefore, O ye kings: be instructed, ye judges of the earth.11 Serve the LORD with fear, and rejoice with trembling.12 Kiss the Son, lest he be angry, and ye perish

from the way, when his wrath is kindled but a little. Blessed are all they that put their trust in him.> <Isa 14:32 What shall one then answer the messengers of the nation? That the LORD hath founded Zion, and the poor of his people shall trust in it.> <Rev 14:6 And I saw another angel fly in the midst of heaven, having the everlasting gospel to preach unto them that dwell on the earth, and to every nation, and kindred, and tongue, and people,7 Saying with a loud voice, Fear God, and give glory to him; for the hour of his judgment is come: and worship him that made heaven, and earth, and the sea, and the fountains of waters.>]

VS4 Thou shalt fall upon the mountains of Israel, thou, and all thy bands, and the people that is with thee: I will give thee unto the ravenous birds of every sort, [Isaiah uses this expression as symbolic of the "man from the east" who does the will of God. < Isa 46:11 Calling a ravenous bird from the east, the man that executeth my counsel from a far country: yea, I have spoken it, I will also bring it to pass; I have purposed it, I will also do it.> Applying it here, it can be related to the "kings of the east" or those who are manifested out of the Sun's rising on whose behalf these things will take place. <Rev 16:12 And the sixth angel poured out his vial upon the great river Euphrates; and the water thereof was dried up, that the way of the kings of the east might be prepared.> These ravenous birds therefore constitute the glorified saints, the royal priesthood of the age to come called out of all nations to reign with Christ <Rev 5:9 And they sung a new song, saying, Thou art worthy to take the book, and to open the seals thereof: for thou wast slain, and hast redeemed us to God by thy blood out of every kindred, and tongue, and people, and nation;10 And hast made us unto our God kings and priests: and we shall reign on the earth.>] **and to the beasts of the field to be devoured.** [Beasts from *chay* or living creatures. It is the word used for them in Ezekiel 1 and thus relates to the Cherubim. The resurrected and immortalized saints or the ravenous birds and the beasts or Cherubim will be the forces who overthrow Gog.]

VS5 Thou shalt fall upon the open field: for I have spoken it, saith the Lord GOD. [God's word is power and what He says, He will do as Ezekiel repeatedly reiterates.]

VS6 And I will send a fire on Magog, [See note 38:2. The Catholic countries of Central Europe are particularly singled out in the verse, likely because of their past brutality against the Jewish people and long heritage of anti-Semitism.] **and among them that dwell carelessly in the isles:** [This expression relates to people who live so far away from the conflict, like Australia, that they feel isolated by distance from the conflict, but this is a false idea. Nations "afar off" will not escape. <Mic 4:3And he shall judge among many people, and rebuke strong nations afar off; and they shall beat their swords into plowshares, and their spears into pruninghooks: nation shall not lift up a sword against nation, neither shall they learn war any more.>] **and they shall know that I am the LORD.** [Conversion will follow the judgment.]

VS7 So will I make my holy name known in the midst of my people Israel; [The full meaning and power of the name will be revealed by these judgments and succeeding acts of mercy and it will be acknowledged by all sides yes some imagine the Divine name is already completely fulfilled and never to be used. Yahweh will reveal his purpose, character and power to all men and by this men will come to appreciate what is incorporate in His name. This will be centered in the midst of Israel because there the house of prayer for all people will be erected and those who came to Jerusalem to fight will come to worship instead.] **and I will not let them pollute my holy name any more:** [Israel has done this in the past, but in the future it will no longer be tolerated. Strong measures will be instituted to preserve the integrity of the Truth. <Zech 13:1 In that day there shall be a fountain opened to the house of David and to the inhabitants of Jerusalem for sin and for uncleanness.2 And it shall come to pass in that day, saith the LORD of hosts, that I will cut off the names of the idols out of the land, and they shall no more be remembered: and also I will cause the prophets and the unclean spirit to pass out of the land.3 And it shall come to pass, that when any shall yet prophesy, then his father and his mother that begat him shall say unto him, Thou shalt not live; for thou speakest lies in the name of the LORD: and his father and his mother that begat him shall thrust him through when he prophesieth.4 And it shall come to pass in that day, that the prophets shall be ashamed every one of his vision, when he hath prophesied; neither shall they wear a rough garment to deceive:5 But he shall say, I am no prophet, I am

an husbandman; for man taught me to keep cattle from my youth.>] **and the heathen shall know that I am the LORD, the Holy One in Israel.** [Even the profane nations will have no choice but to know that Yahweh is God.]

VS8 Behold, it is come, and it is done, saith the Lord GOD; [Rotherman suggests, "Lo it is coming and it is brought to pass." Yahweh's purpose has been plain for 6 thousand years but man has ignored it. That will change.] **this is the day whereof I have spoken.** [That is, the day of the Lord, or the great day of God Almighty, or The Age to Come.]

VS9 And they that dwell in the cities of Israel shall go forth, and shall set on fire and burn the weapons, both the shields and the bucklers, the bows and the arrows, and the handstaves, and the spears, [The symbols of war will be burned in the land of Israel. It was an ordinance in the Law of Moses that all spoils of war were subjected to fire and those metals that survived were to be cleansed and used for <Num 31:21 And Eleazar the priest said unto the men of war which went to the battle, This is the ordinance of the law which the LORD commanded Moses; 22 Only the gold, and the silver, the brass, the iron, the tin, and the lead, 23 Every thing that may abide the fire, ye shall make it go through the fire, and it shall be clean: nevertheless it shall be purified with the water of separation: and all that abideth not the fire ye shall make go through the water.> The weapons of Gog will be treated likewise. The ceremonial and national burning of weapons will testify that there is no further need of such so that lasting peace will ensue. <Isa 2:4 And he shall judge among the nations, and shall rebuke many people: and they shall beat their swords into plowshares, and their spears into pruninghooks: nation shall not lift up sword against nation, neither shall they learn war any more.>] **and they shall burn them with fire seven years:** [Seven is the number of covenant so this speaks to a covenant of peace for a millennium. Seven years of it will likely be occupied in repairing damages of the war and Christ consolidating his power and issuing the ultimatum to the nations. >]

VS10 So that they shall take no wood out of the field, neither cut down any out of the forests; for they shall burn the weapons with

fire: [This is figurative language. In ancient times wooden weapons would have been used as fuel to benefit the people. The same will be true in the future. Whatever can be used will be used.] **and they shall spoil those that spoiled them, and rob those that robbed them, saith the Lord GOD.** [Israel will become the first dominion of the world and all the wealth of the world will flow towards Jerusalem. <Mic 4:8 And thou, O tower of the flock, the strong hold of the daughter of Zion, unto thee shall it come, even the first dominion; the kingdom shall come to the daughter of Jerusalem.> <Isa 60:5 Then thou shalt see, and flow together, and thine heart shall fear, and be enlarged; because the abundance of the sea shall be converted unto thee, the forces of the Gentiles shall come unto thee.> <Isa 60:9 Surely the isles shall wait for me, and the ships of Tarshish first, to bring thy sons from far, their silver and their gold with them, unto the name of the LORD thy God, and to the Holy One of Israel, because he hath glorified thee.>]

VS11 And it shall come to pass in that day, that I will give unto Gog a place there of graves in Israel, [Grave is not *sheol* the general word for grave, but *qeber* a memorial. A memorial will be set up commemorating the overthrow of Gog.] **the valley of the passengers on the east of the sea:** [This is the valley east of the Jordan. Possibly the remnant of Gog's army will retreat north and east across the Jordan. Those who go up from year to year to worship in Jerusalem <Zech 14:16 And it shall come to pass, that every one that is left of all the nations which came against Jerusalem shall even go up from year to year to worship the King, the LORD of hosts, and to keep the feast of tabernacles.> will ascend by such a route east of the Jordan and will turn west along the valley of Achor to enter the Temple city of Jerusalem. To them, as they ascend for the worship and turn into the valley it will be as a door of hope. <Hos 2:15 And I will give her her vineyards from thence, and the valley of Achor for a door of hope: and she shall sing there, as in the days of her youth, and as in the day when she came up out of the land of Egypt.>

There herds will be grazing doubtless for sacrificial proposes in the new Temple. <Isa 65:10 And Sharon shall be a fold of flocks, and the valley of Achor a place for the herds to lie down in, for my people that have sought me.> But, before they come to the valley, they will pass the Memorial to Gog, and will be reminded of the dramatic overthrow of

189

the flesh in political manifestation. It will stand as a warning against following flesh in revolt against God. <Isa 66:24 And they shall go forth, and look upon the carcases of the men that have transgressed against me: for their worm shall not die, neither shall their fire be quenched; and they shall be an abhorring unto all flesh.> It will not die because it is in constant reminder for those visiting the Temple.] **and it shall stop the noses of the passengers: and there shall they bury Gog and all his multitude:** [Stop is *khosam* and means to muzzle. The word nose is in italics and is not in the text. Thus the statement does not mean there is a great stink here. It means that when the pilgrims see the memorial to the great victory of God over flesh, their mouths will be closed or muzzled from speaking against God. They will recognize the righteousness of God's decrees and dare not speak out against Him.] **and they shall call it The valley of Hamon-gog.** [The margin gives the meaning as "the multitude of Gog". The Memorial itself is called a city.]

VS12 And seven months shall the house of Israel be burying of them, that they may cleanse the land. [The object of this close scrutiny and complete burial is that the land might be thoroughly cleansed from the defilement of death. <Num 19:11 He that toucheth the dead body of any man shall be unclean seven days.> <Num 19:22 And whatsoever the unclean person toucheth shall be unclean; and the soul that toucheth it shall be unclean until even.> The long period of time is required to ensure that every last defilement is buried and the land cleansed.]

VS13 Yea, all the people of the land shall bury them; and it shall be to them a renown the day that I shall be glorified, saith the Lord GOD. [The people of Israel will engage in the cleaning with enthusiasm in the knowledge that Yahweh has been glorified in victory, and it will be to their credit or renown.]

VS14 And they shall sever out men of continual employment, passing through the land to bury [To cleans the land, men will be hired to bury any of the slain bones that remain.] **with the passengers those that remain upon the face of the earth, to cleanse it:** [The passengers are visitors but who are they? Those of vs. 11 are doubtless

Gentile visitors who come to worship as suggested by Zechariah. <Zech 14:16 And it shall come to pass, that every one that is left of all the nations which came against Jerusalem shall even go up from year to year to worship the King, the LORD of hosts, and to keep the feast of tabernacles.> But that will be after the Temple is built and will be a considerable time after the destruction of Gog.

It is likely the Temple will take 50 years to build after Christ's return. (See the 40th chapter of Ezekiel and *The Temple of Ezekiel's Prophecy* by H. Sully). These therefore must be those Gentiles in the land before the temple is built. <Isa 60:10 And the sons of strangers shall build up thy walls, and their kings shall minister unto thee: for in my wrath I smote thee, but in my favour have I had mercy on thee.>

The strangers will likely build the city as well as the temple. If they see a bone, as suggested by the next verse, they mark the spot so the burial detail can find it. Thus the entire land is cleansed.] **after the end of seven months shall they search.** [The burial detail will be hired after the main burial has taken place.]

VS15 And the passengers that pass through the land, when any seeth a man's bone, then shall he set up a sign by it, till the buriers have buried it in the valley of Hamon-gog. [See the previous verses]

VS16 And also the name of the city shall be Hamonah. [The city is Gog's tomb or Mausoleum and is call Hamonah or "the multitude" because of the number of slain buried there. Thus it is the city of the dead. <Ps 9:17 The wicked shall be turned into *hell*, (hell here is *sheole* or grave or land of the dead) and all the nations that forget God.> In this prophecy it is contrasted to the city of the living to be erected to the south of Jerusalem and to be named Yahweh Shammah. <Ezek 48:35 It was round about eighteen thousand measures: and the name of the city from that day shall be, The LORD is there.>] **Thus shall they cleanse the land.** [Repeated for emphasis.]

VS17 And, thou son of man, thus saith the Lord GOD; Speak [Typing the Lord Jesus, he speaks in highly symbolic language to the nations imploring them to acknowledge the justice of Yahweh's action against Gog. <Rev 14:6 And I saw another angel fly in the midst of heaven, having the everlasting gospel to preach unto them that dwell on the

earth, and to every nation, and kindred, and tongue, and people,> <Isa 60:12 For the nation and kingdom that will not serve thee shall perish; yea, those nations shall be utterly wasted.>] **unto every feathered fowl, and to every beast of the field, Assemble yourselves, and come;** [As previously shown, theses are used by Daniel and Jeremiah (Dan 4:12, Jer 12:9 to represent the nations.] **gather yourselves on every side to my sacrifice that I do sacrifice** [This is the sacrificial feast that will confirm the millennial covenant into which the nations will enter. As a covenant, it joins two parties in fellowship or mutual agreement. Nations partaking of the sacrifice offered by Yahweh acknowledge that the punishment of Gog is just. Figuratively they will eat the offering implying acceptance of the principle that they would be deserving of similar punishment if they manifested like guilt. This differs from the individual sacrifice for sin when an unblemished animal is slaughtered to acknowledge that the seat of sin is flesh and as a token of his intention to crucify the flesh by trying to obey Yahweh.] **for you, even a great sacrifice upon the mountains of Israel,** [If Yahweh did not intervene, man would destroy itself in its own folly. There is mercy in God's judgment for the redeemable] **that ye may eat flesh, and drink blood.** [The Lord Jesus told his disciples that if they did not eat his flesh and drink his blood they would have no life in themselves. <John 6:53 Then Jesus said unto them, Verily, verily, I say unto you, Except ye eat the flesh of the Son of man, and drink his blood, ye have no life in you.> If nations are to be part of the kingdom Christ will establish, they must figuratively follow that principle as well.]

VS18 Ye shall eat the flesh of the mighty, and drink the blood of the princes of the earth, of rams, of lambs, and of goats, of bullocks, all of them fatlings of Bashan. [These animals are symbols of the rulers and trained men of Gog's forces, all likened to well-fed powerful fatlings of Bashan. The term is used elsewhere for men of the flesh. <Ps 22:12 Many bulls have compassed me: strong bulls of Bashan have beset me round.>]

VS19 And ye shall eat fat till ye be full, and drink blood till ye be drunken, of my sacrifice which I have sacrificed for you. [Under the law, fat or blood was not eaten. <Lev 3:17 It shall be a perpetual statute for your generations throughout all your dwellings, that ye eat neither

fat nor blood.> The command related to the fat of sacrifices <Ex 29:13 And thou shalt take all the fat that covereth the inwards, and the caul that is above the liver, and the two kidneys, and the fat that is upon them, and burn them upon the altar.> But here, the figurative well fattened flesh of the slain is to be figurative eaten in total. And they are to eat until they are full (filled up with the principles of the sacrifice) and it suggests an abundance for as man as will accept it.]

VS20 Thus ye shall be filled [Filled with the covenant] **at my table** [The alter is Yahweh's table. <Mal 1:7 Ye offer polluted bread upon mine altar; and ye say, Wherein have we polluted thee? In that ye say, The table of the LORD is contemptible.> Yahweh figuratively eats with His guests by entering into covenant with them.>]**with horses and chariots, with mighty men, and with all men of war, saith the Lord GOD.** [The covenant will incorporate the cessation of all war. They will not learn war anymore.]

VS21 And I will set my glory among the heathen, [In the Most Holy of the Tabernacle and Solomon's Temple the glory of Yahweh was manifested by a glowing light above the Mercy seat between the Cherubim. Ezekiel saw the glory depart the Temple and the city and the people left on their own. <Ezek 8:4 And, behold, the glory of the God of Israel was there, according to the vision that I saw in the plain.> <Ezek 9:3 And the glory of the God of Israel was gone up from the cherub, whereupon he was, to the threshold of the house. And he called to the man clothed with linen, which had the writer's inkhorn by his side;> <Ezek 10:4 Then the glory of the LORD went up from the cherub, and stood over the threshold of the house; and the house was filled with the cloud, and the court was full of the brightness of the LORD's glory.> <Ezek 10:18 Then the glory of the LORD departed from off the threshold of the house, and stood over the cherubims.> <Ezek 11:23 And the glory of the LORD went up from the midst of the city, and stood upon the mountain which is on the east side of the city.> (These are summary verses. Reading the entire section is beneficial) But he also predicted the return of the Glory at the second advent and a new temple in Chapters 40 to the end of the prophecy.

The Glory will be in a different form as it will be the manifestation of Yahweh in Christ and the multitudinous redeemed. <John 8:12

Then spake Jesus again unto them, saying, I am the light of the world: he that followeth me shall not walk in darkness, but shall have the light of life.> <Ezek 43:2 And, behold, the glory of the God of Israel came from the way of the east: and his voice was like a noise of many waters: and the earth shined with his glory. 3 And it was according to the appearance of the vision which I saw, even according to the vision that I saw when I came to destroy the city: and the visions were like the vision that I saw by the river Chebar; and I fell upon my face. 4 And the glory of the LORD came into the house by the way of the gate whose prospect is toward the east. 5 So the spirit took me up, and brought me into the inner court; and, behold, the glory of the LORD filled the house.> <Isa 43:7 Even every one that is called by my name: for I have created him for my glory, I have formed him; yea, I have made him.> <Isa 40:5 And the glory of the LORD shall be revealed, and all flesh shall see it together: for the mouth of the LORD hath spoken it.> <Isa 66:18 For I know their works and their thoughts: it shall come, that I will gather all nations and tongues; and they shall come, and see my glory. 19 And I will set a sign among them, and I will send those that escape of them unto the nations, to Tarshish, Pul, and Lud, that draw the bow, to Tubal, and Javan, to the isles afar off, that have not heard my fame, neither have seen my glory; and they shall declare my glory among the Gentiles.> <Mal 1:11 For from the rising of the sun even unto the going down of the same my name shall be great among the Gentiles; and in every place incense shall be offered unto my name, and a pure offering: for my name shall be great among the heathen, saith the LORD of hosts.>] **and all the heathen shall see my judgment that I have executed, and my hand that I have laid upon them.** [Not just in Gog's defeat but in the Glory of the multitudinous Christ.]

VS22 So the house of Israel shall know that I am the LORD their God [See notes 36:22]**from that day and forward.** [This shows they do not understand these things when dwelling safely in the land as described in 38:11. See comments vs. 26]

VS23 And the heathen shall know that the house of Israel went into captivity for their iniquity: because they trespassed against me, therefore hid I my face from them, and gave them into the hand of their enemies: so fell they all by the sword. [The Gentiles will realize that the Jews were not dispersed because Yahweh couldn't stop it but as just punishment for their sins. They will recognize that Yahweh had simply withdrawn his support as He said He would do because they broke their covenant with Him. <Deut 31:17 Then my anger shall be kindled against them in that day, and I will forsake them, and I will hide my face from them, and they shall be devoured, and many evils and troubles shall befall them; so that they will say in that day. Are not these evils come upon us, because our God is not among us?> <Lev 26:25 And I will bring a sword upon you, that shall avenge the quarrel of my covenant: and when ye are gathered together within your cities, I will send the pestilence among you; and ye shall be delivered into the hand of the enemy.> They will see the righteousness in his judgments and the need to keep their covenants with Him.>]

VS24 According to their uncleanness and according to their transgressions have I done unto them, and hid my face from them. [See previous verse.]

VS25 Therefore thus saith the Lord GOD; Now will I bring again the captivity of Jacob, [Literally, I will bring back them of the captivity. The full restoration will take place after the defeat of Gog.] **and have mercy upon the whole house of Israel,** [The twelve tribes will be restored to the land. See notes on 37:22. Ezekiel 48 describes how the tribes will be restored and outlines the new borders of and positions of the tribes in the territories given to them.] **and will be jealous for my holy name;** [The Name will be thoroughly vindicated and will enjoy full respect and prominence in the Age to come.]

VS26 After that they have borne their shame, and all their trespasses whereby they have trespassed against me, [The invasion of Gog comprising part of the "time of Jacob's trouble" will be part of his shame. It will help humble them in readiness to accept their Messiah and King who come in the name of Yahweh. <Jer 30:7 Alas! for that day is great, so that none is like it: it is even the time of Jacob's trouble; but he shall be saved out of it.> <Matt 23:39 For I say unto you, Ye shall not see me henceforth, till ye shall say, Blessed is he that cometh in the name of the Lord.>] **when they dwelt safely in their land, and none made them afraid.** [This is the time indicated in 38:8.

Israel today feels secure in its own personal power and ability to achieve success and does not acknowledge dependence on God and their king and look upwards. <Isa 8:21 And they shall pass through it, hardly bestead and hungry: and it shall come to pass, that when they shall be hungry, they shall fret themselves, and curse their king and their God, and look upward.>]

VS27 When I have brought them again from the people, and gathered them out of their enemies' lands, and am sanctified in them in the sight of many nations; [When the people of Israel shall see and recognize Yahweh's goodness towards them they shall become completely converted and will accept him in truth to again be grafted to the good olive. <Rom 11:23 And they also, if they abide not still in unbelief, shall be graffed in: for God is able to graff them in again. 24 For if thou wert cut out of the olive tree which is wild by nature, and wert graffed contrary to nature into a good olive tree: how much more shall these, which be the natural branches, be graffed into their own olive tree? 25 For I would not, brethren, that ye should be ignorant of this mystery, lest ye should be wise in your own conceits; that blindness in part is happened to Israel, until the fulness of the Gentiles be come in. 26 And so all Israel shall be saved: as it is written, There shall come out of Sion the Deliverer, and shall turn away ungodliness from Jacob: 27 For this is my covenant unto them, when I shall take away their sins.>]

VS28 Then shall they know that I am the LORD their God, which cause them to be led into captivity among the heathen: but I have gathered them unto their own land, and have left none of them any more there. [They will see history from the Divine perspective and not the flesh. They will realize that Yahweh had good cause to do what He did and they will loath themselves for their sin. <Ezek 14:23 And they shall comfort you, when ye see their ways and their doings: and ye shall know that I have not done without cause all that I have done in it, saith the Lord GOD.> <Ezek 36:31 Then shall ye remember your own evil ways, and your doings that were not good, and shall lothe yourselves in your own sight for your iniquities and for your abominations.>]

VS29 Neither will I hide my face any more from them: [Their restoration is complete and lasting.] **for I have poured out my spirit upon the house of Israel, saith the Lord GOD.** [By His Spirit is meant the Spirit Word as in 36:26. It will be this that moves the people to understand and acknowledge the full significance of His glorious name.]

CHAPTER 18

Revelation an Introduction

The Book of Revelation, also referred to as the Apocalypse, is seldom the target of organized Bible studies or the subject of sermons from the world's pulpits. It is considered by most a book to difficult to understand and too open to multiple interpretation to be useful for sound doctrine. Nothing could be farther from the truth.

Daniel told us that the wise would understand the prophesies <Dan 10:12 Then said he unto me, Fear not, Daniel: for from the first day that thou didst set thine heart to understand, and to chasten thyself before thy God, thy words were heard, and I am come for thy words.> John, in Patmos was told that the wise who come to understand will be blessed. <Rev 1:3 Blessed is he that readeth, and they that hear the words of this prophecy, and keep those things which are written therein: for the time is at hand.>

In fact this blessing is pronounced seven times in the book. The Apocalypse is a book of sevens; seven messages to the Ecclesias; seven sealed book, seven trumpeters; seven vials and so on. Seven is the number of completion, the number of an oath which seals a matter. The proclamation of seven blessings throughout the book emphasizes the importance of the study of Revelation.

Early Christian scholars were almost unanimous that the book was written in the closing years of John and near the end of the reign of Domitian, that is about AD 95 or 96. The principle testimony comes from Irenaeus, a disciple of Polycarp, overseer of Smyrna, who was himself a disciple of the Apostle John. He had every opportunity of obtaining correct information and expresses the common sentiment of his age on the subject.

His testimony is plain and positive that the book was written during the end of Domitian's reign. He wrote, "The Apocalypse was seen not long ago, but almost in our generation near the end of Domitian's reign." Unless this can be disproved, the evidence is compelling. Internal evidence says it was written on the isle of Patmos during the time of Domitian's well recorded persecution of the Jews. He started this around 93 or 94 and it continued until the emperor's death. The Apocalypse was written in these trying times.

There are three main schools of interpretation of this book, the Immediate, the Futurist and the Historical.

The Immediate sees it all fulfilled prior to the destruction of the Jewish state by the Romans in AD 70. According to this view, the seven kings of Revelation 17:10 are the seven emperors Agustus, Tiberius, Gaius, Claudias, Nero, Balba, Otho, and the number of the beast 666 is the total numeric values of Nero Caesar spelled in Hebrew letters and so on.

The Futurist understands the major part of the book as referring to the future, to the epoch-ending age and beyond. The theory introduces a confused jumble of events unlike anything else in scripture, so Christ is pictured as returning to the earth to wage war and then ascending to heaven again to them come back and finish his work. The saints go forth to fight only to be slain and their bodies lay on the street of the great city, (Rev 11) to be resurrected and ascend to Heaven. This interpretation is quite confusing and filled with unscriptural errors.

The Historic view, that uses Rev. 1:3, 19 as a guide, sees the book as a prophetic program covering the whole of history from AD 96, about the time John was on Patmos, to the end of days, depicting political and ecclesiastical events in cipher, figure or code. In this view, the book unfolds as a history to and through the present age. This is the view which is the most logical and on which this study is based thanks to the works of John Thomas and H. P. Mansfield whose complete works are available from Logos Publications.

Consider the statement of the book itself. <Rev 1:1 The Revelation of Jesus Christ, which God gave unto him, to shew unto his servants things which **must shortly come to pass;** and he sent and signified it by his angel unto his servant John:> Note several things. First, the word Revelation is singular. It is not the book of Revelations, but of Revelation.

Second, whose revelation is it? Not the "Revelation of St. John the Divine" as the King James Version boldly proclaims. This is totally incorrect. It is the "Revelation of Jesus Christ." Christ given to John. Christ himself is revealing the future in prophetic language to his followers.

Third, what time period does this prophecy span? To reiterate, the answer is in verse one of chapter one. The angel, representing Christ, would show John "things which **must shortly come to pass.**" Nothing in the Revelation can be used as proof of anything prior to John's receipt of the prophecy on the Isle of Patmos. All references to devils, Satan and fallen angels, war in heaven and the like are symbols of historic events and forces in opposition to the will of Yahweh and have nothing to do with the historic concept of a superhuman evil spirit.

It is also a timeless document. Christ has interjected a message for every age in the book. The messages to the seven Ecclesias were mainly to the first century churches. His encouraging comments in chapter 13:9-10 particularly concern the faithful of the Middle Ages, who had to endure the Inquisition. Rev 16:15 is directed to those living when he returns. The book has encouragement for believers as well as warnings, exhortation and advice. Above all else it points to the time <Rev 21:4 And God shall wipe away all tears from their eyes; and there shall be no more death, neither sorrow, nor crying, neither shall there be any more pain: for the former things are passed away.> What a glorious thing to contemplate.

The Apocalypse does lend itself to a simple and significant analysis. First, it proclaims that it discusses things from John's time to the end of time and conveniently divides them into three sections, "the things which thou has seen, the things which are, and the things that shall be hereafter." Here is a straightforward outline using these three headings from the work of H.P. Mansfield.

1. Jesus Christ the Redeemed (as alpha and omega.) Things which thou hast seen (Chapter 1)
    a. prologue 1-2
    b. salutation 4-6
    c. introduction 9
    d. the initial vision:

The Multitudinous Christ. 10-20

2. Jesus Christ and the Ecclesia (as head of the body) The things which are (Chapters 2-3)

    a.   Ephesus The Hard Ecclesia Ch. 2:1-7

    b.   Smyrna The Persecuted Ecclesia 8-11

    c.   Pergamos The Embattled Ecclesia 12-17

    d.   Thyatira The Compromising Ecclesia 18-29

    e.   Sardis The Dead Ecclesia Ch. 3:1-6

    f.   Philadelphia The Beloved Ecclesia 7-13

    g.   Laodicea The Complacent Ecclesia 14-22

3 Jesus Christ and the Kingdom (as triumphant one) The things hereafter. (Chapters 4-22)

    1.   Introduction (Chapters 4-5)

        a.   The throne in heaven Chapter 4

        b.   The sealed Scroll & Prevailing Lamb. Chapter 5

    2.   The seven Seals (Chapters 6-7)

        a.   The first seal a white horse Ch. 6 :1-2

        b.   The second seal a red horse 3-4

        c.   The third seal, a black horse 5-6

        d.   The fourth seal a pale horse 7-8

        e.   The fifth seal Souls under alter 9-11

        f.   The sixth seal great earthquake 12

        g.   The seventh seal sealing the servants of God Ch 7:1-8

        h.   The rejoicing redeemed 9-17

    3.   The Seven Angelic Trumpeters (Chapters 8-11)

        a.   Seventh Seal angel prepares to sound Ch 8.1-6

        b.   st Angel fiery storm on the 7

        c.   2nd Angel burning mountain in the sea 8-9

        d.   3rd Angel burning star on the river 10-11

        e.   4th Angel Heavenly Bodies Smitten 12-13

        f.   5th Angel, locusts out of the bottomless pit Ch 9:1-1

        g.   6th Angel loosing angels of the Euphrates 13—21

        h.   Seven sealed thunders of the Rainbow Angel 10:1-11

        i.   Death and resurrection of the witness Ch.11:1-13

        j.   7th Angel Kingdom ceded to Christ 14-19

4. Development and Destruction of the Beast, his image, his organization (Ch 12-14)

a. Birth of the man child Ch.12:1-6
b. War in Heaven 7-12
c. Persecution woman and her seed 13-17
d. Development of the Beast of the Sea Ch.13:1-10
e. Development of the Beast of the Earth & image 11-18
f. he Lamb of Mount Zion Ch.14:1-5
g. Mid-heaven angelic proclamation 6-12
h. Reaping the harvest and vintage 13-20

5. The Seven Vials of Divine Wrath (Chapters 15-16)
a. The rejoicing redeemed Ch.15:1-4
b. The Temple in heaven is opened 5-8
c. First Vial upon the earth Ch.16:1-2
d. Second Vial upon the sea 3
e. Third Vial upon the rivers 4-7
f. Fourth Vial upon the sun 8-9
g. Fifth Vial on the throne of the beast 10-11
h. Sixth Vial upon the Euphrates 12-16
i. Seventh Vial-Armageddon 17-21

6. The Judgment Of The Whore And Triumph Of The Lamb (Ch 17-20)
a. Babylon the Great is Destroyed The system described Ch.17:1-18 The system destroyed Ch.18:1-24
b. The Marriage of the Lamb The Marriage comes Ch.19:1-8 The Marriage celebrated Ch.19:9-10
c. Final Conquest of the Lamb The Beast conquered Ch.19:11-21 Satan Bound Ch. 20:1-6 Satan Destroyed 7-15

7. The New Heavens and the New Earth (Ch 21-22)
a. The Character and Constitution of the New Jerusalem Ch. 21:1-8
b. The Relationship of Jerusalem with the Lamb 9-11
c. Its wall 12-18
d. Its foundation 19-20
e. Its Gates 19:21
f. Its Glory 19:27

g. Its River of Life Ch 22:1-6

h. Epilogue: Final admonition and appeal Ch.22:7-21

Concerning the strange syntax of the Revelation one must realize that it is an introverted Hebrew poem. Hebrew poetry represents a parallelism of ideas rather than of rhyme or rhythm. One idea builds on another until the complete thought or picture is revealed. In introverted Hebrew poetry, which is frequently found in Scripture, the first line is answered by the last, the next by the second to last, and so on. An example is set in the following form found in Psalm 135:15-18.

Ps 135:15 The idols of the heathen are silver and gold, the work of men's hands. 16 They have mouths, but they speak not; eyes have they, but they see not; 17 They have ears, but they hear not; neither is there any breath in their mouths. 18 They that make them are like unto them: so is every one that trusteth in them.>

Couple the first and last lines and the thought of the former is completed in the latter. The idols of the heathen are silver and gold, the work of men's hands. They that make them are like unto them: so is every one that trusteth in them. The general structure of the Apocalypse as a whole seems to be in the form of a long dramatic introverted Hebrew poem, presenting a parallelism of development in which the first harmonizes with the last and so on. The message can be set out in the following form.

1. Introduction: Warning and appeal (Ch 1:1-9)
2. The Multitudinous Son of Man (Ch 1:9-20)
3. The messages to the Ecclesias (Ch 2-3)
4. The heavenly worship and the sealed book (Ch 4-5)
5. The Christianising of Rome (Seals-Ch 6-7)
6. The overthrow of the Roman Empire (Ch 8-9)
7. The development of latter day Communism (Ch 10-11) These thoughts harmonize with:
7. The development of the Holy Roman Empire (Beasts etc. Ch 12-13)
6. The destruction of Babylon the Great (Ch 14)
5. Divine judgment of the Holy Roman Empire (Vials Ch 15-16)
4. The overthrow of false worship (Babylon etc. Ch 17-19)

3. The conquest of sin and death (Ch 20)
2. The Bride as New Jerusalem (Ch 21-22:6)
1. Epilogue: Warning and Appeal (Ch 22:7-21)

The Apocalypse presents an orderly progression of one thought to the next, not a haphazard and unsystematically thrown together vision. This can be summarized as follows.

Section 1 Chapters 1-5
a. Christ in the midst of the ecclesia Ch 1
b. Christ's message to the Ecclesia Ch 2-3
c. Christ's purpose with the Ecclesia Ch 4-5

Section 2 Chapters 6-11
a. The Christianizing of the Roman Empire Ch 6-7
b. The break-up of the Roman Empire Ch 8-9
c. The protest against tyranny and communism Ch 11

This section occupying half of the Apocalypse depicts events that took place in the Roman Empire providing a basis for further developments leading to the end. The Empire was Christianized then broken up into independent nations answering to the toes of the Image of Daniel 2, but held together by the Holy Roman Empire which replaced Pagan Rome.

Simultaneous with that system there were manifested protesting communities both religious and political (The two witnesses of Revelation 11) the political section of which rose to power in the French Revolution and developed modern Communism. Today, the influence of this is manifested in every form of government upon earth and is playing an important part in the development of the crisis of the last days. It has ascended into heaven (political authority Rev. 11:13) and the remnant are affrighted.

Section 3 Chapters 12-19
a. The development and destruction of the Holy Roman Empire Ch 12-14
b. The Divine judgment on the latter day political system Ch 15-16
c. Divine judgment on the latter day religious system Ch 17-19

Section 4 Chapters 20-22
a. Conquest of sin and death Ch 20
b. The Manifestation of the Bride Ch 21
c. The final appeal to the Ecclesia Ch 22

The second half of the Apocalypse follows the first half in orderly fashion. The Holy Roman Empire replaced the former Empire and will be destroyed. The two witnesses developed into political power, (Ch 16) and though used to punish the Beast likewise will be destroyed. The final chapters also follow in proper sequence.

The Book of Revelation appears to be an amplification of that section of Daniel's prophecy which the prophet failed to comprehend. When he was given the vision of the four beasts (Dan 7) with its emphasis upon the fourth beast, Daniel confessed himself as being confused <Dan 7:28 Hitherto is the end of the matter. As for me Daniel, my cogitations much troubled me, and my countenance changed in me: but I kept the matter in my heart.>

Again, in chapter 8, in a prophecy relating to the little horn of the east, or Rome's conquest of the holy land and its subsequent destruction at the hand of the Prince of princes, Daniel stated that none understood the vision. Once more in chapter 12 he confesses to being confused. <Dan 12:8 And I heard, but I understood not: then said I, O my Lord, what shall be the end of these things?> He was not given an interpretation of these visions but they were sealed to the end.

The Book of Revelation was for the time of the end and comprises the additional matter promised. The key to Revelation is in the prophecy of Daniel as we have already touched on. The outline suggested above shows that the entire Apocalypse is an amplification of the fourth beast and the multitudinous man of Daniel chapters 7-12, or the development and decline of Rome both politically and ecclesiastically and the work of the saints in relation to it.

Before plunging into the real message of the Apocalypse, and the true signs of the end of the age as we know it, some keys to prophetic interpretation are necessary. Let's begin with colors. All colors are important, for example white represents purity, or covered sin. Red indicates anger or trial. Grass and trees represent nations and peoples. Horses mean war, since they were used only for that purpose in Christ's time. The sun and moon are governments, principalities and rulers. Analogies and foreshadowing abound. Since prophecy as history has been discussed, the main consideration will be the events of Christ's return and the establishment of the eternal kingdom.

Lastly, there can be no question that Rome is the symbol of the opposition to Christ at the time of the end. But it is also symbolic for all groups that will fail to recognize the Messiah's return. Confused by the apostasy that has confounded the understanding of the scriptures, the political forces that control many of the organized religions of the world will see Christ's return as a threat to their earthly empires. Those that refuse to see the Truth will be destroyed. It is easy for the modern Christian who follows the tenants of a loving, forgiving God to forget that the God of the Old Testament and the God of the New Testament is the same unchanging force who declared in the very beginning, "the soul that sinneth, it shall die."

CHAPTER 19

Revelation Chapter 4

Chapters 4 and 5 are introductions to the section of the Apocalypse which covers the rest of the chapters. It begins with a symbolic description of the Kingdom in its glory and is followed by the visions of the seven seals, trumpets, vials and so on that depicts the historic events leading to its establishment.

The fact that the final events in the Revelation is given first may seem strange, but it is not only the method of this book, but most of prophetic scripture. This method of providing the ultimate picture first emphasizes the importance the Spirit places on the final glory and reminds the readers not to lose sight of that as they live day to day. The section shows The Lord Jesus Christ in relation to the Kingdom, and reveals him as the Triumphant One, victorious over his enemies.

It is divided into 7 sections describing the historic events, each building on its predecessor until the final glory is reached in the establishment of a new heaven and anew earth with the manifestation on earth of the New Jerusalem.

John is now shown a door that opens to heaven (this is the political heaven, not where God lives,) and is invited to go in. He sees a throne sitting upon which is one sits attended by four and twenty elders and the four living creatures. Encircling the throne is a rainbow, while in front are seven lamps of fie and a sea of glass.

In all, the chapter reveals seven distinct characteristics of the throne, which it introduces. The vision in its completeness symbolizes the political order of the future Kingdom of God on earth. It is not a vision of heaven as it exists now or as it existed in John's day, but part of the section of the Apocalypse designed to show things that must come to pass. Next, we will examine this chapter in detail.

VS:1 After this [That is, after the time of the Laodocian epoch, the last Ecclesia mention, until the return of Christ, and the throne of God established on the earth.] **I looked, and, behold, a door was opened** [There is wonder and excitement in John's tone here. At present, this door is closed to those taken out of the Gentiles for his name. But, Christ promised those who overcame power over the nations.

The crisis of Armageddon will result in the door to the political heavens being opened to the saints. <Zech 14:1 Behold, the day of the LORD cometh, and thy spoil shall be divided in the midst of thee. 2 For I will gather all nations against Jerusalem to battle; and the city shall be taken, and the houses rifled, and the women ravished; and half of the city shall go forth into captivity, and the residue of the people shall not be cut off from the city. 3 Then shall the LORD go forth, and fight against those nations, as when he fought in the day of battle. 4 And his feet shall stand in that day upon the mount of Olives, which is before Jerusalem on the east, and the mount of Olives shall cleave in the midst thereof toward the east and toward the west, and there shall be a very great valley; and half of the mountain shall remove toward the north, and half of it toward the south. 5 And ye shall flee to the valley of the mountains; for the valley of the mountains shall reach unto Azal: yea, ye shall flee, like as ye fled from before the earthquake in the days of Uzziah king of Judah: and the LORD my God shall come, and all the saints with thee.>

in heaven: [Heaven is used over 50 times in the Apocalypse, and in the majority of cases applies to the political heavens. It is the heaven spoken of by Isaiah. <Isa 65:17 For, behold, I create new heavens and a new earth: and the former shall not be remembered, nor come into mind. 18 But be ye glad and rejoice for ever in that which I create: for, behold, I create Jerusalem a rejoicing, and her people a joy. Thus the heavens depart for example. <Rev 6:14 And the heaven departed as a scroll when it is rolled together; and every mountain and island were moved out of their places.> A woman births a child in heaven, <Rev 12:1 And there appeared a great wonder in heaven; a woman clothed with the sun, and the moon under her feet, and upon her head a crown of twelve stars: 2 And she being with child cried, travailing in birth, and pained to be delivered.> war occurs in heaven <Rev 12:7 And there was war in heaven: Michael and his angels fought against the dragon; and the dragon fought and his angels,> armies march in heaven <Rev

19:11 And I saw heaven opened, and behold a white horse; and he that sat upon him was called Faithful and True, and in righteousness he doth judge and make war.> These events all happen in the political heaven.] **and the first voice which I heard was** [It is the voice of Rev 1:10, the voice of the perfected multitudinous Christ. Thus this vision is after the resurrection and glorification of the saints. <Rev 5:9 And they sung a new song, saying, Thou art worthy to take the book, and to open the seals thereof: for thou wast slain, and hast redeemed us to God by thy blood out of every kindred, and tongue, and people, and nation; 10 And hast made us unto our God kings and priests: and we shall reign on the earth.>] **as it were of a trumpet talking with me;** [Trumpets called the nation of Israel to judgment or war, see notes 1:10. <Isa 27:13 And it shall come to pass in that day, that the great trumpet shall be blown, and they shall come which were ready to perish in the land of Assyria, and the outcasts in the land of Egypt, and shall worship the LORD in the holy mount at Jerusalem.> **which said, Come up hither,** [The same expression is used in 11:2 for the elevation of the two witnesses to political power, indicating this vision referrers to political ascendancy as well.] **and I will shew thee things which must be hereafter.** [This is the key verse to this part of the Apocalypse. These are future events subsequent to John's lifetime. This is a partial fulfillment of Christ's words John recorded earlier. <John 16:13 Howbeit when he, the Spirit of truth, is come, he will guide you into all truth: for he shall not speak of himself; but whatsoever he shall hear, that shall he speak: and he will shew you things to come.>]

VS2 And immediately I was in the spirit: [There is no definite article in the Greek, it is I was in spirit. This was not a physical thing, but a vision that he saw.] **and, behold, a throne** [The exclamation points out the throne as the center of the vision. It is the throne of the house of David, once desolate, now in its zenith of power.] **was set in heaven,** [So, this is not the heaven where God lives, but where the throne of David is set up, or a political heaven. Daniel describes a similar scene of national judgment. <Dan 7:9 I beheld till the thrones were cast down, and the Ancient of days did sit, whose garment was white as snow, and the hair of his head like the pure wool: his throne was like the fiery flame, and his wheels as burning fire. 10 A fiery stream issued and came forth from before him: thousand thousands ministered unto him, and

ten thousand times ten thousand stood before him: the judgment was set, and the books were opened. 11 I beheld then because of the voice of the great words which the horn spake: I beheld even till the beast was slain, and his body destroyed, and given to the burning flame. 12 As concerning the rest of the beasts, they had their dominion taken away: yet their lives were prolonged for a season and time. 13 I saw in the night visions, and, behold, one like the Son of man came with the clouds of heaven, and came to the Ancient of days, and they brought him near before him. 14 And there was given him dominion, and glory, and a kingdom, that all people, nations, and languages, should serve him: his dominion is an everlasting dominion, which shall not pass away, and his kingdom that which shall not be destroyed.>

The metaphor of placing thrones borrows from the custom of early adjudicators and particularly that of the Great Sanhedrin, where the judges sat in semicircle with the people before them. We get that sense here.] **and one sat on the throne.** [The picture here is drawn from Ezekiel, <Ezek 1:25 And there was a voice from the firmament that was over their heads, when they stood, and had let down their wings. 26 And above the firmament that was over their heads was the likeness of a throne, as the appearance of a sapphire stone: and upon the likeness of the throne was the likeness as the appearance of a man above upon it. 27 And I saw as the colour of amber, as the appearance of fire round about within it, from the appearance of his loins even upward, and from the appearance of his loins even downward, I saw as it were the appearance of fire, and it had brightness round about. 28 As the appearance of the bow that is in the cloud in the day of rain, so was the appearance of the brightness round about. This was the appearance of the likeness of the glory of the LORD. And when I saw it, I fell upon my face, and I heard a voice of one that spake.>

This phrase, one sat on the throne is used throughout as title of Yahweh in manifestation as king. The one on the throne here is Yahweh manifest through His son, Christ. This manifestation allows the comment that Yahweh dwells on earth. He does it through his son. God corporally does not leave his throne in the true heaven. Since Christ already occupies that throne, he is can already claim the title him who sits upon the throne. Christ will bring the extension of that throne to man.]

VS3 And he that sat was to look upon like a jasper and a sardine stone: [Christ is described as the stone of Israel. <1 Peter 2:4 To whom coming, as unto a living stone, disallowed indeed of men, but chosen of God, and precious, 5 Ye also, as lively stones, are built up a spiritual house, an holy priesthood, to offer up spiritual sacrifices, acceptable to God by Jesus Christ. 6 Wherefore also it is contained in the scripture, Behold, I lay in Sion a chief corner stone, elect, precious: and he that believeth on him shall not be confounded. 7 Unto you therefore which believe he is precious: but unto them which be disobedient, the stone which the builders disallowed, the same is made the head of the corner, 8 And a stone of stumbling, and a rock of offence, even to them which stumble at the word, being disobedient: whereunto also they were appointed. 9 But ye are a chosen generation, a royal priesthood, an holy nation, a peculiar people; that ye should shew forth the praises of him who hath called you out of darkness into his marvellous light:> <Gen 49:24 But his bow abode in strength, and the arms of his hands were made strong by the hands of the mighty God of Jacob; (from thence is the shepherd, the stone of Israel:)> <Isa 8:14 And he shall be for a sanctuary; but for a stone of stumbling and for a rock of offence to both the houses of Israel, for a gin and for a snare to the inhabitants of Jerusalem.>

His dual role of Son of God, Son of Man are symbolized by the stones of this verse. Japer, a beautiful cerulean gem is clear as a crystal and symbolizes the Deity's spirit condensed into substance. Sardine is a carnelian with a flesh tone color. In Hebrew Sardin and Adam have the same consonants and since written Hebrew has no vowel points the words would be identical when written. This signifies Christ's human nature. The same stones were in the breastplate of the high priest. Sardis was the first stone and Jasper the last in Aaron's breastplate. <Ex 28:17 And thou shalt set in it settings of stones, even four rows of stones: the first row shall be a sardius, a topaz, and a carbuncle: this shall be the first row.> <Ex 28:20 And the fourth row a beryl, and an onyx, and a jasper: they shall be set in gold in their inclosings.>

This teaches we begin with flesh but may reach spirit, as did Christ. Under the Law, Jasper represented the tribe of Napthali, whose name means wrestling and prevailing, last in the order of march. In the Apocalypse, Jasper is the first stone, <Rev 21:19 And the foundations

of the wall of the city were garnished with all manner of precious stones. The first foundation was jasper; the second, sapphire; the third, a chalcedony; the fourth, an emerald;> thus representing Judah, whose name means praise. The combination suggests the thought that from wresting and prevailing the redeemed give themselves to praise. Under the law, The Sardine represented Judah, but in the new Jerusalem it is the sixth stone representing tribe six or Manasseh whose name means forgetting. Thus praise leads to forgetting. Those who receive the praise will have their sins forgotten.] **and there was a rainbow round about the throne,** [The rainbow was given as a token of God's covenant with the flesh. <Gen 9:11 And I will establish my covenant with you; neither shall all flesh be cut off any more by the waters of a flood; neither shall there any more be a flood to destroy the earth. 12 And God said, This is the token of the covenant which I make between me and you and every living creature that is with you, for perpetual generations: 13 I do set my bow in the cloud, and it shall be for a token of a covenant between me and the earth. 14 And it shall come to pass, when I bring a cloud over the earth, that the bow shall be seen in the cloud: 15 And I will remember my covenant, which is between me and you and every living creature of all flesh; and the waters shall no more become a flood to destroy all flesh.16 And the bow shall be in the cloud; and I will look upon it, that I may remember the everlasting covenant between God and every living creature of all flesh that is upon the earth.>

Raindrops act as a prism to split the pure white sunlight into 7 basic colors. Every detail of this symbol is significant. Seven is the covenant number. The sun is symbolic of the Son of Righteousness, the falling rain the outpouring of the spirit in teaching and power and the clouds are the redeemed. Round about suggests the bow encircled the throne. This is in accordance with nature.

All rainbows are circles, it is only our position on the earth that allows us to see only half of it. If we were in the sky above the earth, we could see the entire circle. This adds to the suggestion of elevation in the political heaven. At present, part of the glory and desirability of eternal life are partly hidden. <1 Cor 13:12 For now we see through a glass, darkly; but then face to face: now I know in part; but then shall I know even as also I am known.> But one day we can join the Queen of Sheba in saying 1 Kings 10:7 Howbeit I believed not the words, until I came, and mine eyes had seen it: and, behold, the half was not told me: thy wisdom and prosperity exceedeth the fame which I heard.>]

in sight like unto an emerald. [In the breastplate the emerald represented Ruben (see a son). In the new Jerusalem it represents Asher (blessed) Together the idea see the son as the channel of true blessing. Though the rainbow has seven colors, green apparently predominated in this one adding strength to the suggestion above.]

VS4 And round about the throne [As in verse 3 to encircle.] **were four and twenty seats:** [In Greek the word for seats is thrones. This is the royal priesthood of the Age to Come and these are the seats of judgment to be set, or established in the future age. <Rev 5:9 And they sung a new song, saying, Thou art worthy to take the book, and to open the seals thereof: for thou wast slain, and hast redeemed us to God by thy blood out of every kindred, and tongue, and people, and nation; 10 And hast made us unto our God kings and priests: and we shall reign on the earth.> <Ps 122:3 Jerusalem is builded as a city that is compact together: 4 Whither the tribes go up, the tribes of the LORD, unto the testimony of Israel, to give thanks unto the name of the LORD. 5 For there are set thrones of judgment, the thrones of the house of David.>] **and upon the seats I saw four and twenty elders sitting,** [Yahweh intends to restore the tabernacle of David as it was in olden days. <Amos 9:11 In that day will I raise up the tabernacle of David that is fallen, and close up the breaches thereof; and I will raise up his ruins, and I will build it as in the days of old:> David divided the priests and Levites into 24 orders based upon the job they were to do. <1 Chron 24:4 And there were more chief men found of the sons of Eleazar than of the sons of Ithamar; and thus were they divided. Among the sons of Eleazar there were sixteen chief men of the house of their fathers, and eight among the sons of Ithamar according to the house of their fathers.> Thus these are the 24 royal priests of the Age after the pattern of David Yahweh vowed to retore.] **clothed in white raiment;** [see prior notes for significance here. The clothing of righteousness.] **and they had on their heads crowns of gold.** [Gold is the symbol of faith tried, and the way to true and lasting victory. <1 John 5:4 For whatsoever is born of God overcometh the world: and this is the victory that overcometh the world, even our faith.> The crown here is Stephanos, the laurel wreath given to winners of games. Made of vegetation they would not last. God would. And symbolizes the eternal victory.]

VS5 And out of the throne proceeded lightnings and thunderings and voices: [Lightning and thunder are symbols of the Spirit's wrath or of war. <2 Sam 22:14 The LORD thundered from heaven, and the most High uttered his voice. 15 And he sent out arrows, and scattered them; lightning, and discomfited them.> <Ps 144:6 Cast forth lightning, and scatter them: shoot out thine arrows, and destroy them.> <Zech 9:14 And the LORD shall be seen over them, and his arrow shall go forth as the lightning: and the LORD GOD shall blow the trumpet, and shall go with whirlwinds of the south.>

They symbolize the ultimatums, decrees and declarations of war that shall issue forth from Christ against a disobedient world. These same tools were used by Yahweh at Sinai. <Ex 19:16 And it came to pass on the third day in the morning, that there were thunders and lightnings, and a thick cloud upon the mount, and the voice of the trumpet exceeding loud; so that all the people that was in the camp trembled.>

Yahweh then made his divine decree and Israel accepted. So too will some nations when they see His power manifest at Armageddon. <Isa 60:9 Surely the isles shall wait for me, and the ships of Tarshish first, to bring thy sons from far, their silver and their gold with them, unto the name of the LORD thy God, and to the Holy One of Israel, because he hath glorified thee.> The rest will be compelled to do so by war and conquest. <Isa 60:12 For the nation and kingdom that will not serve thee shall perish; yea, those nations shall be utterly wasted.>

The voices are the multitudinous Christ fulfilling Isaiah. <Isa 2:2 And it shall come to pass in the last days, that the mountain of the LORD's house shall be established in the top of the mountains, and shall be exalted above the hills; and all nations shall flow unto it. 3 And many people shall go and say, Come ye, and let us go up to the mountain of the LORD, to the house of the God of Jacob; and he will teach us of his ways, and we will walk in his paths: for out of Zion shall go forth the law, and the word of the LORD from Jerusalem.>] **and there were seven lamps of fire burning before the throne, which are the seven Spirits of God.** [The 7 spirits represent the complete manifestation of the one spirit through the Redeemed, 7 because of its diverse nature. They are at the throne because it is via the spirit that the nations will be brought into subjugation. <Zech 4:5 Then the angel that talked with me answered and said unto me, Knowest thou not what these be? And I said, No, my lord. 6 Then he answered and spake unto me, saying, This is the word of the LORD unto Zerubbabel, saying, Not by might, nor by power, but by my spirit, saith the LORD of hosts.>

David had an inner council of seven <1 Chron 27:32 Also Jonathan David's uncle was a counseller, a wise man, and a scribe: and Jehiel the son of Hachmoni was with the king's sons: 33 And Ahithophel was the king's counseller: and Hushai the Archite was the king's companion: And after Ahithophel was Jehoiada the son of Benaiah, and Abiathar: and the general of the king's army was Joab.> who assisted him in manners of state and of war. That council typed the seven lamps seen here. The guidance and power of the spirit will be certain that all that is done by the Redeemed is in concert with the will of the one on the throne.]

VS6 And before the throne there was a sea of glass like unto crystal:
[The seven spirits act as intermediary between the throne and the sea of crystal like glass. But today nations are in a different state,. <Isa 57:20 But the wicked are like the troubled sea, when it cannot rest, whose waters cast up mire and dirt.> The use of Scripture to represent nations as waters or seas reveals a progression from one state to another. From their troubled condition, <Isa 17:13 The nations shall rush like the rushing of many waters: but God shall rebuke them, and they shall flee far off, and shall be chased as the chaff of the mountains before the wind, and like a rolling thing before the whirlwind.> <Ezek 26:3 Therefore thus saith the Lord GOD; Behold, I am against thee, O Tyrus, and will cause many nations to come up against thee, as the sea causeth his waves to come up.> <Dan 7:2 Daniel spake and said, I saw in my vision by night, and, behold, the four winds of the heaven strove upon the great sea.>

Subject to the discipline of Christ their raging will cease. <Rev 15:2 And I saw as it were a sea of glass mingled with fire: and them that had gotten the victory over the beast, and over his image, and over his mark, and over the number of his name, stand on the sea of glass, having the harps of God.>

When the fire has cleansed all impurities, they are hardened to pure crystal. At the end of Christ's millennium, when death and sin are no more, all will meld into one perfected kingdom for ever and every and the symbolic sea of different nations will cease to exist. <Rev 21:1 21:1 And I saw a new heaven and a new earth: for the first heaven and the first earth were passed away; and there was no more sea.>]
and in the midst of the throne, and round about the throne, were four beasts [The beasts didn't occupy the throne but were in its midst, in the sense they were beneath the center of it an encircled it in the sense one looked in each direction facing outwards so they saw all around, in every direction. They therefore occupy the same position that the Cherubim did in Ezekiel's vision. <Ezek 1:25 And there was a voice from the firmament that was over their heads, when they stood, and had let down their wings. 26 And above the firmament that was over their heads was the likeness of a throne, as the appearance of a sapphire stone: and upon the likeness of the throne was the likeness as the appearance of a man above upon it. 27. And I saw as the colour of amber, as the appearance of fire round about within it, from the appearance of his loins even upward, and from the appearance of his loins even downward, I saw as it were the appearance of fire, and it had brightness round about.>

Beasts is an unfortunate translation. The word is zoon from zoe or life. Living creatures, as the AV describes the cherubim of Ezekiel's vision would be a better translation. They represent the universal and complete vigilance in the Kingdom. The one on the throne would see all, know all and be in complete control. Why four living creatures? Because four is the number of perfect administration as exhibited in Israel. When they marched out of Egypt they did so in groups of fjour tribes each and when they camped one foursome camped on each side with the tabernacle in the middle to foreshadow the situation in the new Jerusalem. At the head of each group flew the standard of the principle tribe. Judah (a lion) Ruben (a man) Ephraim (a bullock) and Dan (an Eagle) (See Num 2:3, 10, 18,25)] **full of eyes before and behind.** [Angels are the eyes of Yahweh supervising conditions on earth. <Gen 11:5 And the LORD came down to see the city and the tower, which the children of men builded.> <Gen 18:20 And the LORD said, Because the cry of Sodom and Gomorrah is great, and because their sin is very grievous; 21 I will go down now, and see whether they have

done altogether according to the cry of it, which is come unto me; and if not, I will know.> In each of these passages, Lord is Elohim or the might ones or angels. <Dan 4:17 This matter is by the decree of the watchers, and the demand by the word of the holy ones: to the intent that the living may know that the most High ruleth in the kingdom of men, and giveth it to whomsoever he will, and setteth up over it the basest of men.> These living creatures represent omniscience and identify with the Ezekiel's vision of the Cherubim.]

VS7 And the first beast was like a lion, and the second beast like a calf, and the third beast had a face as a man, and the fourth beast was like a flying eagle. [In the Apocalypse, the saints are represented as an encampment. <Rev 20:9 And they went up on the breadth of the earth, and compassed the camp of the saints about, and the beloved city: and fire came down from God out of heaven, and devoured them.>

The four faces here are identical to the faces seen by Ezekiel in the first chapter of his prophecy. They represent the standards of the principle tribes as described in the last verse that were always around the Ark when it stopped and the tabernacle erected. The lion represents loyalty, the ox service, the eagle draws attention toward heaven, and the man is humanity.

The four gospels and the four prophets portray Christ in those four particulars as King (Isaiah and Matthew) Servant (Jeremiah and Mark) Son of Man (Ezekiel and Luke) and as Divine (Daniel and John). There is a message in them as well. If you would rule (lion) you must serve (calf). As you are flesh (man) this can only be done with help from heaven (eagle).]

VS8 And the four beasts had each of them six wings about him; and they were full of eyes within: [This identifies the beasts also with the seraphim of Isaiah. <Isa 6:2 Above it stood the seraphims: each one had six wings; with twain he covered his face, and with twain he covered his feet, and with twain he did fly. 3 And one cried unto another, and said, Holy, holy, holy, is the LORD of hosts: the whole earth is full of his glory.>

Seraphim comes from a word to burn, or consume. When applied to the redeemed they teach that their mission is to burn or consume all that evil in the kingdom. <2 Thess 2:8 And then shall that Wicked be revealed, whom the Lord shall consume with the spirit of his mouth, and shall destroy with the brightness of his coming:>

Why six wings. Six is the number of man. Adam was born on the sixth day. Six wings make 24 in all, identifying them with the 24 elders. The beasts have to do with man, since they represent the Deity in fleshly manifestation. The military aspect of the saints represented by the four beasts, will be joined with the priestly functions indicated by the number 24. The wings completely cover yet allow mobility, speaking to the spirit covering of the saints in the Age to Come. The will be able to speedily go wherever they desire to go.] **and they rest not day and night,** [Under Mosaic law, priests were on duty day and night. <Ps 134:1 Behold, bless ye the LORD, all ye servants of the LORD, which by night stand in the house of the LORD.> These immortal priests, needing not to rest, will do so as well.] **saying, Holy, holy, holy,** [There were three stages to holiness in the temple, the court, the holy place and the most holy place. So, this phrase means most holy. This is the exact phrase from Isaiah. <Isa 6:1 In the year that king Uzziah died I saw also the Lord sitting upon a throne, high and lifted up, and his train filled the temple. 2 Above it stood the seraphims: each one had six wings; with twain he covered his face, and with twain he covered his feet, and with twain he did fly. 3 And one cried unto another, and said, Holy, holy, holy, is the LORD of hosts: the whole earth is full of his glory.>]

Lord God Almighty, which was, and is, and is to come. [Here the name Lord God Almighty is Yahweh Elohim of Armies, the belligerent name of the Deity, He who will be the mighty ones of armies used when his power is unleashed to subdue the flesh.]

VS9 And when those beasts give glory and honour and thanks to him that sat on the throne, [When here is better rendered as in the RSV at all times. The giving of thanks is not sporadic but continuous.] **who liveth for ever and ever,** [The phrase represents Christ as the ancient of days. <Dan 7:9 I beheld till the thrones were cast down, and the Ancient of days did sit, whose garment was white as snow, and the hair of his head like the pure wool: his throne was like the fiery flame, and his wheels as burning fire. <7:13 I saw in the night visions, and, behold, one like the Son of man came with the clouds of heaven, and came to the Ancient of days, and they brought him near before him.<7:22 Until the Ancient of days came, and judgment was given to the saints of the most High; and the time came that the saints possessed the kingdom.>]

VS10 The four and twenty elders fall down before him that sat on the throne, and worship him that liveth for ever and ever, [They worship the father manifest in the son and acknowledge that all the Son is stems from the Father.] **and cast their crowns before the throne, saying,** [An act of both submission and homage.]

VS11 Thou art worthy, O Lord, to receive glory and honour and power: [Christ is worthy because of who he is and what he has done and represents the manifestation of God in all His diversity. This is not a Trinitarian vision, but manifestation of the multitudinous Christ.] **for thou hast created all things,** [Echoes of the words of Paul. <Col 1:16 For by him were all things created, that are in heaven, and that are in earth, visible and invisible, whether they be thrones, or dominions, or principalities, or powers: all things were created by him, and for him:> This is not a rambling that would suggest Christ was alive before we saw him on earth. What heavens and earths did Christ bring into being? Those of the future Age, of course. <2 Peter 3:13 Nevertheless we, according to his promise, look for new heavens and a new earth, wherein dwelleth righteousness.> Without Christ's sacrifice, this new heaven and earth would not be.] **and for thy pleasure they are and were created.** [This is true of all forms of creation, for everything so formed is designed for the pleasure of their Creator, whether Yahweh or his Son.]

CHAPTER 20

Revelation Chapter 5

John notices a scroll in the hand of the man on the throne that is so completely sealed that it appears no one could ever open it. He is distraught until it is announced that the Lion of Judah has prevailed and can open it. This announcement triggers a scene of joyous celebration. Expecting to see a lion he sees a lamb. As the lamb is given the scroll, onlookers break into songs of adoration and praise. John hears first the song of the redeemed, then the praise of angels and lastly of the whole world.

VS:1 And I saw in the right hand of him that sat on the throne [The one on the throne is God manifest in the flesh or the Lord Jesus. The book is in his right hand (the hand of strength and power) because the one on the throne directs the things written in the book. <1 Peter 3:22 Who is gone into heaven, and is on the right hand of God; angels and authorities and powers being made subject unto him **a book written within and on the backside,** [This is similar to the little book handed to Ezekiel. <Ezek 2:9 and when I looked, behold, an hand was sent unto me; and, lo, a roll of a book was therein; 10 And he spread it before me; and it was written within and without: and there was written therein lamentations, and mourning, and woe.> The events on the scroll relate to things both within the ecclesia as well as the world, therefore events both within and without covenant.] **sealed with seven seals.** [Seven is the number of completeness. The scroll is completely sealed from human knowledge. <Isa 29:11 And the vision of all is become unto you as the words of a book that is sealed, which men deliver to one that is learned, saying, Read this, I pray thee: and he saith, I cannot; for it is sealed:> <Dan 12:4 But thou, O Daniel, shut up the words, and seal

the book, even to the time of the end: many shall run to and fro, and knowledge shall be increased.>]

VS2 And I saw a strong angel [All angels are strong, but it emphasizes that God and Christ are stronger. <1 Peter 1:12 Unto whom it was revealed, that not unto themselves, but unto us they did minister the things, which are now reported unto you by them that have preached the gospel unto you with the Holy Ghost sent down from heaven; which things the angels desire to look into.>] **proclaiming with a loud voice,** [So that anyone who wanted to hear could.] **Who is worthy to open the book, and to loose the seals thereof?** [Daniel was told the book was sealed till the end. <Dan 12:4 But thou, O Daniel, shut up the words, and seal the book, even to the time of the end: many shall run to and fro, and knowledge shall be increased. 5 Then I Daniel looked, and, behold, there stood other two, the one on this side of the bank of the river, and the other on that side of the bank of the river. 6 And one said to the man clothed in linen, which was upon the waters of the river, How long shall it be to the end of these wonders? 7. And I heard the man clothed in linen, which was upon the waters of the river, when he held up his right hand and his left hand unto heaven, and sware by him that liveth for ever that it shall be for a time, times, and an half; and when he shall have accomplished to scatter the power of the holy people, all these things shall be finished. 8 And I heard, but I understood not: then said I, O my Lord, what shall be the end of these things? 9 And he said, Go thy way, Daniel: for the words are closed up and sealed till the time of the end.>

Now, at the end of Hebrew times it will be open and read. At the end of Gentile times, the things in the scroll will be fulfilled. <Luke 21:24 And they shall fall by the edge of the sword, and shall be led away captive into all nations: and Jerusalem shall be trodden down of the Gentiles, until the times of the Gentiles be fulfilled.> <Rom 11:25 For I would not, brethren, that ye should be ignorant of this mystery, lest ye should be wise in your own conceits; that blindness in part is happened to Israel, until the fulness of the Gentiles be come in.> <Dan 12:1 And at that time shall Michael stand up, the great prince which standeth for the children of thy people: and there shall be a time of trouble, such as never was since there was a nation even

to that same time: and at that time thy people shall be delivered, every one that shall be found written in the book. 2 And many of them that sleep in the dust of the earth shall awake, some to everlasting life, and some to shame and everlasting contempt. 3 And they that be wise shall shine as the brightness of the firmament; and they that turn many to righteousness as the stars for ever and ever.>]

VS3 And no man in heaven, nor in earth, neither under the earth, was able to open the book, neither to look thereon. [No one living or dead, angelic or human could unloose the seals. The unfolding of the divine purpose and its glorious consummation required the sacrifice and resurrection to glory of one coming in sinful flesh and yet rendering perfect obedience in order to accomplish this. The future was all dependent upon the victory of Calvary.]

VS4 And I wept much, because no man was found worthy to open and to read the book, neither to look thereon. [This illustrates John's keen anxiety to understand the will of Yahweh. There is blessing for those who "hunger and search after righteousness." <Matt 7:7 Ask, and it shall be given you; seek, and ye shall find; knock, and it shall be opened unto you:> <James 1:5 If any of you lack wisdom, let him ask of God, that giveth to all men liberally, and upbraideth not; and it shall be given him.> <Rev 1:3 Blessed is he that readeth, and they that hear the words of this prophecy, and keep those things which are written therein: for the time is at hand.>]

VS5 And one of the elders saith unto me, Weep not: [Words of comfort from one of the 24 elders. It is appropriate that one of them should be represented in the vision of this chapter for their future glory and position is dependent upon the prevailing of the lam. As John was an elder then, <2 John 1:1 The elder unto the elect lady and her children, whom I love in the truth; and not I only, but also all they that have known the truth;> and will be part of the eldership in the future, this verse depicts him speaking with the symbol of his own glorified state even as Christ as the Lamb is depicted as taking the book from Christ, the manifestation of Yahweh.] **behold, the Lion of the tribe of Juda, the Root of David,** [The root of David is Yahweh, for all his promised greatness stemmed from God. Since Christ is God manifest, he represents the root and the offspring of Jesse. As the manifest Yahweh he is the root, as Jesus son of Mary, he is the offspring.] **hath prevailed to open the book, and to loose the seven seals thereof.** [Christ's victory over the flesh opened a new phase in the divine purpose. He prevailed personally, guaranteeing that he will do so nationally and universally. He will prevail over the fourth beast of Daniel's prophecy (Dan 7) and the serpents head will be finally bruised. Now the words of Hebrews are about to be fulfilled. <Heb 2:8 Thou hast put all things in subjection under his feet. For in that he put all in subjection under him, he left nothing that is not put under him. But now we see not yet all things put under him.>]

VS6 And I beheld, and, lo, in the midst of the throne and of the four beasts, and in the midst of the elders, [The Lamb is said to be on the throne for it is the center of Yahweh's purpose in the earth. <Heb 2:14 Forasmuch then as the children are partakers of flesh and blood, he also himself likewise took part of the same; that through death he might destroy him that had the power of death, that is, the devil;> Christ's purpose was to provide the means to end all opposition to the will of God] **stood a Lamb as it had been slain, having seven horns and seven eyes, which are the seven Spirits of God sent forth into all the earth.** [This is a dramatic moment in the Apocalypse. John, expecting the Lion of Judah, finds a resurrected lamb, teaching that to rule we must serve. The term is used 28 times in relation to the Lord in the book. Throughout the Apocalypse, the Lamb is shown to be:

1. The center of divine rule on earth the object of the adoration and veneration of all created beings. <Rev 5:8 And when he had taken the book, the four beasts and four and twenty elders fell down before the Lamb, having every one of them harps, and golden vials full of odours, which are the prayers of saints.> <Rev 5:12 Saying with a loud voice, Worthy is the Lamb that was slain to receive power, and riches, and wisdom, and strength, and honor, and glory, and blessing. 13 And every creature which is in heaven, and on the earth, and under the earth, and such as are in the sea, and all that are in them, heard I saying, Blessing, and honour, and glory, and power, be unto

him that sitteth upon the throne, and unto the Lamb for ever and ever.>

2. <u>The one who unlooses the seals and guides the destiny of the nations</u>. <Rev 6:1 And I saw when the Lamb opened one of the seals, and I heard, as it were the noise of thunder, one of the four beasts saying, Come and see.> <Rev 6:16 And said to the mountains and rocks, Fall on us, and hide us from the face of him that sitteth on the throne, and from the wrath of the Lamb:>

3. <u>The acknowledged channel of divine love and salvation.</u> <Rev 7:9-10 After this I beheld, and, lo, a great multitude, which no man could number, of all nations, and kindreds, and people, and tongues, stood before the throne, and before the Lamb, clothed with white robes, and palms in their hands; 10 And cried with a loud voice, saying, Salvation to our God which sitteth upon the throne, and unto the Lamb.> <Rev 7:14 And I said unto him, Sir, thou knowest. And he said to me, These are they which came out of great tribulation, and have washed their robes, and made them white in the blood of the Lamb.>

4. <u>The Shepherd Shepherding the flock</u> <Rev 7:17 For the Lamb which is in the midst of the throne shall feed them, and shall lead them unto living fountains of waters: and God shall wipe away all tears from their eyes.>

5. <u>The inspiration for victory in the hearts of others</u> <Rev 12:11 And they overcame him by the blood of the Lamb, and by the word of their testimony; and they loved not their lives unto the death.>

6. <u>The recorder of the Book of Life</u> <Rev 13:8 And all that dwell upon the earth shall worship him, whose names are not written in the book of life of the Lamb slain from the foundation of the world.> <Rev 21:27 And there shall in no wise enter into it any thing that defileth, neither whatsoever worketh abomination, or maketh a lie: but they which are written in the Lamb's book of life>

7. <u>Leader and shepherd of the redeemed</u> <Rev 14:114:1 And I looked, and, lo, a Lamb stood on the mount Sion, and with him an hundred forty and four thousand, having his Father's name written in their foreheads. 2 And I heard a voice from

heaven, as the voice of many waters, and as the voice of a great thunder: and I heard the voice of harpers harping with their harps: 3 And they sung as it were a new song before the throne, and before the four beasts, and the elders: and no man could learn that song but the hundred and forty and four thousand, which were redeemed from the earth. 4 These are they which were not defiled with women; for they are virgins. These are they which follow the Lamb whithersoever he goeth. These were redeemed from among men, being the firstfruits unto God and to the Lamb.>

8. <u>Conqueror of the beast</u>. <Rev 14:10 The same shall drink of the wine of the wrath of God, which is poured out without mixture into the cup of his indignation; and he shall be tormented with fire and brimstone in the presence of the holy angels, and in the presence of the Lamb:>

9. <u>Choir-Leader of the victorious saints</u> <Rev 15:3 And they sing the song of Moses the servant of God, and the song of the Lamb, saying, Great and marvellous are thy works, Lord God Almighty; just and true are thy ways, thou King of saints.>

10. <u>The captain of the victorious warriors who conquer the Catholic confederacy</u>. <Rev 17:14 These shall make war with the Lamb, and the Lamb shall overcome them: for he is Lord of lords, and King of kings: and they that are with him are called, and chosen, and faithful.>

11. <u>The bridegroom of the saints.</u> <Rev 19:7 Let us be glad and rejoice, and give honour to him: for the marriage of the Lamb is come, and his wife hath made herself ready. 8 And to her was granted that she should be arrayed in fine linen, clean and white: for the fine linen is the righteousness of saints. 9 And he saith unto me, Write, Blessed are they which are called unto the marriage supper of the Lamb. And he saith unto me, These are the true sayings of God.> <Rev 21:9 And there came unto me one of the seven angels which had the seven vials full of the seven last plagues, and talked with me, saying, Come hither, I will shew thee the bride, the Lamb's wife.>

12. <u>The foundation stone and light of the New Jerusalem</u>. <Rev 21:14 And the wall of the city had twelve foundations, and in them the names of the twelve apostles of the Lamb.> <Rev

21:22 And I saw no temple therein: for the Lord God Almighty and the Lamb And the city had no need of the sun, neither of the moon, to shine in it: for the glory of God did lighten it, and the Lamb is the light thereof.>

13. Ruler of the Age to Come <Rev 22:1 And he shewed me a pure river of water of life, clear as crystal, proceeding out of the throne of God and of the Lamb. 2. In the midst of the street of it, and on either side of the river, was there the tree of life, which bare twelve manner of fruits, and yielded her fruit every month: and the leaves of the tree were for the healing of the nations. 3 And there shall be no more curse: but the throne of God and of the Lamb shall be in it; and his servants shall serve him:> If we put to death the flesh, as he did, we will rise to future greatness as the Lamb slain. The slain and resurrected Lamb is represented in the Apocalypse as the center and foundation of all of Yahweh's purpose.]

VS7 And he came and took the book [The Lamb (Christ manifesting the triumph over flesh) takes the book from the one on the throne (Christ the manifestation of Yahweh suggesting the unity in all things in Yahweh.] **out of the right hand** [The hand of power and privilege. <Ps 80:17 Let thy hand be upon the man of thy right hand, upon the son of man whom thou madest strong for thyself.> <Ps 110:1 The LORD said unto my Lord, Sit thou at my right hand, until I make thine enemies thy footstool.>] **of him that sat upon the throne.** [The principle of God manifestation is summarized in John. <John 17:21 That they all may be one; as thou, Father, art in me, and I in thee, that they also may be one in us: that the world may believe that thou hast sent me.> Isaiah, in his vision in chapter 6 sees Yahweh seated on a throne surrounded by the Seraphim who proclaimed the words repeated in Rev 4:8 The prophet was then sent with a warning message to the people. John declared that what Isaiah saw and said was prophetic of the ministry of Jesus. <John 12:38 That the saying of Esaias the prophet might be fulfilled, which he spake, Lord, who hath believed our report? and to whom hath the arm of the Lord been revealed? 39 Therefore they could not believe, because that Esaias said again, 40 He hath blinded their eyes, and hardened their heart; that they should not see with their eyes, nor understand with their heart,

and be converted, and I should heal them. 41 These things said Esaias, when he saw his glory, and spake of him.> He thus represented Christ as being both Yahweh on the throne surrounded by Seraphim and as the messenger with the warning. Christ indeed fills both roles. The duality of symbolism is here in this chapter too.]

VS8 And when he had taken the book, [This symbolizes the performance of the things written.] **the four beasts and four and twenty elders fell down before the Lamb,** [They paid homage to the one who opened the book and revealed its contents that comprise the assurance of their own ultimate salvation.] **having every one of them harps, and** [Temple priests prophesied with harps. <1 Chron 25:1 Moreover David and the captains of the host separated to the service of the sons of Asaph, and of Heman, and of Jeduthun, who should prophesy with harps, with psalteries, and with cymbals: and the number of the workmen according to their service was:> The use of the analogy here and in 14:2 identifies the four living creatures and 24 elders with the 144,000 rejoicing saints in glory.] **golden vials full of odours,** [Margin gives odors as incense. <Ex 30:7 And Aaron shall burn thereon sweet incense every morning: when he dresseth the lamps, he shall burn incense upon it. 8 And when Aaron lighteth the lamps at even, he shall burn incense upon it, a perpetual incense before the LORD throughout your generations.> It was symbolic of prayers of the saints and when the priests burned the incense every morning, true Israelites gave themselves to prayer. Golden vials suggest the prayers of faith. <James 5:15 And the prayer of faith shall save the sick, and the Lord shall raise him up; and if he have committed sins, they shall be forgiven him.>] **which are the prayers of saints.** [Leaving no doubt what is meant.]

VS9 And they sung a new song, [New is from *kainos* meaning new as to form, quality or information and not a new point in time. Neos would have been used for that. If we have the words to the song in this verse, how can they be "new". Simply, although we can ascribe to the sentiments of the song, when the redeemed are actually there, with the glory around them, will they grasp the full and complete meaning of the words.

The term new song appears often in the Psalms expressing prophetic utterances that will not be fully appreciated until they are fulfilled. <Ps 98:1 O sing unto the LORD a new song; for he hath done marvelous things: his right hand, and his holy arm, hath gotten him the victory. 2 The LORD hath made known his salvation: his righteousness hath he openly shewed in the sight of the heathen.> < Ps 149:1Praise ye the LORD. Sing unto the LORD a new song, and his praise in the congregation of saints.> The words of the new song in this verse mirror the intent of the Psalms.] **saying, Thou art worthy to take the book, and to open the seals thereof:** [Acknowledges the power of the lamb to open the book and cause the prophecies in it to be fulfilled.] **for thou wast slain,** [Implying the sacrificial offering of the Lamb is the basis for his power and greatness.] **and hast redeemed us to God** [Some experts challenge the fact that the singers are the Redeemed, since the RV translates this Thou didst purchase by thy blood, *men* of every tribe. Men is in italics because the word is in dispute among translators. That aside, these must be the redeemed because, they use harps, <Rev 14:2 And I heard a voice from heaven, as the voice of many waters, and as the voice of a great thunder: and I heard the voice of harpers harping with their harps:> <Rev 15:2 And I saw as it were a sea of glass mingled with fire: and them that had gotten the victory over the beast, and over his image, and over his mark, and over the number of his name, stand on the sea of glass, having the harps of God.>] **by thy blood** [<Acts 20:28 Take heed therefore unto yourselves, and to all the flock, over the which the Holy Ghost hath made you overseers, to feed the church of God, which he hath purchased with his own blood.>] **out of** [Greek *ek*, first part of Ekklesia. <Acts 15:14 Simeon hath declared how God at the first did visit the Gentiles, to take out of them a people for his name.>] **every kindred, and tongue, and people, and nation;** [This all embracing expression comprises family, language, districts and nations. It is used frequently in the Apocalypse.]

VS10 And hast made us unto our God kings and priests: [A better translation here would be a kingdom of priests, and identifies the song with the foreshadowing words of Exodus. <Ex 19:6 And ye shall be unto me a kingdom of priests, and an holy nation. These are the words which thou shalt speak unto the children of Israel. **and we shall reign**

on the earth. [Note where the reign is, on earth, not in the heaven of popular theology.]

VS 11 And I beheld, and I heard the voice of many angels [Heaven will have representatives at the epoch of Christ's triumph who will raise angelic voices in his honor. <Luke 12:9 But he that denieth me before men shall be denied before the angels of God.> <Heb 1:6 And again, when he bringeth in the firstbegotten into the world, he saith, And let all the angels of God worship him.>

The heavenly angels will be supplemented by the redeemed, now equal unto angels. <Luke 20:36 Neither can they die any more: for they are equal unto the angels; and are the children of God, being the children of the resurrection.>] **round about the throne and the beasts and the elders:** [Thus identifying with them.] **and the number of them was ten thousand times ten thousand, and thousands of thousands;** [This strange enumeration seems to divide the angels into two groups, (1) 10,000 x 10,000 and (2) thousands of thousands. The statement is drawn from Daniel. <Dan 7:10 A fiery stream issued and came forth from before him: thousand thousands ministered unto him, and ten thousand times ten thousand stood before him: the judgment was set, and the books were opened.>

The 10,000 is used in relation to the Redeemed and is a figure used in Scripture to denote a large, undefined number, for ten has that spiritual significance. <Deut 33:2 And he said, The LORD came from Sinai, and rose up from Seir unto them; he shined forth from mount Paran, and he came with ten thousands of saints: from his right hand went a fiery law for them> <Ps 68:17 The chariots of God are twenty thousand, even thousands of angels: the Lord is among them, as in Sinai, in the holy place.> and for the figurative use of ten as signifying a large number, <Ps 3:6 I will not be afraid of ten thousands of people, that have set themselves against me round about.> <1 Cor 4:15 For though ye have ten thousand instructors in Christ, yet have ye not many fathers: for in Christ Jesus I have begotten you through the gospel.> <1 Cor 14:19 Yet in the church I had rather speak five words with my understanding, that by my voice I might teach others also, than ten thousand words in an unknown tongue.>

Then 10,000 x 10,000 represents a very large number encompassing all of the redeemed. The thousands of thousands refer to the angels of heaven. Though the Redeemed number is larger, it does not mean there are more of them than there are angels. It suggests that all of the redeemed will be involved in the judgments written in the book, while only a token number of angels will be involved in it.]

VS12 Saying with a loud voice, [Loud enough for all the earth to hear.] **Worthy is the Lamb that was slain to receive power, and riches, and wisdom, and strength, and honour, and glory, and blessing.** [All these things are laid at the feet of the lamb, while a similar hymn is directed to the one upon the throne, showing the two are one.]

VS13 And every creature [All creatures, angels, redeemed, mortals both Jew and Gentile will praise the Lamb. First redeemed v. 910, then angels, v. 11, finally everyone in this verse.] **which is in heaven, and on the earth, and under the earth, and such as are in the sea, and all that are in them,** [These terms are symbolic, not literal. Heavenly represents the ruling places, the dominion which will ben be held by Israel <Mic 4:8 And thou, O tower of the flock, the strong hold of the daughter of Zion, unto thee shall it come, even the first dominion; the kingdom shall come to the daughter of Jerusalem.> The bottomless pit of nations denotes specifically the Roman Empire, <Rev 11:7 And when they shall have finished their testimony, the beast that ascendeth out of the bottomless pit shall make war against them, and shall overcome them, and kill them.> while the sea is the rest of the Gentiles. <Rev 13:1And I stood upon the sand of the sea, and saw a beast rise up out of the sea, having seven heads and ten horns, and upon his horns ten crowns, and upon his heads the name of blasphemy.> <Rev 17:5and upon her forehead was a name written, MYSTERY, BABYLON THE GREAT, THE MOTHER OF HARLOTS AND ABOMINATIONS OF THE EARTH.> Thus all mankind give homage to the One it ignored so long.>] **heard I saying, Blessing, and honour, and glory, and power, be unto him that sitteth upon the throne, and unto the Lamb for ever and ever.** [All aspects of praise have the definite article in this statement. The honor, the glory, the praise. For rest of the statement see notes on 4:2 For ever and ever see notes on 1:6]

VS14 And the four beasts said, Amen. [Christ is the Amen of the Divine purpose.] **And the four and twenty elders fell down and worshipped** [In so doing, they endorsed the words of the four living ones.] **him that liveth for ever and ever.** [These word are missing from the best text of the Greek and are supplied from Rev. 4:9]

CHAPTER 21

Revelation Chapter 20

Time and space do not allow a study of the entire Book of Revelation. For a complete look at this wonderful book, the reader is referred to the Christadelphian Expositor volume *A Study of the Book of Revelation* by H.P. Mansfield and available through Logos Publications (Logos.org.au). However, three more chapters should be examined to complete the true story of the end of time.

As our story opens, Christ has returned; the world has been conquered; the great temple of Ezekiel's prophecy is functioning in Jerusalem; immortal teachers and priests teach the mortals who have survived the destruction of society as we know it in the Truth of God. But to accomplish this, sin must be put on hold. That is the subject of the chapter before us.

VS:1 And I saw an angel come down from heaven, [These are the angles that will now distribute divine law and teaching from the new political heaven where Christ rules.] **having the key of the bottomless pit** [The Greek here is Abusson or abyss. In the original, there is no word for bottomless. The abyss is the deep or the ocean and as has been shown, the nations. A key is a symbol of power, so this angel has power over the nations.] **and a great chain in his hand.** [This is used for restraint to limit the action of a madman or criminal as with the example of Legion. <Mark 5:4 Because that he had been often bound with fetters and chains, and the chains had been plucked asunder by him, and the fetters broken in pieces: neither could any man tame him.>]

VS2 And he laid hold on the dragon, [The dragon is used throughout the Apocalypse to represent political sin. Christ and the Redeemed will restrain all political opposition to Christ for 1000 years and then will be relaxed to allow people to demonstrate their loyalty. Again, human nature will rebel.] **that old serpent,** [See Rev. 12:9. In the beginning the serpent incited rebellion against the expressed commands of God and the spirit of such has been manifested by flesh and its institutes ever since.] **which is the Devil, and Satan,** [The false accuser and the adversary. Devil is often used for sins of the flesh, but one of its manifestations is political opposition to Gods way, the symbol of the dragon. Devil is sometime used for political opposition to the Truth. False accuser and adversary are suitable descriptions of the flesh in political manifestations for it has falsely accused and opposed in the brethren of Christ. It in no way relates to a supernatural being.] **and bound him a thousand years,** [The righteous controls are suggested <Zech 14:17 And it shall be, that whoso will not come up of all the families of the earth unto Jerusalem to worship the King, the LORD of hosts, even upon them shall be no rain. 18 And if the family of Egypt go not up, and come not, that have no rain; there shall be the plague, wherewith the LORD will smite the heathen that come not up to keep the feast of tabernacles. 19 This shall be the punishment of Egypt, and the punishment of all nations that come not up to keep the feast of tabernacles.>

The Redeemed will be able to read the hearts of the people. <Isa 30:20 And though the Lord give you the bread of adversity, and the water of affliction, yet shall not thy teachers be removed into a corner any more, but thine eyes shall see thy teachers: 21 And thine ears shall hear a word behind thee, saying, This is the way, walk ye in it, when ye turn to the right hand, and when ye turn to the left.>

Through the Holy Spirit, Peter was able to detect the motive of Ananias, <Acts 5:3 But Peter said, Ananias, why hath Satan filled thine heart to lie to the Holy Ghost, and to keep back part of the price of the land? 4 While it remained, was it not thine own? and after it was sold, was it not in thine own power? why hast thou conceived this thing in thine heart? thou hast not lied unto men, but unto God. 5 And Ananias hearing these words fell down, and gave up the ghost: and great fear came on all them that heard these things. 6 And the young men arose, wound him up, and carried him out, and buried him. 7 And it was about the space of three hours after, when his wife, not knowing what was done, came in. 8 And Peter answered unto her, Tell me whether ye

sold the land for so much? And she said, Yea, for so much. 9 Then Peter said unto her, How is it that ye have agreed together to tempt the Spirit of the Lord? behold, the feet of them which have buried thy husband are at the door, and shall carry thee out.> And Elisha, by the same means knew of the deception of Gehazi <2 Kings 5:25 But he went in, and stood before his master. And Elisha said unto him, Whence comest thou, Gehazi? And he said, Thy servant went no whither. 26 And he said unto him, Went not mine heart with thee, when the man turned again from his chariot to meet thee? Is it a time to receive money, and to receive garments, and oliveyards, and vineyards, and sheep, and oxen, and menservants, and maidservants? 27 The leprosy therefore of Naaman shall cleave unto thee, and unto thy seed for ever. And he went out from his presence a leper as white as snow.> Under Christ it will be much more, as a period of divine Truth, peace and justice are established.]

VS3 And cast him into the bottomless pit, [As seen, this pit is humanity. The dragon will be shut up in the hearts of men and they will not be able to see or hear evil.] **and shut him up, and set a seal upon him,** [The seal officially prohibits any opposition. The government will be a Divine dictatorship. The redeemed will command the forces of omnipotence and will silence all those who would otherwise oppose their will.] **that he should deceive the nations no more,** [No deception will be permitted.] **till the thousand years should be fulfilled:** [This begins after the nations are subdued, not when Christ returns.] **and after that he must be loosed a little season.** [This is a test permitted at the close of an epoch of great benefit to humanity. How long is the little season? It could be for a jubilee of 50 years to balance the 50 years between Christ's return and the beginning of the millennium, during which the dragon is restrained. This would seem fitting, but is only an educated guess.]

VS4 And I saw thrones, [These are the thrones of Judgment] **and they sat upon them,** [The reference is to the Redeemed.] **and judgment was given unto them:** [This honor is reserved for the redeemed.]**and I saw the souls of them that were beheaded for the witness of Jesus, and for the word of God,** [These are the souls last seen under the Christ altar (Rev.6:9) then in persecution now in glory. The prayers of that section are now answered by the judgment dispensed.] **and which had not worshipped the beast, neither his image, neither had received his mark upon their foreheads, or in their hands;** [The expressions denote complete separation politically, socially, ecclesiastically. Salvation is dependent upon such separation. <2 Cor 6:17 Wherefore come out from among them, and be ye separate, saith the Lord, and touch not the unclean thing; and I will receive you, 18 And will be a Father unto you, and ye shall be my sons and daughters, saith the Lord Almighty.>] **and they lived and reigned with Christ a thousand years.** [Through resurrection, they live again and reign with Christ.]

VS 5 But the rest of the dead lived not again until the thousand years were finished. This is the first resurrection. [This cannot be those who died before Christ's coming for vast multitudes of those shall never rise from the grave. <Ps 49:17 For when he dieth he shall carry nothing away: his glory shall not descend after him. 18 Though while he lived he blessed his soul: and men will praise thee, when thou doest well to thyself. 19 He shall go to the generation of his fathers; they shall never see light. 20 Man that is in honour, and understandeth not, is like the beasts that perish.> <Ps 88:5 Free among the dead, like the slain that lie in the grave, whom thou rememberest no more: and they are cut off from thy hand.> <Isa 26:15 They are dead, they shall not live; they are deceased, they shall not rise: therefore hast thou visited and destroyed them, and made all their memory to perish.> <Eph 2:12 That at that time ye were without Christ, being aliens from the commonwealth of Israel, and strangers from the covenants of promise, having no hope, and without God in the world:> The responsible wicked for they will rise with the righteous to be judged at Christ's coming. <Dan 12:2 And many of them that sleep in the dust of the earth shall awake, some to everlasting life, and some to shame and everlasting contempt.> These dead are those who die after Christ's return. Thus it appears no one else will get immortality until after the end of the 1000 years.]

VS6 Blessed and holy is he that hath part in the first resurrection: [These are the firstfuits. They are the Redeemed.] **on such the second death hath no power,** [See 2:14 and 21:8] **but they shall be priests**

of God and of Christ, and shall reign with him a thousand years.
[See Rev 1:6 and 3:12]

VS7 And when the thousand years are expired, [After the
Millennium.] **Satan shall be loosed out of his prison,** [Each mortal
will be permitted to exercise his own desire and be self-judged on the
way he reacts, just as mankind did after Eden.]

**VS8 And shall go out to deceive the nations which are in the four
quarters of the earth,** [All over the world, human nature will again
oppose the will of God.] **Gog and Magog, to gather them together
to battle:** [In Gen 10:2 Magog appears as a son of Japhet. In Ezekiel
38, Magoag is a general name for the northern nations and Gog is
their prince. Magog means from the top, and God means roof. The
Gog and Magog of Ezekiel 38 represents political antagonism towards
God and therefore type the form of Rebellion that will be manifested
at the end of the 1000 year reign of Christ.] **the number of whom is
as the sand of the sea.** [An unspecified number. It does not denote
an entire population. <2 Sam 17:11 Therefore I counsel that all Israel
be generally gathered unto thee, from Dan even to Beer-sheba, as the
sand that is by the sea for multitude; and that thou go to battle in thine
own person.> This suggests many will rebel at the restrictions placed
on them.]

VS 9 And they went up on the breadth of the earth, [There is no
mention of armies here, but more of a large group moving to the Holy
City to demand their rights as they see them.] **and compassed the
camp of the saints about,** [Throughout the millennium the saints
will guard the temple in Jerusalem acting as guards to keep out those
without the correct attitude. Now the city will be surrounded by an
unruly mob who would challenge the immortal leadership.] **and the
beloved city:** [It may be that the Redeemed have withdrawn to the
beloved city during the period of relaxation of the divine rule.] **and
fire came down from God out of heaven, and devoured them.** [Fire
from the political heaven will destroy the rebels as it did at Sodom. The
fire is the manifestation of the Spirit wielded by the saints so that the
destruction of the revels will be an act of judicial execution.]

VS10 And the devil that deceived them [Human nature is the devil of the Bible and is a great deceiver. <Mark 7:20 And he said, That which cometh out of the man, that defileth the man. 21 For from within, out of the heart of men, proceed evil thoughts, adulteries, fornications, murders, 22 Thefts, covetousness, wickedness, deceit, lasciviousness, an evil eye, blasphemy, pride, foolishness: 23 All these evil things come from within, and defile the man.> In this verse, the devil signifies the spirit of revolt that will dominate the rebels who will converge on the beloved city.] **was cast into the lake of fire and brimstone, where the beast and the false prophet are,** [Just as Sodom and Gomorrah which is set forth as an example of suffering the vengeance of eternal fire. Now the opposition and its apocalyptic associates will be consumed in like manner.] **and shall be tormented day and night for ever and ever.** [Paul declares that the value of a person's works will be determined by fire at the judgment. <1 Cor 3:13 Every man's work shall be made manifest: for the day shall declare it, because it shall be revealed by fire; and the fire shall try every man's work of what sort it is.>

This is not literal fire of course, but the fierce and purging scrutiny of divine inspection. The analogy is drawn from the Law. The ordinance delivered Moses required that all things taken by Israel in conquest had to be tested by fire. <Num 31:23 Every thing that may abide the fire, ye shall make it go through the fire, and it shall be clean: nevertheless it shall be purified with the water of separation: and all that abideth not the fire ye shall make go through the water.> When put to the test, inflammable material is inevitably destroyed, whereas by the same means gold, silver and the like is purified. Therefore a person is either destroyed or purified by divine judgment. This is a fitting end to sin.]

VS11 And I saw a great white throne, [The white throne of righteous judgment. The figure is drawn from Solomon's great white throne. <2 Chron 9:17 Moreover the king made a great throne of ivory, and overlaid it with pure gold. 18 And there were six steps to the throne, with a footstool of gold, which were fastened to the throne, and stays on each side of the sitting place, and two lions standing by the stays: 19 And twelve lions stood there on the one side and on the other upon the six steps. There was not the like made in any kingdom.> From there Solomon administered justice stemming from his wisdom. Christ will do likewise.] **and him that sat on it, from whose face the earth and the heaven fled away; and there was found no place for them.** [The one on the throne is described in 4:2 and represents Yahweh manifest in the flesh. All prior systems of government will be overshadowed by the rule of God in the flesh.]

VS12 And I saw the dead, small and great, [The dead are those mortals who have died during the millennium. Remember during this thousand years there are both mortals and immortals on earth, and among the mortals, life goes on as it did before.] **stand before God;** [Actually they stand before Christ the judge.] **and the books were opened:** [These are the ledgers or the accounts of daily life, separate from the book of life. A number of books are mentioned in the Bible.

A book of death in which all enter by virtue of birth. <Gen 5:1 This is the book of the generations of Adam. In the day that God created man, in the likeness of God made he him;>

A book of Condemnation in which the rebellious are recorded, <Isa 30:8 Now go, write it before them in a table, and note it in a book, that it may be for the time to come for ever and ever: 9 That this is a rebellious people, lying children, children that will not hear the law of the LORD:>

A book of Remembrance based on the custom of the times in which kings recorded incidents under their reign in order to reward their friends. <Mal 3:16 Then they that feared the LORD spake often one to another: and the LORD hearkened, and heard it, and a book of remembrance was written before him for them that feared the LORD, and that thought upon his name.> At the judgment seat these symbolic books will be opened and their contents revealed.] **and another book was opened, which is the book of life:** [The most important book for only those whose names are written therein will receive eternal life. <Ex 32:32 Yet now, if thou wilt forgive their sin; and if not, blot me, I pray thee, out of thy book which thou hast written.> <Luke 10:20 Notwithstanding in this rejoice not, that the spirits are subject unto you; but rather rejoice, because your names are written in heaven.> <Phil 4:3 And I intreat thee also, true yokefellow, help those women which laboured with me in the gospel, with Clement also, and with other my fellow labourers, whose names are in the book of life.>]

and the dead were judged out of those things which were written in the books, according to their works. [This second judgment at the end of the millennium is based on methods adopted at the first, pre-millennium judgment.]

VS13 And the sea gave up the dead which were in it; [The living mortals are judged at the same time as the dead are resurrected for the same purpose. Sea here remains consistent to the analogy of the nations.] **and death and hell delivered up the dead which were in them:** [A bodily resurrection will take place at the same time.] **and they were judged every man according to their works.** [Their works based upon their faith will determine their destiny.]

VS14 And death and hell were cast into the lake of fire. [Death and the grave are personified and represented as being destroyed in the lake of fire. The wicked are destroyed, and the righteous are granted immortality. Death and the grave become redundant. Paul taught that the last enemy to be destroyed by Christ will be death. <1 Cor 15:26 The last enemy that shall be destroyed is death.>] **This is the second death.** [This is a death from which there will be no awakening. The Lake of Fire is likened to such an end.]

VS15 And whosoever was not found written in the book of life was cast into the lake of fire. [This happens in both the pre and post millennial judgment]

CHAPTER 22

Revelation Chapter 21

The world is now full of immortal saints and these last two chapters tell us of the glorious new government and the joy it will bring to the immortal faithful

VS:1 And I saw a new heaven and a new earth: [This is not the literal heaven and earth but the new state of divine society on earth, < Isa 65:17 For, behold, I create new heavens and a new earth: and the former shall not be remembered, nor come into mind.> <Dan 12:3 And they that be wise shall shine as the brightness of the firmament; and they that turn many to righteousness as the stars for ever and ever.> because the literal earth will remain forever. < Eccl 1:4 One generation passeth away, and another generation cometh: but the earth abideth for ever.> <Ps 125:1 A Song of degrees. They that trust in the LORD shall be as mount Zion, which cannot be removed, but abideth for ever.> <Ps 148:5 Let them praise the name of the LORD: for he commanded, and they were created. 6 He hath also stablished them for ever and ever: he hath made a decree which shall not pass.>] **for the first heaven and the first earth were passed away;** [As described in 20:11 The firsts in this passage would be better rendered former, as they are in the Diaglott, This is the third heaven referred to by Paul in his vision of future glory. < 2 Cor 12:2 I knew a man in Christ above fourteen years ago, (whether in the body, I cannot tell; or whether out of the body, I cannot tell: God knoweth;) such an one caught up to the third heaven.>

In the former heaven and earth there was death and sin, and in the new one there is none. This is the second heaven and earth.

The third heaven and earth will be at the Close of Christ's reign when he delivers a perfect kingdom to God. < 1 Cor 15:24 Then cometh the end, when he shall have delivered up the kingdom to God, even the Father; when he shall have put down all rule and all authority and power.>] **and there was no more sea.** [There will be no more sin, death multitudes nations or tongues as seen in Rev. 17:15. We have seen the sea of nations dirty stirring up mire, at peace after fire judgments and calm and purified as glass. Now it is removed completely when independent national existence is no longer necessary.]

VS2 And I John saw the holy city, [The term city is often used in the Bible to describe its inhabitants, and that is the case here. The city is now holy in contrast to the ungodliness of Babylon.] **new Jerusalem,** [New is *kainos* meaning new in form or quality, not new in time which would be neos. The Greek suggests a change in an existing city. The Temple and Jerusalem will have been there a thousand years by this time. Now, all the redeemed will be gathered together within its walls.] **coming down from God out of heaven,** [Only those born from above will be there. < John 3:3 Jesus answered and said unto him, Verily, verily, I say unto thee, Except a man be born again, (from above *margin*) he cannot see the kingdom of God.> < James 1:17 Every good gift and every perfect gift is from above, and cometh down from the Father of lights, with whom is no variableness, neither shadow of turning.> Thus the city, now made up totally of immortals is said to come out of heaven for it is born from above.] **prepared as a bride adorned for her husband.** [This suggests that the city is not a material city but the symbol of the elect. < 2 Cor 11:2 For I am jealous over you with godly jealousy: for I have espoused you to one husband, that I may present you as a chaste virgin to Christ.> The adornment is a perfection of character and nature that Christ desires to see in all those who he will take to himself as his own.]

VS3 And I heard a great voice out of heaven [The voice makes a proclamation outlining the new constitution of things.] **saying, Behold, the tabernacle of God is with men,** [The tabernacle was God's dwelling place in Israel < Ex 25:8 And let them make me a sanctuary; that I may dwell among them.> and ws a type of the elect in whom He chooses to dwell. < Heb 9:11 But Christ being come an high priest of good things to come, by a greater and more perfect tabernacle, not made with hands, that is to say, not of this building;>

Jack L. Summers

<2 Cor 6:16 And what agreement hath the temple of God with idols? for ye are the temple of the living God; as God hath said, I will dwell in them, and walk in them; and I will be their God, and they shall be my people.> The tabernacle was a parable of the New Jerusalem and foreshadowed the tabernacle made not with hands.] **and he will dwell with them,** [Yahweh will not personally leave his heavenly throne to come to earth, but will be dwell with men in the terms of God manifestation by revealing Himself through the redeemed. Similar words are used to describe His dwelling in the sanctuary in the midst of Israel. < Ex 29:45 And I will dwell among the children of Israel, and will be their God.> The token of His presence was the Shekinah (dwelling) glory which shone above the Mercy Seat and between the Cherubim. < 80:1 To the chief Musician upon Sho-shan'-nim-E'-duth, A Psalm of A'-saph. Give ear, O Shepherd of Israel, thou that leadest Joseph like a flock; thou that dwellest between the cherubims, shine forth.> His glory will shine forth in the multitude of the Redeemed, each one individually reflecting the glory of God.] **and they shall be his people,** [People, *la oi* is peoples, plural. Abraham was promised that he would be the father of many nations, pleural. At the end of the millennium, all nations will be incorporated into Christ and the New Jerusalem.] **and God himself shall be with them, and be their God.** [This comprises the foundation of New Jerusalem, God manifested in each individual and each one recognizing His status.]

VS4 And God shall wipe away all tears from their eyes; [The final victory will reproduce the conditions following the first judgment. < Isa 25:8 He will swallow up death in victory; and the Lord GOD will wipe away tears from off all faces; and the rebuke of his people shall he take away from off all the earth: for the LORD hath spoken it.>] **and there shall be no more death,** [At the end of the millennium, it is the last enemy destroyed.] **neither sorrow, nor crying, neither shall there be any more pain: for the former things are passed away.** [Greatly reduced during the millennium, these too will be gone after it.]

VS5 And he that sat upon the throne said, [See Rev 4:2] **Behold, I make all things new.** [A new political order, a perfect kingdom fit for the Father.] **And he said unto me, Write: for these words are true and faithful.** [They will come to pass.]

242

VS6 And he said unto me, It is done. [A similar statement is made at the beginning of the millennium and at its conclusion, a similar statement is made. It has come to pass.] **I am Alpha and Omega, the beginning and the end.** [See note Rev. 1:8] **I will give unto him that is athirst of the fountain of the water of life freely.** [The water of life is not given to everyone only those who thirst for it. < Isa 55:1 Ho, every one that thirsteth, come ye to the waters, and he that hath no money; come ye, buy, and eat; yea, come, buy wine and milk without money and without price.> Christians must always be athirst.]

VS7 He that overcometh shall inherit all things; [This was a promise of creation. < Gen 1:28 And God blessed them, and God said unto them, Be fruitful, and multiply, and replenish the earth, and subdue it: and have dominion over the fish of the sea, and over the fowl of the air, and over every living thing that moveth upon the earth.> But sin delayed that until by war and conquest Christ and the immortals produced a perfect world.] **and I will be his God, and he shall be my son.** [The Redeemed now join Christ as true sons of God. < Rom 1:3 Concerning his Son Jesus Christ our Lord, which was made of the seed of David according to the flesh; 4 And declared to be the Son of God with power, according to the spirit of holiness, by the resurrection from the dead:>]

VS8 But the fearful, [The Truth demands mental and physical courage. All cowards are excluded from the kingdom.] **and unbelieving,** [This caused the children of Israel to fail in the wilderness. A person can believe a doctrine academically but be faithless. That was Israel's failure.] **and the abominable,** [That which causes one to turn away in disgust. That which is highly esteemed in the site of man but abhorred by God. A similar word is used in Luke. < Luke 16:15 And he said unto them, Ye are they which justify yourselves before men; but God knoweth your hearts: for that which is highly esteemed among men is abomination in the sight of God.>] **and murderers,** [Even those who hate their brother without cause. < 1 John 3:15 Whosoever hateth his brother is a murderer: and ye know that no murderer hath eternal life abiding in him.>] **and whoremongers,** [The unfaithful who made friends with the world and are described as adulteresses. < James 4:4 Ye adulterers and adulteresses, know ye not that the friendship of the world is enmity with God? whosoever therefore will be a friend of the world is the enemy of God.>] **and sorcerers,** [Those who drug the mind with doctrines of unbelief.] **and idolaters,** [Those who refuse the word of God or covertly serve self to the exclusion of the truth.] **and all liars,** [An errorist is counted as a liar. < 1 John 2:4 He that saith, I know him, and keepeth not his commandments, is a liar, and the truth is not in him.>] **shall have their part in the lake which burneth with fire and brimstone: which is the second death.** [They share the fate of the world they love so much.]

VS9 And there came unto me one of the seven angels which had the seven vials full of the seven last plagues, [The appearance of this angel suggests that the fulfillment of his vial is after the return of Christ. It will be during the period of the seventh vial that New Jerusalem will be revieled.] **and talked with me, saying, Come hither, I will shew thee the bride, the Lamb's wife.** [This reveals that new Jerusalem constitutes the company of the Redeemed. See Rev. 19:7]

VS10 And he carried me away in the spirit [Ezekiel was carried in spirit from captivity in Babylonia to view the literal city of Jerusalem in its future glory. < Ezek 40:2 In the visions of God brought he me into the land of Israel, and set me upon a very high mountain, by which was as the frame of a city on the south.> John is take from his place of captivity on Patmos to view the New Jerusalem in similar fashion.] **to a great and high mountain,** [Ezekiel saw the literal mountain as it will be after the earthquake will elevate Zion. < Zech 14:4 And his feet shall stand in that day upon the mount of Olives, which is before Jerusalem on the east, and the mount of Olives shall cleave in the midst thereof toward the east and toward the west, and there shall be a very great valley; and half of the mountain shall remove toward the north, and half of it toward the south.> <Zech 14:10 All the land shall be turned as a plain from Geba to Rimmon south of Jerusalem: and it shall be lifted up, and inhabited in her place, from Benjamin's gate unto the place of the first gate, unto the corner gate, and from the tower of Hananeel unto the king's winepresses.>

John saw the spiritual Zion after the political earthquake will elevate it. The symbol of the kingdom of God is a mountain filling the whole earth. < Dan 2:35 Then was the iron, the clay, the brass, the silver, and the gold, broken to pieces together, and became like the chaff of the summer threshingfloors; and the wind carried them away, that no place was found for them: and the stone that smote the image became a great mountain, and filled the whole earth.>] **and shewed me that great city, the holy Jerusalem,** [The adjective holy suggests John saw a temple city. Like the literal counterpart seen by the prophets, a city built unto Yahweh < Jer 31:38 Behold, the days come, saith the LORD, that the city shall be built to the LORD from the tower of Hananeel unto the gate of the corner.> The one seen by John is made up of living persons, the Redeemed. < 2 Cor 6:16 And what agreement hath the temple of God with idols? for ye are the temple of the living God; as God hath said, I will dwell in them, and walk in them; and I will be their God, and they shall be my people.> <1 Peter 2:4 To whom coming, as unto a living stone, disallowed indeed of men, but chosen of God, and precious, 5 Ye also, as lively stones, are built up a spiritual house, an holy priesthood, to offer up spiritual sacrifices, acceptable to God by Jesus Christ. 6 Wherefore also it is contained in the scripture, Behold, I lay in Sion a chief corner stone, elect, precious: and he that believeth on him shall not be onfounded. 7 Unto you therefore which believe he is precious: but unto them which be disobedient, the stone which the builders disallowed, the same is made the head of the corner,] **descending out of heaven from God,** [Appropriately both pre and post millennial houses come from the political heaven.]

VS11 Having the glory of God: [That glory is promised the saints and will be revealed at the coming of the Lord.< John 17:22 And the glory which thou gavest me I have given them; that they may be one, even as we are one:> <2 Thess 1:10 When he shall come to be glorified in his saints, and to be admired in all them that believe (because our testimony among you was believed) in that day.>] **and her light was like unto a stone most precious,** [The stone relate to the Lord Jesus, of whose likeness the Bride of Christ will partake. He is the measuring rod of glory and light for all the elect for he comes to be glorified in his sight. The word light is luminary or light giver. It is used figuratively of believers as shining in spiritual darkness of the world. Here it is used of Christ as the light reflected in and shining through the New Jerusalem his Bride. These who shine as lights today, will do so in the future.]

even like a jasper stone, clear as crystal; [The Jasper is representative of Christ see note Rev 4:3.]

VS12 And had a wall great and high, [This wall is not the height of the city mentioned in vs 16. The true meaning is revealed in the specifications of the Temple of Ezekiel's prophecy. This had a wall to separate the Holy from the profane. <Ezek 40:5 And behold a wall on the outside of the house round about, and in the man's hand a measuring reed of six cubits long by the cubit and an hand breadth: so he measured the breadth of the building, one reed; and the height, one reed.> <Ezek 42:20 He measured it by the four sides: it had a wall round about, five hundred reeds long, and five hundred broad, to make a separation between the sanctuary and the profane place.>

The first principle demonstrated by the symbol therefore is that of separation for without holiness no man shall see the Lord. The word for gates if pulonas and signifies a porch or vestibule then the gateway or gate tower of a walled town. The figure is thus drawn from the literal gates seen by Ezekiel in his vision of a literal Temple-city. <Ezek 40:5 And behold a wall on the outside of the house round about, and in the man's hand a measuring reed of six cubits long by the cubit and an hand breadth: so he measured the breadth of the building, one reed; and the height, one reed. 6 Then came he unto the gate which looketh toward the east, and went up the stairs thereof, and measured the threshold of the gate, which was one reed broad; and the other threshold of the gate, which was one reed broad.>] **and had twelve gates, and at the gates twelve angels,** [The messengers at the gates are the symbolic porters of the spiritual Temple. They grant access to believers and keep out the unworthy.] **and names written thereon, which are the names of the twelve tribes of the children of Israel:** [Following Ezekiel <Ezek 48:31 And the gates of the city shall be after the names of the tribes of Israel: three gates northward; one gate of Reuben, one gate of Judah, one gate of Levi. 32 And at the east side four thousand and five hundred: and three gates; and one gate of Joseph, one gate of Benjamin, one gate of Dan. 33 And at the south side four thousand and five hundred measures: and three gates; one gate of Simeon, one gate of Issachar, one gate of Zebulun. 34 At the west side four thousand and five hundred, with their three gates; one gate of Gad, one gate of Asher, one gate of Naphtali.>

First looking at the meaning of the names on the east, Joseph-adding; Benjamin-Son of his right hand; Dan-judge: on the north Reuben—see a son; Juday-Praise; Levi-Join: On the south Simeon-hearing; Issachar-Reward; Zebulun-Dwelling On the west Gad-Company; Asher-blessed; Naphtali-Wrestling. This sentence emerges stating the purpose of God.

East: There shall be adding to the Son of His Right Hand after Judgment.

North: See a son. Praise him. Join him.

South: To those who hear he will reward with a dwelling.

West;   The company of the blessed have gone through wrestling. But in the Apocalypse, Dan s replaced with Manasseh. Dan is judging and Manasseh is forgetting. After the judgment, there will be a forgetting of the past in the joy of deliverance. Adjustment accordingly can be made to the above.]

VS13 On the east three gates; on the north three gates; on the south three gates; and on the west three gates.[The new Jerusalem being also the antitypical Cherubim faces all directions.]

VS14 And the wall of the city had twelve foundations, [See Eph 2:20] **and in them the names of the twelve apostles of the Lamb.** [The apostles are to be the twelve rulers of Israel and upon their authority will rest the administration of the Land of the future. <Matt 19:28 And Jesus said unto them, Verily I say unto you, That ye which have followed me, in the regeneration when the Son of man shall sit in the throne of his glory, ye also shall sit upon twelve thrones, judging the twelve tribes of Israel.> <Acts 28:20 For this cause therefore have I called for you, to see you, and to speak with you: because that for the hope of Israel I am bound with this chain.>]

VS15 And he that talked with me had a golden reed to measure the city, and the gates thereof, and the wall thereof. [The reed measured both Ezekiel's temple and this one. Golden reed symbolizes tried faith. Without faith it is impossible to please God.]

VS 16 And the city lieth foursquare, [This is the shape of the breastplate <Ex 28:16 Foursquare it shall be being doubled; a span shall be the length thereof, and a span shall be the breadth thereof.> the altar and Israel's encampment as seen in Numbers 2. The holy city will be a breastplate from whence shone forth the divine glory the altar which consumed the sacrifice, the encampment emphasizing the Israelitish nature of the hope.] **and the length is as large as the breadth: and he measured the city with the reed, twelve thousand furlongs.** [Each side is 12,000 furlongs or 1500 miles or 6000 miles around precluding a literal city. It is a symbol for the Lamb's wife. 6000 speaks of the measure of the multitudinous man for six is the number of man. It also points to the length of time during which the materials of the New Jerusalem have been gathered from the Gentiles. At the end of the millennium, it will fill the whole earth.

The number 12,000 is significant. 12 is the number of perfect government and we have seen its use in a figurative sense in Rev. 7. It has also a most interesting relationship to the Tabernacle.

The walls of the Tabernacle were formed of boards ending in two tenons that fitted into silver sockets. Each socket was made of a talent of silver and represented the redemption money of six thousand men so that each double socket represented 12,000 redeemed men. The talent represented the measure of redemption as seen in a multitude.

The sockets provided the foundation in which the tenons took hold and the Hebrew word for sockets is *Edonim* the pleural of Adon the word used for God as Ruler. Tehons is from *Yadoth* the feminine gender of the word for hands. The thought suggests that the Bride takes hold upon the Lord to form a dwelling place for Yahweh.

The double sockets being the redemption measure of 12000 men and the foundation wall of the New Jerusalem 12000 furlongs in estent the measurement of the former provides a type of the latter.< Ex 25:15 The staves shall be in the rings of the ark: they shall not be taken from it. 16 And thou shalt put into the ark the testimony which I shall give thee. 17 And thou shalt make a mercy seat of pure gold: two cubits and a half shall be the length thereof, and a cubit and a half the breadth thereof. 18 And thou shalt make two cherubims of gold, of beaten work shalt thou make them, in the two ends of the mercy seat. 19 And make one cherub on the one end, and the other cherub on the other end: even of the mercy seat shall ye make the cherubims on the two ends thereof.> <Ex 38:25 And the silver of them that were numbered of the congregation was an hundred talents, and a thousand seven hundred and threescore and fifteen shekels, after the shekel of the sanctuary: 26 A bekah for every man, that is, half a shekel, after the shekel of the sanctuary, for every one that went to be numbered, from twenty years old and upward, for six hundred thousand and three thousand and five hundred and fifty men. 27 And of the hundred talents of silver were cast the sockets of the sanctuary, and the sockets of the vail; an hundred sockets of the hundred talents, a talent for a socket.>] **The length and the breadth and the height of it are equal.** [The city is a cube. The Most High was also a cube. <1 Kings 6:20 And the oracle in the forepart was twenty cubits in length, and twenty cubits in breadth, and twenty cubits in the height thereof: and he overlaid it with pure gold; and so covered the altar which was of cedar.> and as such pointed to the perfect love of God as Paul observes. < Eph 3:17 That Christ may dwell in your hearts by faith; that ye, being rooted and grounded in love,>The ground area or surface of this cube is divisible into 144 equal parts of 1000 furlongs each pointing to the symbolic number of its citizens. <Rev 7:4 And I heard the number of them which were sealed: and there were sealed an hundred and forty and four thousand of all the tribes of the children of Israel.> <Rev 14:1 And I looked, and, lo, a Lamb stood on the mount Sion, and with him an hundred forty and four thousand, having his Father's name written in their foreheads.>]

VS17 And he measured the wall thereof, an hundred and forty and four cubits, [The Temple in Jerusalem in the days of Christ had a wall of separation dividing the Jews from the Gentiles known as the middle wall or partition. <Eph 2:14 For he is our peace, who hath made both one, and hath broken down the middle wall of partition between us;>

A notice on the wall warned Gentiles that if they strayed beyond this point could blame themselves for their own death that would ensue. The measure of the 144 is made up of the square of 12 x 12 for perfect government. The whole city as well as the wall is divisible into 12 for the multitudinous Christ will administer the perfect government.

The cubit is the length between elbow and middle fingertip or 18 inches. The Apocalypse is not interested in the cubit as a unit of measure so why use it? Because it represents that part of the human body that is known for power and work, the arm and hand. These are used as divine attributes of manifestation in the active governing of the nations. Yahweh's hand can be stretched out to help or to rule. <Isa 40:10 Behold, the Lord GOD will come with strong hand, and his arm shall rule for him: behold, his reward is with him, and his work before him.> This is the figurative cubit the fore-arm of Yahweh manifested by the multitudinous Christ in the age to come.] **according to the measure of a man, that is, of the angel.** [This angelic man is the one of Rev 1:13 as one like to the son of man. The measure of this perfect man made like unto angels is thus 144 cubits. In the Apocalypse he stands in contrast to the man whose number is 666.]

VS18 And the building of the wall of it was of jasper: [Building is from *endomesis* to build or that which is built or the building materials of which the wall is constructed. Speaking of the literal Temple city yet to be built at Jerusalem, Yahweh through Zechariah declared, <Zech 2:5 For I, saith the LORD, will be unto her a wall of fire round about, and will be the glory in the midst of her.> That wall of fire will separate the holy from the profane.

The jasper stone is appropriate for God manifestation will provide the basic material of this spiritual city. It will be the glory in the midst of her.] **and the city was pure gold,** [Gold is tried faith which is the basic requirement to please God. <1 Peter 1:7 That the trial of your faith, being much more precious than of gold that perisheth, though it be tried with fire, might be found unto praise and honour and glory at the appearing of Jesus Christ:>] **like unto clear glass.** [The word rendered glass in this place *hualos* occurs in the NT only here and v. 21. It signifies anything transparent. Here the meaning is the golden city would be so bright and burnished that it would seem to be glass reflecting the brilliance of the sun. How appropriate to the figure of a city formed of the glorified redeemed. The general picture of reflecting Divine light is conveyed by the description in this verse. <Matt 13:43 Then shall the righteous shine forth as the sun in the kingdom of their Father. Who hath ears to hear, let him hear.>]

VS19 And the foundations of the wall of the city were garnished with all manner of precious stones. [As the foundation of the walls comprise 12 basic gems representing the apostles to garnish or decorate them. This will be done in that all the Redeemed will find a place in the Lamb's bride the New Jerusalem.

The 12 foundations are identified with the Apostles because the the doctrines they proclaimed involved things concerning the Kingdom of God and the name of Christ Jesus that forms the basis of New Jerusalem. As the wall lies foresquare and comprises 12 gems the general shape and formation of the walls of New Jerusalem answers to the Urim and Thummim of the High Priest's breastplate representing the Lights and Fullness of the perfected Israel. It is logical that the gems of the breastplate were set in order in such a way as to reproduce the encampment of Israel, leaving the square in the centre to represent the Tabernacle.

This is strongly implied in that Moses was instructed to place the gems in the breastplate according to the twelve tribes. <Ex 28:21 And the stones shall be with the names of the children of Israel, twelve, according to their names, like the engravings of a signet; every one with his name shall they be according to the twelve tribes.>

This suggests the stones were place in the order the tribes encamped around the tabernacle. That is also the order of the gems around new Jerusalem linking the Tabernacle of the past with the symbolic city of the future. The gems are not only identified with the Apostles but the tribe over which they will rule but their various colors reproduce the sevenfold colors of the rainbow, the token of the covenant. When these colors combine they form white light of the sun figurative of the light of righteousness. To bring out their beauty, the stones must be cut and polished to bring out the beauty of them. This is the process of obtaining righteousness that accomplished this.] **The first foundation was jasper;** Symbolizing divine light and glory. In the breastplate it represented Napthali. In the Apocalypse the gems correspond to the enumeration of the tribes given in Rev. 7. A comparison of the two will show that Jasper in this verse is Judah meaning praise, while Napthali means striving. In new Jerusalem, striving will be replaced by praise.] **the second, sapphire;** [Hebrew *sappeer*, to scratch, polish, write, number. The deep blue color suggests God manifestation. The pavement under the feet of the Elohim seen by Moses was sapphire as was the throne of glory associated with the Cherubim.< Ex 24:10 And they saw the God of Israel: and there was under his feet as it were a paved work of a sapphire stone, and as it were the body of heaven in his clearness.> <Ezek 1:26 And above the firmament that was over their heads was the likeness of a throne, as the appearance of a sapphire stone: and upon the likeness of the throne was the likeness as the appearance of a man above upon it.> <Ezek 10:1 Then I looked, and, behold, in the firmament that was above the head of the cherubims there appeared over them as it were a sapphire stone, as the appearance of the likeness of a throne.>

Both were visions of glory of the coming Kingdom the foundation and throne of which will manifest the divine glory in the earth. In the breastplate the sapphire was Simeon and in Revelation Ruben. Simeon is hearing and Ruben seeing. In new Jerusalem, we will see the word that to that point we have only heard.] **the third, a chalcedony;** [This gem is found in different colors among which is a golden yellow variety speaking to faith. It is found only here where it stands for Gad. Gad is a company, for example faithful ones. Through lack of faith Israel failed to obtain that which the elect has and will obtain.] **the fourth, an emerald;** [The bright green gem was Reuben in the breastplate but in Revelation it is Asher. Ruben is see a son, Asher is blessed. When Christ walked the earth we saw the son. In the millennium, we see the blessed son.]

VS 20 The fifth, sardonyx; [The rarest variety of onyx. Pliny defines it as originally signifying a white mark in a sard (cornelian) like the human nail (onyx) placed in flesh and both of them transparent. Onyx is so called for its resemblance of its white and yellow veins resembling the shades in human finger nails. Vine define it as a name which indicates the formation of the gem a layer of sard and a layer of onyx mark ed by the red of the sardis and the white of the onyx. In the apocalypse, the gem is related to Naphtali to wrestle with the hands the red of flesh contrasting with the whit of righteousness. The Hebrew word for onyx denotes a flashing forth of splendor. Those who successfully wrestle with the flesh will ultimately flash forth in splendor. The gem was not used in the breastplate.]

the sixth, sardius; [*Sardius* is *odem* similar to Adam and relates to flesh with its red color. Judah or praise in the breastplate while in the apocalypse Manasseh means forgetting. Those who praise Christ will forget the flesh in the future.]

the seventh, chrysolite; [Means yellow stone. It is not in the breastplate but represents Simeon] **the eighth, beryl;** [*Tharshish* means beat or subdue translated beryl. The wheels of the Cherubim were of beryl mighty in subduing the nations as is the body of the multitudinous Christ. <Ezek 1:16 The appearance of the wheels and their work was like unto the colour of a beryl: and they four had one likeness: and their appearance and their work was as it were a wheel in the middle of a wheel.> <Dan 10:6 His body also was like the beryl, and his face as the appearance of lightning, and his eyes as lamps of fire, and his arms and his feet like in colour to polished brass, and the voice of his words like the voice of a multitude.>

In the breastplate beryl was Dan or judge and in Apocalypse its Levi.or joining. The nations will be humbled and subdued by the judgments of Christ and then will be joined to him in fellowship.] **the ninth, a topaz;** [Mainly yellow it comes in many colors. In both the breastplate and Apocalypse it is Issachar whose name means reward. The reward that was set before Israel after the flesh will be reaped by Israel after the spirit.] **the tenth, a chrysoprasus;** [The word in Greek is a combination of the words for gold and leek and is a greenish gold in color similar to the apple green of the leek. It combines the symbolism of a tried faith gold and the glory of everlasting life by the green color. The stone is for Zebulen whose name means dwelling. Saints of faith will dwell in New Jerusalem.] **the eleventh, a jacinth;** [Same word as hyacinth and is deep purple or reddish blue. Purple stands for God manifest in the flesh being a combination of red and blue. In the breastplate Ephraim meansdouble fruit while here it is Joseph is increaser. Those who develop double fruit will find an abiding place in the new Jerusalem and will bring forth increased fruit in the millennium.] **the twelfth, an amethyst.** [Violet or purple again suggesting God in the flesh as well as the color of royalty. It was also supposed to help prevent intoxication. In both instances it represents Benjamin the son of the right hand. Those associated with the Son will find an antidote against the intoxicating doctrines of Babylon the Great and will be incorporated into the new Jerusalem in due time.

VS21 And the twelve gates were twelve pearls; [The pearl makes a perfect analogy for the redeemed. A pearl is hidden away in the depths of the ocean until it is harvested. So the Redeemed are hidden in the sea of nations until revealed at the resurrection. A pearl forms when an irritant like a grain of sand invades the oyster who covers it with a nacreous substance that is the pearl. So it is through much tribulation that the Redeemed are formed. <Acts 14:22 Confirming the souls of the disciples, and exhorting them to continue in the faith, and that we must through much tribulation enter into the kingdom of God.>

Before the pearl is beautiful, it must be exposed by stripping away the outer covering and exposing it to the light of the sun. The Redeemed must shed their coats of flesh and bask in the light of the Sun of Righteousness to show their luster. >] **every several gate was of one pearl:** [The entrance to new Jerusalem is adorned with the symbol of the gospel, <Matt 13:4545 Again, the kingdom of heaven is like unto a merchant man, seeking goodly pearls: 46 Who, when he had found one pearl of great price, went and sold all that he had, and bought it.> The value of that pearl must be acknowledged by all who enter New Jerusalem.] **and the street of the city was pure gold,** [Street here is the word for broad space. It was not a street as we understand street, but the broad quadrangle within the Temple wall which accommodates the worshipers. As often said before it's the symbol of tried faith, and without such faith we will not be among the Redeemed.] **as it were transparent glass.** [See note vs. 18]

VS 22 And I saw no temple therein: [In both the Tabernacle and the Temple there was a Holy of Holies, or a temple within a temple. In new Jerusalem there is not such distinction. The reason is that the Holy place in the Tabernacle or Temple was for mortals and the Most Holy or Holy of Holies, represented the dwelling of the immortal state. In new Jerusalem this will not be needed since only immortals will be there.] **for the Lord God Almighty and the Lamb are the temple of it.** [God in manifest glory though Christ and the Redeemed now equal to angels are the living Most Holy. This is foreshadowed in the Tabernacle and Temple for in them are found the Mercy Seat pointing to Christ, the Cherubim representing the Redeemed and the Shekinah Glory being the token of Yahweh's indwelling presence. All this is summed up by the statement in this section of the verse.]

VS 23 And the city had no need of the sun, neither of the moon, to shine in it: [The need for political suns and moons has past and are no longer needed in new Jerusalem.] **for the glory of God did lighten it,** [The Redeemed will manifest the glory of God in the age to come. <John 17:22 And the glory which thou gavest me I have given them; that they may be one, even as we are one>] **and the Lamb is the light thereof.** [As the Bride of Christ, the Redeemed will reflect his light.]

VS24 And the nations of them which are saved [Those which accepted Christ and joined the Redeemed rather than oppose him and be destroyed.] **shall walk in the light of it:** [That is the light of the law and instruction that is dispensed throughout the world by the saints. <Isa 2:2 And it shall come to pass in the last days, that the mountain of the LORD's house shall be established in the top of the mountains, and shall be exalted above the hills; and all nations shall flow unto it. 3 And many people shall go and say, Come ye, and let us go up to the mountain of the LORD, to the house of the God of Jacob; and he will teach us of his ways, and we will walk in his paths: for out of Zion shall go forth the law, and the word of the LORD from Jerusalem.>] **and the kings of the earth do bring their glory and honour into it.** [These are not the rebellious kings of the earth of Rev. 16:14, for they are here replaced by the Redeemed kings of Rev. 5:9-10. who are the kings of the age to come.]

VS25 And the gates of it shall not be shut at all by day: [This was foreshadowed by the Temple priests who worked in shifts night and day so the worship of God was continual.] **for there shall be no night there.** [The light of the world will constantly shine in the new Jerusalem. <Mal 4:1 For, behold, the day cometh, that shall burn as an oven; and all the proud, yea, and all that do wickedly, shall be stubble: and the day that cometh shall burn them up, saith the LORD of hosts, that it shall leave them neither root nor branch. 2 But unto you that fear my name shall the Sun of righteousness arise with healing in his wings; and ye shall go forth, and grow up as calves of the stall.]

VS26 And they shall bring the glory and honour of the nations into it. [<Hag 2:7 And I will shake all nations, and the desire of all nations shall come: and I will fill this house with glory, saith the LORD of hosts.> Only those nations who accept him and honor him will be there in the Glory.]

255

VS27 And there shall in no wise enter into it any thing that defileth, [To defile is to render for common purpose what Yahweh has claimed as his own. Israel did this in the past but in the future, will see Yahweh's requirements respected. <Ezek 44:7 In that ye have brought into my sanctuary strangers, uncircumcised in heart, and uncircumcised in flesh, to be in my sanctuary, to pollute it, even my house, when ye offer my bread, the fat and the blood, and they have broken my covenant because of all your abominations.> Those who defiled God's holy things will not be here.] **either whatsoever worketh abomination,** [See note v. 8] **or maketh a lie:** [False teaching is equivalent to a lie, and those who indulge in it are endangering their future inheritance.] **but they which are written in the Lamb's book of life.** [See notes Rev. 20:12. By continuance in well doing we shall find a place in the book of life and will be incorporated into the symbolic Holy Jerusalem, forming the multitudinous Bride of the Lamb.]

CHAPTER 23

Revelation Chapter 22

This marvelous chapter ends the word of God with a picture of a world so filled with glory of Yahweh that the joy it describes is nearly unimaginable.

VS1 And he shewed me a pure river of water of life, clear as crystal, [This symbol is based on the literal temple prophesied by Ezekiel (Chapter 47) who saw a stream of living water in his vision proceeding from the Altar and flowing eastward to heal the waters of the Dead Sea. In symbolic new Jerusalem, Christ is the Altar, < Heb 13:10 We have an altar, whereof they have no right to eat which serve the tabernacle.> and form him flows the doctrine of life represented as living water. This will refresh the arid minds of man and heal the Dead Sea of nations. < Isa 57:20 But the wicked are like the troubled sea, when it cannot rest, whose waters cast up mire and dirt. 21 There is no peace, saith my God, to the wicked.>] **proceeding out of the throne of God and of the Lamb.** [This will be done by the Redeemed.]

VS2 In the midst of the street of it, [This is again the broad space, since there will be no streets in the Temple. It is the square where the Redeemed gather to worship.] **and on either side of the river, was there the tree of life,** [We cannot have a tree inside and outside the city on both sides of the river if it is a single tree. The word tree here is *xulon* is woods. John saw a forest of trees just like Ezekiel did. < Ezek 47:12 And by the river upon the bank thereof, on this side and on that side, shall grow all trees for meat, whose leaf shall not fade, neither shall the fruit thereof be consumed: it shall bring forth new fruit according to his months, because their waters they issued out of the sanctuary: and the fruit thereof shall be for meat, and the leaf thereof for medicine.>

The roots of these trees draw water from the River of Life and produce leaves that bear fruit, or the Redeemed who will carry forth the gospel. < Ps 1:1 Blessed is the man that walketh not in the counsel of the ungodly, nor standeth in the way of sinners, nor sitteth in the seat of the scornful. 2 But his delight is in the law of the LORD; and in his law doth he meditate day and night. 3 And he shall be like a tree planted by the rivers of water, that bringeth forth his fruit in his season; his leaf also shall not wither; and whatsoever he doeth shall prosper.>] **which bare twelve manner of fruits, and yielded her fruit every month:** [This confirms it is a forest John sees. These fruits are; < Gal 5:22 But the fruit of the Spirit is love, joy, peace, longsuffering, gentleness, goodness, faith, 23 Meekness, temperance: against such there is no law.>Twelve links the fruits with the hope of Israel and suggests the monthly pilgrimage and services that will form part of the ministry of saints in the age to come. < Isa 66:22 For as the new heavens and the new earth, which I will make, shall remain before me, saith the LORD, so shall your seed and your name remain. 23 And it shall come to pass, that from one new moon to another, and from one sabbath to another, shall all flesh come to worship before me, saith the LORD.>] **and the leaves of the tree were for the healing of the nations.** [Figuratively these leaves relate to the administration of the saints in the age to come. All creatures need plants and their leaves since they are a major food source, even for fish. Chlorophyll is derived from light energy. Leaves breath in carbon dioxide and purify the air. As the saints derive energy from the Sun of Righteous and carry the Word forward to feed the nations, they also purify the political, moral and social aspect of the age to come. Could there be a more perfect analogy?"]

VS3 And there shall be no more curse: [The Genesis curse of death for sin is removed from those who have put on immortality.] **but the throne of God and of the Lamb shall be in it;** [This limits beneficiaries from the lifting of the curse to those in new Jerusalem, though eventually all the world will have the curse removed.] **and his servants shall serve him:**[The Redeemed will minister as a royal priesthood on behalf of humanity. Servants here is *latreuo* towork for hire or job. Their job will be to serve him.]

VS4 And they shall see his face; [They will see the full glory of God revealed in Christ. < Isa 33:17 Thine eyes shall see the king in his beauty: they shall behold the land that is very far off.><Matt 5:8 Blessed are the pure in heart: for they shall see God.> <John 14:9 Jesus saith unto him, Have I been so long time with you, and yet hast thou not known me, Philip? he that hath seen me hath seen the Father; and how sayest thou then, Shew us the Father?> <1 Tim 6:14 That thou keep this commandment without spot, unrebukeable, until the appearing of our Lord Jesus Christ: 15 Which in his times he shall shew, who is the blessed and only Potentate, the King of kings, and Lord of lords;>] **and his name shall be in their foreheads.** [See Rev 14:1]

VS5 And there shall be no night there; [See Rev. 21:25] **and they need no candle,** [Candle from *lunchos*, a portable oil lamp that burns for a time and then goes out. Such is the state of the saints in their mortal existence. In the age to come, they will shine forth like the sun. < Matt 13:43 Then shall the righteous shine forth as the sun in the kingdom of their Father. Who hath ears to hear, let him hear.>] **neither light of the sun;** [See Rev. 21:23] **for the Lord God giveth them light:** [The Redeemed will have a divine light within.] **and they shall reign for ever and ever.** [See notes 1:6; 20:4]

VS6 And he said unto me, See notes Rev. 19:11; 20:4] **These sayings are faithful and true: and the Lord God of the holy prophets sent his angel to shew unto his servants the things which must shortly be done.** [The same spirit that moved the prophets inspired the Apocalypse. Among the chief function of prophets of the old Testament was comforting, exhorting and edifying believers. Revelation does that as well as foretells the future.]

VS7 Behold, I come quickly: [Significantly, this warning occurs seven times in the Apocalypse. In Rev. 2:5,16; 3:11; 11:4; 22:7, 12, 20] **blessed is he that keepeth the sayings of the prophecy of this book.** [Blessed signifies happy, and happy are those who keep the sayings. Keep if form a word meaning to watch over, preserve, guard from loss or injury. If we keep God's word in that way we will all be blessed.]

VS8 And I John saw these things, and heard them. [John authenticates the visions revealed to him.] **And when I had heard and seen, I fell down to worship before the feet of the angel which shewed me these things.** [See Rev. 19:10]

VS9 Then saith he unto me, See thou do it not: for I am thy fellowservant, and of thy brethren the prophets, and of them which keep the sayings of this book: worship God. [Awe and joy overcome him in direct contrast to the misery he felt when he was unable to open the book. (Rev 5:4) The angel gives an apt warning. No matter how brilliant, charismatic or insightful any human being or even divine being is, they are not to be worshiped.]

VS10 And he saith unto me, Seal not the sayings of the prophecy of this book: [The Apocalypse is given to be understood.] **for the time is at hand.** [See Rev. 1:3]

VS11 He that is unjust, let him be unjust still: [This associates with the Behold I come quickly. When Christ leaves the right hand of the Father, his role as mediator will be temporarily close, as in the days of Noah, when the ark was closed, those outside were doomed and there was too late to change for a time. The unjust are those who refuse Christ.] **and he which is filthy, let him be filthy still:** [Filthy, *rhuparos* is the term used for vial clothing in James. < James 2:2 For if there come unto your assembly a man with a gold ring, in goodly apparel, and there come in also a poor man in vile raiment;> It is those who have embraced Christ but failed to keep their garments clean. Whereas the unjust refuse Christ, the filthy disgrace him.] **and he that is righteous, let him be righteous still:** [True righteousness is a matter of actions. See Rev. 19:8. These are justified by both faith and works.] **and he that is holy, let him be holy still.** [Separation is necessary if one would please Christ.]

VS12 And, behold, I come quickly; [See v. 7] **and my reward is with me, to give every man according as his work shall be.** [Christ comes with the reward, man does not go to heaven to get it. He rewards at the resurrection of the just as the result of judgment based on faith in action and not a mere academic understanding of the Truth.]

VS13 I am Alpha and Omega, [Appropriately this appears at both the beginning and the end of the Apocalypse.] **the beginning and the end,** [See Rev. 1:8] **the first and the last.** [See Rev. 1:11]

VS14 Blessed are they that do his commandments, [The Diaglott reads "Blessed are they who wash their robes." This would be in preparation of his coming.] **that they may have right to the tree of life,** [That which was forbidden to Adam and Eve is now made available to the elect.] **and may enter in through the gates into the city.** [To the exclusion of all others, they will enter the gates of new Jerusalem.]

VS15 For without are dogs, [Dogs are unclean animals and it was a term of reproach by which Israel described unjustified Gentiles. < Matt 15:26 But he answered and said, It is not meet to take the children's bread, and to cast it to dogs. 27 And she said, Truth, Lord: yet the dogs eat of the crumbs which fall from their masters' table.> Under the law it denounced moral perversion with male prostitutes. <Deut 23:18 Thou shalt not bring the hire of a whore, or the price of a dog, into the house of the LORD thy God for any vow: for even both these are abomination unto the LORD thy God.>

Paul used the term for Judaisers who acted as Gentiles. < Phil 3:2 Beware of dogs, beware of evil workers, beware of the concision.> The herds of ownerless dogs that infest eastern cities, eating the filth and garbage on the streets and attacking passers-by completes the image of these to be excluded.] **and sorcerers, and whoremongers, and murderers, and idolaters, and whosoever loveth and maketh a lie.** [Maketh a lie is better rendered doeth a lie. This class of excluded people live the lie.]

VS16 I Jesus have sent mine angel to testify unto you these things in the churches. [Christ himself now speaks to verify the and confirm all that has been communicated to John by the angels.] **I am the root and the offspring of David,** [David's greatness came from God, as did Christ's, and he is offspring for he is in David's line of succession. The Hebrew for Nazarene is *netzer* to sprout. < Isa 11:1 And there shall come forth a rod out of the stem of Jesse, and a Branch shall grow out of his roots:>

The oak that grows in Israel is of a nature that if cut down will grow again. < Job 14:7 For there is hope of a tree, if it be cut down, that it will sprout again, and that the tender branch thereof will not cease. 8 Though the root thereof wax old in the earth, and the stock thereof die in the ground; 9 Yet through the scent of water it will bud, and bring forth boughs like a plant.> The oak was a national symbol of Israel. < Isa 6:13 But yet in it shall be a tenth, and it shall return, and shall be eaten: as a teil tree, and as an oak, whose substance is in them, when they cast their leaves: so the holy seed shall be the substance thereof.>

In contrast, the overthrow of Gog is likened to cutting down a forest of cedars. < Isa 10:33 Behold, the Lord, the LORD of hosts, shall lop the bough with terror: and the high ones of stature shall be hewn down, and the haughty shall be humbled. 34 And he shall cut down the thickets of the forest with iron, and Lebanon shall fall by a mighty one.> The cedar throws out no new suckers and once cut down dies. But, the root of the Israel-oak will sprout again to even greater glory.] **and the bright and morning star.** [This bright star shines forth as the night ends and unseen sun is about to rise. What a marvelous comparison the new age.]

VS17 And the Spirit and the bride say, Come. And let him that heareth say, Come. [The invitation is from those who will take the message to the world, the Redeemed or the bride. But the message must be heard to be accepted.] **And let him that is athirst come.** [See note 21:6. Living water is only for those who thirst after it.] **And whosoever will, let him take the water of life freely.** [Will is from *Thelon* or desire. Those who desire to change can do so through the matchless grace of Christ.]

VS18 For I testify unto every man that heareth the words of the prophecy of this book, [This begins a solemn warning against tampering with the words of the book.] **If any man shall add unto these things, God shall add unto him the plagues that are written in this book:** [The Bible opens and closes with such warnings. < Deut 4:2 Ye shall not add unto the word which I command you, neither shall ye diminish ought from it, that ye may keep the commandments of the LORD your God which I command you.> Both Moses and Christ representing Law and Grace testify as one against adding to the words of the divine Revelation. Judaizers try to do it anyway.]

VS19 And if any man shall take away from the words of the book of this prophecy, [To take away is not merely to reject, but to reduce the power of its teaching by a wrong interpretation of it, or by discouraging others from studying it.] **God shall take away his part out of the book of life, and out of the holy city, and from the things which are written in this book.** [There is a solemn obligation then to read and understand the book.]

VS20 He which testifieth these things saith, Surely I come quickly. [Jesus once again testifies to the truth of the Apocalypse.] **Amen. Even so, come, Lord Jesus.** [The words even so doesn't appear in the Greek. It is simply, Amen (so be it) come Lord Jesus. It is the fervent prayer of all those who love the Lord. < 2 Tim 4:8 Henceforth there is laid up for me a crown of righteousness, which the Lord, the righteous judge, shall give me at that day: and not to me only, but unto all them also that love his appearing.>]

VS21 The grace of our Lord Jesus Christ be with you all. [John adds this blessing to all those who read and study the book. He opens and closes the book with a call for grace and divine favor on all who read it. (Rev. 1:4) **Amen.** This concluding word is omitted from the Greek, but it would make an appropriate close to the Apocalypse. SO BE IT. COME LORD JESUS. May God bless the study of His Word.

CHAPTER 24

Caveats

This work has been a means to an end. The concern about the end of the world sweeping certain segments of the world's population deserves a reasonable answer to that concern that might help to allay those fears. It is truly a shame that entities such as the United States government helps fan those flames with this thinly veiled article that appeared in the news.

"(Oct. 25, 2010)—If an asteroid were on a collision course with Earth, would we be ready to defend against its destructive impact or would we be helpless and defenseless?

NASA, America's space agency, is being charged with leading the way to protect not only the U.S. but the entire world in the event of such a horrifying scenario. And a top White House science adviser says we have to be prepared.

In separate 10-page letters to the House Committee on Science and Technology and the Senate Committee on Commerce, Science and Transportation, John Holdren, director of the White House Office of Science and Technology Policy, or OSTP, outlines plans for "(A) protecting the United States from a near-Earth object that is expected to collide with Earth; and (B) implementing a deflection campaign, in consultation with international bodies, should one be necessary."

The White House has asked Congress to consider how to best deal with the potential threat to Earth of an impact with an asteroid from space. While Holdren indicates that no large asteroid or comet presents an immediate hazard to our planet, the fact that devastating impacts have occurred on Earth in the distant past is enough to warrant safety precautions for the future.

Indeed, a steady stream of these objects enters the Earth's atmosphere on a daily basis, consisting mostly of dust-sized particles and estimated to total some 50 to 150 tons each day," Holdren wrote. As remote as it may seem that Earth could be the target of a giant rock from space, nevertheless, Holdren insists that "the possibility of a future collision involving a more hazardous object should not be ignored."

No Christian, young or old, who believes in the Truth and that the Bible is the word of the one and only true God should be uncertain about the future or convinced, as the Mayana tell us that at 11:11 on the 21st of December, 2012 the world as we know it will end. Hopefully, the reader now has some doubts about the accuracy of that prediction.

Admittedly, this is not the ideal way to study the word of God. One should not skip about from place to place to prove a point, but without reviewing the entire books of Daniel, Ezekiel and the Revelation, as well as other large portions of scripture that is not possible. As cited throughout this work, an abundance of reference material exists and is available at Logos.org.au., as well as other web sites. If nothing else, it is the hope that this humble volume will encourage the study of the word of God because it is the only way to find eternal salvation. Yesterday is history; tomorrow and adventure; today is a gift. Use the gift God has given you to study his word.

APPENDIX 1

End of Time Promises

1. AD 30 Jesus. Some say that according to Matthew 16:28, Jesus himself predicted his second coming and the end of the world within the lifetime of his contemporaries. (Matt 16:28 Verily I say unto you, There be some standing here, which shall not taste of death, till they see the Son of man coming in his kingdom.) Unfortunately, this verse has been taken out of context and used as proof for Jesus predicting his return during the lifetime of his disciples. In fact, Jesus meant that those standing by did not believe he would come again to establish his kingdom. Jesus predicted that many of them would come to that realization before they died.

2. About AD 90: Saint Clement 1 predicted that the world end would occur at any moment.

3. AD 156 A man named Montanus declared himself to be the "Spirit of Truth," the personification of the Holy Spirit, mentioned in the Gospel of John, who was to reveal all truth. Montanus quickly gathered followers, including a pair of far-seeing "prophetesses", who claimed to have visions and ecstatic experiences supposedly from God. They began to spread what they called "The Third Testament, a series of revelatory messages which foretold of the soon-coming Kingdom of God and "The New Jerusalem," which was about to descend from heaven to land in Montanus' city of Pepuza, in Phrygia (modern-day Turkey), where it would be home for all "true" believers. The word was spread, and all were urged to come to Phrygia to await the Second Coming. The movement divided Christians into two camps, even after the New Jerusalem didn't appear. Whole communities were fragmented, and continuous

discord resulted. Finally, in AD 431, the Council of Ephesus condemned Chiliasm, or belief in the Millennium, as a dangerous superstition, and Montanus was declared to be a heretic. Despite the failure of the prediction, the cult survived several centuries until it was ordered exterminated by Pope Leo I.—SSA pg 54

3. AD 247, Christian prophets declare that the persecutions by the Romans are a sign of the impending return of Jesus.

4. AD 300 Lactantius Firmianus (AD c260—AD c340), called the "Christian Cicero", from his Divinae Institutiones: "The fall and ruin of the world will soon take place, but it seems that nothing of the kind is to be feared as the city of Rome stands intact." Rome would fall in AD 410.—TEOTW pg 27

5. AD 365, Hilary of Poitiers predicted the world would end in 365.

6. AD 380, The Donatists, a North African Christian sect, predicted the world would end in 380.

7. AD 387 St. Ambrose, Bishop of Milan, identified the Goths with Ezekial's Gog. The Goths had just destroyed the Imperial army at Adrianople, prompting Ambrose to say, " . . . the end of the world is coming upon us."—TEOTW pg 27

8. AD 300 St. Martin, Bishop of Tours: "Non est dubium, quin antichristus . . . There is no doubt that the Antichrist has already been born. Firmly established already in his early years, he will, after reaching maturity, achieve supreme power."—TEOTW pg 27

9. AD 410 When Rome was sacked, some proclaimed, (as reported by St. Augustine of Hippo) "Behold, from Adam all the years have passed, and behold, the 6,000 years are completed." This alludes to the Great Week theory, held by many millennialists, that the God-allotted time of man on earth was 6,000 years, to be followed by a thousand years of peace under the earthly reign of Christ.—TIME pg 30

10. AD 500 At the mid-fifth century, Vandal invasions recalled calculations that the world would end in the year 500, 6000 years after Creation, and spurred new calculations to show that the name of the Vandal king Genseric represented 666: the number of the Beast.—Apoc pg 34

11. AD 500 Hippolytus of Rome, a third-century theologian supported the oft-accepted (for the day) view of the end of the world occuring sometime around the year AD 500. He used a mass of scriptural evidence, including the dimensions of the ark of the covenant.—TIME pg 31

12. AD 500 Roman theologian Sextus Julius Africanus (ca. 160-240) predicted the second coming of Jesus in the year 500.

13. AD 500 The theologian Irenaeus predicted the second coming of Jesus in the year 500.

14. AD 590 Bishop Gregory of Tours, who died in AD 594, calculated the Time of the End for sometime between 799 and 806.—Apoc pg 48

15. AD 793 Elipand, bishop of Toledo, accused Beatus, abbot of Liebana, of having prophesied the end of the world. Beatus made the prediction on Easter Eve, predicting the end of the world that very night, spraking a riot.—Apoc 49-50

16. AD 800 Sextus Julius Africanus predicted the second coming of Jesus in the year 800.

17. AD 800 Beatus of Liébana, not having learned anything from the riot he started in 793, wrote in his Commentary on the Apocalypse that the world would end in the year 800 at the latest.

18. AD 806 Bishop Gregory of Tours predicted the world would end between 799 and 806.

19. Ad 848 The Christian prophetess Thiota predicted the world would end in 848.

20. AD 900 Adso of Montier-en-lDer, a celbrated 10th-century apocalyptic writer, a Frankish emperor of Rome who was 'the last and greatest of rulers' would, after governing his empire, go to Jerusalem and put off his scepter and crown at the Mount of Olives; this would be the end and consummation of the Christian empire and the beginning of the reign of Antichrist.—TIME pg

21. AD 970 Lotharingian mathematicians foresaw the End on Friday, March 25, 970, when the Annunciation and Good Friday fell on the same day. They believed that it was on this day that Adam was created, Isaac was sacrificed, the Red Sea was parted, Jesus was conceived, and Jesus was crucified.

22. AD An eclipse was interpreted as a prelude to the end of the world by the army of the German Emperor Otto III

23. AD Jan.1,1000 Many European Christians predicted the end of the world on this date. As the date approached, Christian armies waged war against some Pagan countries in Northern Europe. The motivation was to convert them all to Christianity, by force if need be, before Christ returned in the year 1000. Meanwhile, many Christians gave their possessions to the Church in anticipation of the end. Fortunately, the level of education was so low that many people were unaware of the year. They didn't know enough to be afraid. Otherwise, the panic might have been far worse than it was. Jesus did not return and the church kept the gifts, resulting in serious criticism of the Church. The church reacted by extermination some heretics, bringing a swift end to the uproar.

24. AD May, 1000: A legend stated that an emperor would rise from his sleep to fight the Antichrist, so the body of Charlemagne was disinterred on Pentecost, but the emperor refused to wake up.

25. AD 1005-1006 A terrible European famine was interpreted as being a sign of the nearness of the end.

26. AD 1033 When the world did not end in 1000, the same Christian authorities claimed they had forgotten to add in the length of Jesus' life and revised the prediction to 1033. The writings of the Burgundian monk Radulfus Glaber described a rash of mass hysterias during the period from 1000-1033.

27. AD 1033 The roads to Jerusalem fill up with an unprecedented number of pilgrims. Asked why this is happening, the 'more truthful of that time . . . cautiously responded that it presaged nothing else but the coming of the Lost One, the Antichrist, who, according to divine authority, stands ready to come at the end of the age."—TIME pg 47

28. AD 1100 Guibert of Nagent (1064-1125) informed would-be crusaders that they should seize Jerusalem as a necessary prelude to its eventual capture by Antichrist. "The end of the world is already near!," he explained.—TIME pg 61-62

29. 1147 CE: Gerard of Poehlde decided that the millennium had actually stared in 306 CE during Constantine's reign. Thus the world was expected to end on 1306.]

30. AD 1184 Various Christian prophets predicted the end of the world in the year 1184. Nobody seems to remember just why.

31. AD 1186 Certain prophecies, during the time of the Third Crusade, began circulating in 1184, telling of a "new world order." These were believed to have been written by astrologers in Spain, and one of them, the "Letter of Toledo,"(John of Toledo predicted the end of the world during 1186 based on the alignment of many planets), urged everyone to flee to caves and other remote places, because the world was soon to be devastated by terrible storms, famine, earthquakes, and more. Only a few true belivers would be spared. —SSA pg 55

32. AD 1205 Joachim of Fiore predicted in 1190 that the Antichrist was already in the world and that King Richard of England would

Jack L. Summers

defeat him. The Millennium would then begin sometime before 1205

33. AD 1260 The year, according to Joachim of Flores'(c1145-1202) prophecies, when the world was supposed to pass throught the reign of Antichrist and enter the Age of the Holy Spirit. Joachim was an Italian mystic theologian who wrote, in his Expositio in Apocalypsia, that history was to be divided into three ages: The Age of the Law (the Father), The Age of the Gospel (the Son), and the final Age of the Spirit. He had indicated at the end of the 12th Century that the Antichrist was already born in Rome.—DOOM pg 87, TEOTW pg 125

34. AD 1260 A Dominican monk named Brother Arnold gained a following when he wrote that the end was about to take place. According to his scenario, he would call upon Christ, in the name of the poor, to judge the Church leaders, including the Pope. Christ would then appear in judgement, revealing the Pope to be the heralded Antichrist.—SSA pg 56

35. AD 1284 Pope Innocent III predicted the end of the world in the year 1284, 666 years after the founding of Islam

36. AD 1290 When Joachim of Fiore's predicted end of the world had not happened by 1260, members of his order (the Joachites) simply re-scheduled the end another 30 years later to 1290

37. AD 1297 Writing in 1297, the friar Petrus Olivi predicted Antichrist's coming between 1300 and 1340, after which the world would enter the Age of the Holy Spirit, which itself would end around the year 2000 with Gog and the Last Judgement.—Apoc pg 54

38. AD 1300 A Frenchman, Jean de Roquetaillade, published a guide to the tribulation. Imprisoned for most of his adult life, he predicted Antichrist in 1366, to be followed in 1369 or 1370 by a millennial Sabbath. Jerusalem, under a Jewish king, would become the center of the world.—Apoc pg 55

39. AD 1300 Many Germans were living in fearful expectation of the return of the Emperor Frederick II, who had been considered a century earlier as the Antichrist, the terrible ruler who was to chastise the Church before the return of Christ.

40. AD 1306 Gerard of Poehlde, believing that Christ's Millennium actually began when the emperor Constantine came to power, predicts the end of the world 1000 years after the start of Constantine's reign, in 1306.

41. AD 1307 fra Dolcino founds a society, the Apostolic Bretheren, in 1260. He preached that authority had passed from the Roman Church to themselves. The Pope and clergy would soon be exterminated by the forces of the Last Empoeror in a tremendous battle leading to the age of the spirit. Dolcino and his followers perished in a battle at Monte Rebello in 1307.—TIME pg 68

42. AD 1335 The Joachites again re-scheduled the end of the world, this time to the year 1335.

43. AD 1346 and later: The black plague spread across Europe killing one third of the European population, and was interpreted as an immediate prelude to an immediate end of the world. Unfortunately, Christians had killed many of the cats in Europe, feeling that they might be familiars of Witches. The fewer the cats the more the rats. It was the rat flea that spread the black death.

44. AD 1348 Agnolo di Tura, called "the Fat," writing during the time of the Black Death: "And I . . . buried my five children with my own hands, and so did many others likewise . . . And nobody wept no matter what his loss because almost everyone expected death . . . People said and believed, 'This is the end of the world.'"—TEOTW pg 115

45. AD 1349 The group known as the Flagellants claimed that their movement must last thirty-three and a half years, culminating in the Second Coming. They persuaded many people that their assertions were true. One chronicle states: "Many persons, and

even young children, were soon bidding farewell to the world, some with prayers, others with praises on their lips."—TEOTW 125-129

46. AD 1366 Jean de Roquetaillade, a French ascetic, predicted the Antichrist was to come in 1366, with the end of the world a few years after that.

47. AD 1367 Czech archdeacon Militz of Kromeriz claimed the Antichrist was alive and well and would show up no later than 1367, bringing the end of the world with him.

48. AD 1378 The Joachites again re-scheduled the end of the world, this time to the year 1378.

49. AD 1420 Martinek Hauska, near Prague, led a following of priests to announce the soon Second Coming of Christ. They warned everyone to flee to the mountains because between February 1 and February 14, 1420, god was to destroy every town with Holy Fire, thus beginning the Millennium. Hauska's band then went on a rampage to "purify the earth", ridding the world of, in their eyes, false clergymen in the Church. They occupied an abandoned fortress which was named Tabor, and defied the religious powers of the day, ultimately succumbing to the Bohemians in 1452—SSA pg 56, TIME pg 75-77

50. AD 1476 Hans Bohm was burnt at the stake for heresy, after proclaiming the village of Nikleshausen the center of imminent world salvation.—Apoc pg 151

51. AD 1490 Girolamo Savonarola, a Dominican visionary, attracted large crowds with his prophecies of Antichrist. He began preaching that his city of Florence would soon be "The reformation of all Italy . . ." and that its people would take on the mantle of God's elect, saved from destruction to play a glorious new role. This would only be accomplished, however, if Florence submitted peacefully to the invading Charles VIII of France. They did so, and for a short time became what has been called a 'proto-Messianic republic.' But

when the corrupt Pope Alexander VI regained Florence, Savanarola was publicly executed in May, 1498.—TIME pg 79-81

52. AD 1496 Several 15th Century prophets predict the end of the world for the year 1496. This was about 1500 years after the birth of Jesus, and some mystics in also predicted that the millennium would begin during this year.

53. AD 1499 A mathemetician in Tubingen, Germany, had foretold of a coming alignment of the planets in 1524, which would bring a disastrous world-wide flood. This was generally rejected because such would violate God's covenant with Noah. the uneasiness, though, did not pass, and in 1523, printing presses in Germany churned out 51 pamphlets which added fuel to the speculative fire.

54. AD 1500 Martin Luther, Protestant reformer, stated: "I persuade myself verily, that the day of judgment will not be absent full three hundred years. God will not, cannot, suffer this world much longer . . . the great day is drawing near in which the kingdom of abominations shall be overthrown."

55. AD 1500 The Italian artist Botticelli captioned his painting, "The Mystical Nativity" with a message warning that the end of the world would occur within three years, based on the predictions of Girolamo Savonarola.

56. AD 1520 Nicholas Storch was a former weaver who was a self-proclaimed expert on the Bible. He began warning groups of workers that all of Christendom was about to be annihilated by the Turks. Not only did he quote from the Scriptures, but insisted that God spoke to him directly through dreams and visions. Ultimately rejected by reformer Martin Luther, Storch vanishes from history at the end of 1522.—TEOTW pg 155

57. AD 1520 Thomas Muntzer, another self-appointed prophet in Germany, who made bold predictions based upon the book of Daniel, and called for the overthrow by the peasantry of those in power. "The time of the harvest is at hand," he declared. ". . . I

have sharpened my sickle." Muntzer proclaimed that is was the Last Days, and whoever resisted his preaching would be, ". . . slain by the Turks when they come next year." He was executed in 1525, after leading a peasant army in rebellion. TEOTW pg 153-158

58. AD 1520 Melchior Hoffman (c1498-1543/4) was one of the most influential of the self-appointed prophets. A Swabian furrier by trade, Hoffman had converted to Lutheranism in 1522 and became a wandering preacher. In 1526 Hoffman published a detailed pamphlet on the twelfth chapter of Daniel which proclaimed that the world would end in seven years, at Easter of 1533. The seven year period was to be divided into two parts. The first part would see the appearance of Elijah and Enoch, who would overthrow the Pope. They would, however, be martyred and all the saints would then be persecuted. After forty-two months of tribulation, Christ would appear. Hoffman referred to himself as Elijah, and embarked on the fulfillment of his vision. He was imprisoned for his views, however, in Strasburg, later dying in the 1540s.—TEOTW pg 160-162

59. AD 1524 Prophets in England predicted a flood on February 1, 1524 (Julian) to strike at London. 20,000 people abandoned their homes in fear. Yet another prophet, citing an alignment of planets in the constellation Pisces, set the date for the flood for February 20th. Both days turned out to be sunny with not even a drop of rain.

60. AD 1525 Anabaptist Thomas Müntzer, thinking that he was living at the "end of all ages," in 1525, incited a spectacularly unsuccessful revolt of the peasantry.

61. AD 1526 Anabaptists in St. Gallen, Switzerland, excited by various leaders and events, began running through the streets and shouting that the Last Day would arrive in exactly one week. Many were baptized, stopped work, abandoned their homes and set off into the hills, singing and praying in expectant furvor. After a week had passed with no sign of their returning Lord, they returned to their homes.—TEOTW pg 145-153

62. AD 1527 A German bookbinder named Hans Nut said that he was a prophet of God sent by Christ to herald the Second Coming. This would occur exactly three and a half years after the start of the Peasant's War, in 1527. The Lord's arrival would be followed, according to Nut, by a thousand years of free food, love, and free sex. He amassed some followers, but was killed during an attempted prison escape in 1527.—SSA pg 56

63. AD 1528 Hans Romer insisted that Christ was coming within the year, so he organized his own rebellion to attack the city of Erfurt on New Year's Day of 1528. He was betrayed, however, and arrested.—TEOTW 159

64. AD 1528 Prophets in England, having failed in their February 20th, 1524 prediction for a massive flood, reschedule the prediction to 1528.

65. AD 1528 Reformer Hans Hut predicted the end would occur on Pentecost (May 27, Julian calendar) 1528.

66. AD 1532 Bishop Frederick Nausea (yes, that is his name), predicted that the world would end in 1532 after hearing a single report of bloody crosses appearing in the sky alongside a comet.

67. AD 1533 Anabaptist prophet Melchior Hoffman predicted the end of the world in 1533. he also predicted that Jesus would reappear in Strasbourg, to save 144,000 people from the world's end.

68. AD 1533 Mathematician Michael Stifel, a devout Christian, calculated that the Day of Judgement would begin at exactly 8:00am on October 19, 1533.

69. AD 1534 A message out of the besieged city of Munster, where fanatic Anabaptists, originally led by one Jan Matthys, self-proclaimed Enoch, second witness (after Hoffman's Elijah) to the coming end of all things, read: "God has made known to us that all should get ready to go to the New Jerusalem (Munster), the city of saints, because he is going to punish the world . . . flee out of Babylon,

and deliver every man his soul . . . for this is the time of the Lord's vengeance." Matthys had also fancied himself a second Gideon, leading 30 followers out in an attack on the city's besiegers. He and his band of thirty were annhilated. The movement's new leader, Jan Beukels, or Bockholdt, known to history as John of Leyden, had declared himself King of the World, a position he would hold until Christ's return. Berhardt Rothmann published two pamphlets proclaiming the triumph of the saints at Munster, but the Catholic bishop whose town was held, eventually retook it, executing most of the rebels.—SSA pg 57, TEOTW pg 163-175

70. AD 1532 Michael Stiefel, mathematician and follower of Luther, published Apocalypse on the Apocalypse: A Little Book of Arithmetic about the Antichristwhich computed the Day of Judgement for 8AM on October 9, 1533. when nothing happened on that day, the local peasants siezed the minister and tookhim to nearby Wittenburg, where some sued him for damages. Stiefel survived this misadventure and, twenty years later, published a "recalculation."—Apoc pg 91-92

71. AD 1537 French astrologer Pierre Turrel, a devout Christian, wanting to avoid the Jaochites' embarrassment, hedges his bets and predicts the end of the world in 1537, 1544, 1801 or 1814.

72. AD 1555 French theologian Pierre d'Ailly predicted the end of the world in 1555. Christopher Columbus' own apocolyptic views were based on this prediction.

73. AD 1556 Rumors of the end of the world swept through the churches of Switzerland on Magdalene's Day in 1556, source unknown.

74. AD 1583 Several astrologers and clergy cite a conjunction of Jupiter with Saturn

75. AD 1584 Above prophecy is revised one year later.

76. AD 1588 Philip Melanchthon, ally of Martin Luther, claimed that a divine numerical cycle, chiefly utilizing the numbers 7 and 10, would culminate in 1588, which was 10x7, years from Luther's 1518 defiance of the Pope. It was then that the seventh seal would be opened, Antichrist be would be overthrown, and the Last Judgement would occur.—The Armada pg 175

77. AD 1588 The sage Johann Müller (aka Regiomontanus) predicts the second coming of Christ in 588.

78. AD 1594 John Napier, mathematician extraordinaire, published A Plaine Discoverie of the Whole Revelation of St. John, in which he predicted the Last Judgement either for 1688, according to Revelation, or 1700, according to Daniel.—Apoc pg 92

78. AD 1600 The Fifth Monarchy Men, an extreme Puritan sect in England, believed that the time of the monarchy which would succeed the Biblical Assyrian, Persian, Greek, and Roman monarchies was at hand. During this time Christ would appear to reign on earth with his saints for 1000 years. After the fall of the Commonwealth, the sect first supported Oliver Cromwell, but later were at odds with the Lord Protector. Their extreme violence led to the arrest of their leaders. Despite attempted uprisings, the movement eventually died out.—Brit 1957, vol 9, pg 227

80. AD 1600 Martin Luther predicted that the world would end no later than the year 1600.

81. AD 1603 Dominican monk Tomasso Campanella wrote that the sun would collide with the Earth in 1603.

82. AD 1623 Eustachius Poyssel used numerology to pinpoint 1623 as the year of the end of the world.

83. AD 1624 The same astrologers who failed in predicting a great flood in 1524, finally moved their predictions safely beyond their own deaths, to 1624.

84. AD 1648 Sabbatai Zevi, a rabbi from Smyrna, Turkey, predicted that the Messiah would come in 1648. When 1648 arrived, Zevi announced thet he was the Messiah.

85. AD 1651 The date selected for the end of the world by fifteenth century "prophet" Johann Hilten.—TIME pg 89

86. AD 1654 In 1578, physician Helisaeus Roeslin of Alsace, basing his prediction on a nova that occurred in 1572, predicted the world ending in 1654 in a blaze of fire.

87. AD 1656 The date the world would end, according to predictions put forth by Christopher Columbus in his "Book of Prophecies". Columbus held that his explorations were fulfillment of prophecy. He was to have led a Christian army in a great final crusade that would eventually convert the entire world to Christendom. The date wes chosen because supposedly 1656 years passed between the time of the creation and Noah's flood.—99R pg 13

88. AD 1657 The Fifth Monarchy Men, a group of radical Christians intending to force the British Parliament to base all laws on the Bible (much like Christians are trying to do to the United States) predicted the world would end in 1657.

89. AD 1660 Joseph Mede, whose writings influenced James Ussher and Isaac Newton, claimed that the Antichrist appeared way back in 456, and the end of the world would come in 1660.

90. AD 1666 During a period of strife, English clergy announce that the year 1666 will bring the end of the world, a prediction thought to be coming true when a great fire strikes London.

91. AD 1666 Few believe Rabi Sabbatai Zevi is the Messiah, so he changes his prediction for the appearence of the Messiah to 1666. He is arrested for disturbing the peace with his prophecies, and when given the choice between execution and conversion to Islam, eagerly converts.

92. 1669 C.E. The Old Believers in Russia believed that the end of the world would occur in this year. Twenty thousand burned themselves to death between 1669 and 1690 to protect themselves from the Antichrist.

93. AD 1673 Deacon William Aspinwall, a leader of the Fifth Monarchy movement, predicts the end of the world for 1673.

94. AD 1680 The supposed founder of Rosicrucianism, Christian Knorr von Rosenroth, told in his Proper Exposition of the Aspects of the Book of Revelation of the fall of the idolatrous Roman church and the establishment of Christ's Millennium in 1860.—Apoc pg 122

95. AD 1686 Frenchman Pierre Jurieu published his work L'Accomplissement des propheties, in which he predicted the end of the persecution of the Protestant Huguenots, and the fall of Babylon (the Roman Catholic Church, according to Jurieu) for 1689.

96. AD 1688 John Napier, the mathematician who discovered logarithms, applies his new mathematics to the Book of Revelations and predicts the end of the world for 1688.

97. AD 1689 Pierre Jurieu, a Camisard prophet, predicted that Judgement Day would occur in 1689. The Camisards were Huguenots of the Languedoc region of southern France.

98. 1689 C.E. Benjamin Keach, a 17th century Baptist leader predicted the end of the world in t7his year

99. AD 1694 Anglican rector John Mason and German theologian Johann Alsted both predict the end of the world for 1694. Another German prophet Johann Jacob Zimmerman, predicted that Jesus would reappear in America and organized an expedition of Christians to sail across the Atlantic and welcome their savior when he reappeared. Although Zimmerman himself died on the day

of departure, his followers completed the journey and remained encamped in the wilderness of North America until it became obvious that Jesus had stood them up.

100. AD 1697 Anglican rector Thomas Beverly predicts the end of the world for 1697.

101. AD 1697 Notorious witch chaser Cotton Mather predicts the end of the world for 1697.

102. AD 1697 Napier tries again, predicts the end of the world for 1697.

103. AD 1697 Henry Archer, a Fifth Monarchy Manpredicts the end of the world for 1697.

104. AD 1700 The Camisards were a radical movement of French peasantry that engaged in organized military resistance to the renunciation of the Edict of Nantes. They were supposedly accompanied by miracles, such as lights in the sky which guided them, and resistance to wounding. They also purportedly spoke in tongues and prophesied in ecstatic trances, foretelling the soon destruction of the Roman Catholic Church, the supposed Satan and Babylon. Due to pressures they fled to England where they became known as the "French Prophets," forecasting doom and a new world ahead. They gained large numbers of followers, and much attention. Their prophecies failed to materialize, however, and their numbers soon dwindled. Their movement influenced many later groups, though, including the Shakers.—SSA pg 57

105. AD 1700 Immanuel Swedenborg, though never claiming the desire to found a sect, said that dreams, visions, and direct communications from God had led him to believe he had been given a new, divine, interpretation of Scripture. Swedenborg claimed to have witnessed the Second Advent, which was manifested in the inauguration of his "New Church."—HOD pg 236-238, Brit 1957, vol 21

106. AD 1700 Sir Isaac Newton, the great scientist, was himself not immune to missed prophecy. He developed a carefully constructed grand scenario which predicted that the Jews would return to reclaim Jerusalem in 1899, and that the second coming of Christ would occur precisely forty-nine years later.

107. AD 1700 Jonathan Edwards, premier evangelist, was fascinated by the Apocalypse, noted all signs of the times, and calculated and recalculated its coming. He concluded that Antichrist's rule would end when the papacy ended in 1866, and that old serpent, the Devil, would finally be vanquished in the year 2000, when the Millennium would begin.—Apoc pg 171

108. AD 1701 The prophetic writer Mory Cary, writing in 1647, expected the conversion of the Jews in 1656 and the Millennium in 1701, and thought that there would be a prophetic outpouring before then. "Not only men, but women shall prophesy . . . Not only superiors but inferiors; not only those that have university learning but those that have it not, even servants and handmaids."—TIME pg 90

109. AD 1736 A sea captain witnessing the disaster of the Lisbon quake wrote: " . . . if one went through the broad places of squares, nothing to be met with but people wringing their hands, and crying 'the world is at an end.'"—TEOTW pg 179-189

110. AD 1755 AD. British theologian and mathematician William Whitson predicted a great flood similar to Noah's for October 13th of that year. Another who never read Genesis

111. AD 1785 Jean-Baptiste Ruere, a professed descendant of King David, claimed that heavenly sources assured him he was destined to rule as king in Jerusalem, and likewise foretold of revolution, kingdoms overthrown, the Jews returning to the Holy Land, and Jesus returning to launch the Third Age.—Apoc pg 107

112. AD 1789 The forecast year for the end of the world, or at least of Christendom, by Cardinal Pierre d-Ailly, Canon Roussart,

Dijon Academy rector Pierre Turel, and the Londoner Peter Pearson.—Apoc pg 109

113. 1792 C.E. This was the date of the end of the world calculated by some believers in the Shaker movement

114. 1794: C.E. Charles Wesley, one of the founders of Methodism though Doomsday would be in this year. 115. AD 1799 Esther Thrale Piozzi recorded how many found the First Consul of France, Napoleon Buonaparte to be "the Devil Incarnate," the Appolyon mentioned in Scripture. The name of Antichrist had become clear, and it was (in the Corsican dialect) N'Apollione, the Destroyer "coming forwards followed by a cloud of locusts from ye bottomless Pit."—Apoc pg 114-115

116. AD 1800 Mother Ann Lee, leader of the "Shaker" movement, claimed that in her the female principle of Christ was manifested, and the promise of the Second Coming fulfilled. Christ's kingdom on earth, according to Lee, began with the establishment of the Shaker Church.

117. AD 1800 The Rev Edward Bishop Elliot, fellow of Trinity College, Cambridge, provided a massive work in four volumes, wherein he stated that the French Revolution had been the "pouring out of the 1st vial (of Revelation)" There was to be a short time, he warned, before the end of all things.—TSOR pg 11

118. AD 1820 In England, Edward Irving preached on the imminent appearance of Christ as witnessed by the apparent revival of "apostolic gifts", and Irving's own intense study of prophetical books, especially Revelation.

119. AD1830. Margaret McDonald, a Christian prophetess predicted that Robert Owen would be the Antichrist. Owen helped found New Harmony Indiana.

120. AD 1832 Mormon founder Joseph Smith prophesied under "divine revelation" the gathering of the saints and the coming of the New Jerusalem, the temple of which would be built in Missouri

and "reared in this generation." Smith added "Pestilence, hail, famine, and earthquake will sweep the wicked of this generation from off the face of the land, to open and prepare the way for the return of the lost tribes of Israel from the north country . . . . there are those now living upon the earth whose eyes shall not be closed in death until they see all these things which I have spoken, fulfilled."—99R pg 120

121. AD 1840 Dr. John Cumming, eloquent preacher of apocalypse, drew audiences of many thousands to his lectures. Cumming, while preparing for the publications of these lectures, warned that the seventh and final vial of God's wrath was now being poured out. "We are about to enter on the Last Woe . . . and to hear the nearly-spent reverberations of the Last Trumpet."—TSOR pg 84

122. AD 1843 People stared in wonder and uneasiness at the parahelia, a great halo that circled the sun. They also looked with fear at the night sky where a giant comet with a fiery tail rushed through the darkness. Some said that the comet was racing toward mankind, bringing "the end of the world."—Thief pg 1

123. AD 1844 William Miller, a Massachussetts farmer, after a years-long study of the Bible, chiefly Revelation and Daniel, concurred that the Second Coming of Christ would take place between 21 March, 1843, and 21 March, 1844. When this time passed, Miller and his followers set up new dates, again with failure. Eventually the movement collapsed, but gave birth to Seventh Day Adventism, while also influencing the formation of several others, including the Jehovah's Witnesses.—SSA pg 58, TSOR pg 16, Doom pg 92-111

124. AD 1847 Joseph Wolff, a converted Jew living in Palestine, predicted the Advent for 1847.—Thief pg 1

125. AD 1850 Chinese schoolteacher Hung Hsiu-ch'uan, failing a government job examination for the third time, suffered an emotional collapse during which he professed to have had visions of an old man in a golden beard, as well as a younger man. These

two told Hung that the world was overrun by demons and that he, Hung, was to be the instrument in their eradication. Later, after returning to his home village, Hung reread a Chinese Christian missionary's book and discovered the meaning for the vision which he had experienced. The old man had seen God, and the younger man, Jesus. Hung further understood that he was the second Son of God, sent to save China. Eventually his charisma and teachings began to gather a following and he became the leader of a group known as the Pai Shang-ti Hui (God Worshipper's Society). By 1850 the movement had grown into open rebellion. In 1851 Hung proclaimed the new dynasty the T'ai-p'ing T'ien-kun (Heavenly Kingdom of Great Peace), and assumed the title of Heavenly King. His ragtag group of thousands grew into a disciplined army of over a million. Full scale war erupted across the Chinese countryside. Chinese imperial troops were defeated in pitched battle on more than one occasion. Hung captured the city of Nanking, making it his capital. Eventually he fell ill, and committed suicide in 1864. Chinese forces lay siege to Nanking, and in taking it inflicted a terrible slaughter of over 100,000 people. The rebellion gradually faded across China. As many as 20,000,000 people died as a result of this, the T'ai-p'ing Rebellion, and Hung Hsiu-ch'uan's misprophetic delusions.—Brit 1977, vol 8

126. AD1850 Ellen White, founder of the Seventh Day Adventist movement, made many predictions of the timing of the end of the world. All failed. On June 27,1850 she prophesized that only a few months remained before the end. She wrote: *"My accompanying angel said, 'Time is almost finished. Get ready, get ready, get ready.' . . . now time is almost finished . . . and what we have been years learning, they will have to learn in a few months."*

127. AD 1856 C.E. or later: At Ellen White's last prediction, she said that she was shown in a vision the fate of believers who attended the 1856 SDA conference. She wrote *"I was shown the company present at the Conference. Said the angel: 'Some food for worms, some subjects of the seven last plagues, some will be alive and remain upon the earth to be translated at the coming of Jesus."* That is, some of the attendees would die of normal diseases; some would die from

plagues at the last days, others would still be alive when Jesus came. *"By the early 1900s all those who attended the conference had passed away, leaving the Church with the dilemma of trying to figure out how to explain away such a prominent prophetic failure."*

128. AD 1858 The Rev Richard Shimeall of New York identified Napolean III as the Beast of the Apocalypse.—TSOR pg 78

129. AD 1870 Cyrus Read Teed, a former corporal in the Union medical corps, said that he was the "seventh messenger of God", and adopted "Koresh" as his new surname. Teed claimed that an angel had visited him, giving him new spiritual awareness. He was now the reincarnated Messiah, and it was his job to gather the 144,000 faithful to await the Last Judgment. Teed's legacy would bear bitter fruit in the 1990s, with the rise of another Koresh, David, who would lead his followers into an apocalyptic death near Waco, Texas.

130. AD 1874 Charles Taze Russell, founder of what would become the Jehovah's Witnesses, first announced that the Last Days had definitely begun in 1874, then that the end would come in 1914. Succeeding Witnesses placed the date in 1925, 1936, 1953, 1973 . . .—99R pg 20

131. AD 1881 A prophecy in rhyme by Mother Shipton: "The world to an end shall come,/in Eighteen hundred and eighty one." Purportedly written by a 15th century witch, it was actually penned by Charles Hindley of Brighton, who profitted greatly from the double false prediction.—TSOR pg 99

132. AD 1890 A native American known as Kicking Bear claimed to have received a certain divine revelation. Christ had returned to earth, given his followers a new spiritual magic, the "Ghost Dance", which they were to engage in until Christ came again to "take them up into the air," eventually to be set down among the ghosts of their ancestors on the new earth, where only Indians would live. The movement spread quickly among the various tribes on

and off the reservations, especially among the Sioux.—Bury pg 431-435

133. AD 1891 or before: On Feb. 14,1835, Joseph Smith, the founder of the Mormon church, attended a meeting of church leaders. He said that the meeting had been called because God had commanded it. He announced that Jesus would return within 56 years—i.e. before Feb. 15th, 1891 *(History of the Church* 2:182)

134. AD 1897 Brazil—Antonio Conselheiro (The Counsellor), a sixty-year old, half crazy ascetic, became spiritual leader of Canudos, a "New Jerusalem" of tumbledown shacks in the remote state of Bahia. The residents were largely peasants who fled the decline of the northeast coffee and sugar economies. They practiced a mixture of Catholicism, Indian rites, and witchcraft. conselheiro had seen the overthrow of the Emperor Pedro II as an act of disobedience to God, and a shattering of the patriarchal order so wicked that it must foreshadow the apocalypse. After several violent encounters with local police and government soldiers, in which the Canudos zealots inflicted severe defeats on their foes, an army of 10,000 men surrounded Canudos, and on October 5, 1897 took by force the last smoking huts. The defenders had died by enemy bullets and by fire, the latter set by their own hands.

135. AD 1900 Paris priest Pierre Lacheze published several apocalyptic works, and predicted the restoration of the Jerusalem temple for 1892 and Doomsday in 1900.—Apoc pg 136

136. AD 1900 Philosopher Vladimir Solovyev, eminent Russian theologian, foretold in his work, War, Progress, and the End of History, of a war with the Japanese in which the Japanese would win, conquering much of the world, but eventually being driven back by the Europeans. Then there would arise a brilliant writer and thinker who would unite the world and decree everlasting peace, ultimately summoning all religious leaders of the world, promising them everything they wanted if they would bow down and accept his sovereignty. The Jews would accept him as the Messiah, until they learn that he is not a Jew. Then would begin

the revolt that would lead to the final battle north of Jerusalem, as well as the eruption of a volcano from the bottom of the Dead Sea. Said Solovyev: "The approaching end of the world strikes me like some obvious but quite subtle scent—just as a traveler nearing the sea feels the sea breeze before he sees the sea."—TEOTW pg 221-227

137. AD 1901 In 1889, the Rev. Michael Baxter, editor of the London Christian Herald, announced in a book called The End of This Age about the End of This Century that 1896 would witness the Rapture of 144,000 devout Christians, and that the world would end in 1901.—TIME pg 120-121

138. AD 1901 Sergei Nilus, Russian magistrate, in a book titled The Great in the Small, prophesied "the coming of the Antichrist and the rule of Satan on earth." He later stated in 1905, "The king born of the blood of Zion—the Antichrist is near to the throne of universal power."—TEOTW pg 234-237

139. AD 1906 H.G.Wells shows that apocalyptic fever was prevalent in his day: "Like most people of my generation . . . I was launched into life with Millennial expectations . . . it might be in my lifetime or a little after it, there would be trumpets and shoutings and celestial phenomena, a battle of Armageddon and the judgement."—TSOR pg 177

140. AD 1908 When a terrible explosion rocked Siberia, a newspaper correspondent present reported . . ."All the inhabitants of the village ran out into the streets in panic. The old women wept. Everyone thought the end of the world was approaching."—TEOTW pg 274

141. AD 1910 In Pittsburgh, a clergyman announced that the arrival of Haley's Comet would herald Armageddon and the Second Coming.

142. AD 1914 C.E. was one of the more important estimates of the start of the war of Armageddon by the *Jehovah's Witnesses (Watchtower*

Bible and Tract Society). They based their prophecy of 1914 from prophecy in the book of Daniel, Chapter 4. The writings referred to "seven times". The WTS interpreted each "time" as equal to 360 days, giving a total of 2520 days. This was further interpreted as representing 2520 years, measured from the starting date of 607 BCE. This gave 1914 as the target date. When 1914 passed, they changed their prediction; 1914 became the year that Jesus invisibly began his rule. 1914, 1915, 1918, 1920, 1925, 1941, 1975 and 1994, C.E. etc. were other dates that the Watchtower Society (WTS) or its members predicted. Since late in the 19th century, they had taught that the *"battle of the Great Day of God Almighty"* (Armageddon) would happen in 1914 CE. It didn't. The next major estimate was 1925. Watchtower magazine predicted: *"The year 1925 is a date definitely and clearly marked in the Scriptures, even more clearly than that of 1914; but it would be presumptuous on the part of any faithful follower of the Lord to assume just what the Lord is going to do during that year."* ₆The Watchtower Society selected 1975 as its next main prediction. This was based on the estimate *"according to reliable Bible chronology Adam was created in the year 4026 BCE, likely in the autumn of the year, at the end of the sixth day of creation."* They believed that the year 1975 a promising date for the end of the world, as it was the 6,000th anniversary of Adam's creation. Exactly 1,000 years was to pass for each day of the creation week. This prophecy also failed. The current estimate is that the end of the world as we know it will happen precisely 6000 years after the creation of Eve. There is no way of knowing when this happened. The "Rapture" must take place at least 7 years before that . . . It may have been 4075 years, instead of 4004 (as generally given) from Adam to Christ. In that case we are living in the year 5993 from the creation of Adam, or on the eve of the Rapture."

143. AD 1918 Clarence Larkin, in his book Dispensational Truth, writes, " . . . at no time in the history of the Christian Church have the conditions necessary to the Lord's return been so completely fulfilled as at the present time, therefore his coming is imminent, and will not probably be long delayed

144. AD 1919 Meteorologist Albert Porta predicted that the conjunction of 6 planets would generate a magnetic current that would cause the sun to explode and engulf the earth on December 17th.

145. AD 1940 William Marrion Branham, a Pentecostal faith healer declared himself to be God's end-time prophet, and urged all Christians to come out of their corrupt denominations before the Lord's return.—99R pg 115-116

146. AD 1945 A Protestant minister in Hiroshima upon the dropping of the first atomic bomb: "The feeling I had was that everyone was dead. The whole city was destroyed . . . I thought all of my family must be dead—it doesn't matter if I die . . . I thought that this was the end of Hiroshima, of Japan, of humankind . . . This was God's judgment on man."—TEOTW pg 337

147. AD 1973 The "Children of God" cult claimed that its leader, David Berg, was "God's end-time prophet to the world." They fled America in 1973 due to Berg's prediction that Comet Kohoutek would destroy the country.—99R pg 117

148. AD 1976 Prophecy teacher Doug Clark announced that President Jimmy Carter would be "the president who will meet Mr. 666 (the Antichrist) SOON!" A flier announcing Clark's new book that year claimed, "The Death of the United States and the Birth of One World Government under President Carter."—SSA pg 24

148. AD 1980 North Carolina prophecy teacher Colin Deal has set dates for the return of Christ for 1982 or 1983, 1988, 1989, and in a March 17, 1989 radio broadcast, "about eleven years away." If at first you don't succeed . . .—SSA pg 38

150. AD 1980 Prophecy promoter Charles Taylor predicted a 1988 rapture: "This new book (Watch 1988—The Year of Climax) is being written with the expectation that it will be the last book I will ever write . . . with the millennial reign of Christ due to begin

in 1995, the rapture must surely occcur in 1988 to coordinate with many other prophecies!" Not surprisingly, Taylor also made similar predictions for 1975, 1976, 1980, 1982, 1983, 1985, 1986, 1987, and, of course, 1989.—SSA pg 134-142

151. AD 1981 May 25. About fifty members of a group called the Assembly of Yahweh gathered at Coney Island, NY, in white robes, awaiting their "Rapture" from a world about to be destroyed between 3PM and sundown. A small crowd of onlookers watched and waited for something to happen. The members chanted prayers to the beat of bongo drums until sunset. The end did not come.

152. AD 1982 Full-page advertisements in many major newspapers for the weekend of April 24-25, 1982, announced: "The Christ is Now Here!" and predicted that he was to make himself known "within the next two months." That date passed, but the Tara Centers that placed the ad said that the dalay was only because the "consciousness of the human race was not quite right . . ."—99R pg 154-155

153. AD 1980 Psychic Jeanne Dixon predicted a world holocaust for the 1980s, and the rise of a powerful world leader, born in the Middle-East in 1962.—99R pg 120-

154. AD 1988 Edgar C. Whisenant, in his book 88 Reasons Why the Rapture Will Be in 1988, gave a three day period in September for the saints to be "caught up with the Lord." When this failed, he issued another book claiming that he was a year off, and urging everyone to be ready in 1989.—SSA pg 28-33, DOOM pg 134

155. AD 1990 Southwest Radio Church's David Webber and Hoah Hutching's book, "Prophecy in Stone" contained a chart which set dates for the rebuilding of the Jewish Temple in 1974-1978, and the Great Tribulation for sometime between 1981 and 1992. A later book, "New Light on the Great Pyramid," had another chart which revised these figures, tentatively setting dates of

1988, 1992, and 1996, for the Tribulation, the abomination of desolation, and Christ's return, respectively.—SSA pg 37

156. AD 1990 Elizabeth Clare Prophet predicted the end of the world by nuclear war in 1990. Her church has since seen a decline in membership.

157. AD 1991 Reginald Dunlop, end-times author, stated that "The Antichrist would be revealed" around the year 1989 or 1990, perhaps sooner." The Rapture he predicted for 1991. Says dunlop, God verified this "through many prayers . . . I am MORE than positive that this is THE YEAR that the Rapture will occur."—SSA pg 36

158. AD 1992 "Rapture, October 28, 1992, Jesus is coming in the Air." Full page add in the October 20, 1991, issue of USA Today, placed by followers of the Hyoo-go (Rapture) movement, a loose collection of Korean "end-times" sects. When the prophesied events failed to pass, much turmoil broke out among the sects. Some believers were distraught, while others tried to attack their doomsday preachers with knives. The founder of one church was later charged with swindling four million dollars from his parishioners.—99R pg 11, 168-169

159. AD 1993 David Koresh, self-proclaimed little lamb of Isaiah 16, and the Second Coming of Christ, dies in a fiery conflagration with some 80 of his followers. These members of the Branch Dividians, an offshoot of the Seventh-Day Adventists had faced a botched ATF raid on their compound near Waco, Texas, and a subsequent 51-day siege by the FBI. A devastating fire broke out when the FBI attempted to fire gas into the group's buildings.—99R pg 122-124

160. AD 1994 Arab Christian prophet Om Saleem claimed that the antichrist was born November 23, 1933, that his unveiling would come in 1993 and the rapture in 1994.—99R pg 149

161. AD 1994 Harold Camping, a radio evangelist, wrote a book entitled "1994?" In it, Camping says, "if this study is accurate, and I believe with all my heart that it is, there will be no extensions of time. There will be no time for second guessing. When September 6, 1994, arrives, no one else can be saved, the end has come." Thousands believed Camping's distorted biblical teachings, but again, the end did not come as Camping had wished.—99R pg 12, 48-50

162. AD 1997 Mary Stewart Relfe wrote in 1983 that she had been praying to "know the year" of the Lord's coming, and that subsequently she received detailed "divine revelations" from God. She released a chart showing World War III beginning in 1989, the Great Tribulation starting in 1990, and that Jesus Christ will come back in 1997, just after Armageddon."—SSA pg 35

163. AD 1998 Larry Wilson, a former Seventh-day Adventist pastor, predicted four massive global earthquakes beginning around 1994 and ending in 1998 with the Second Coming.—99R pg 77

BIBLIOGRAPHY

The following is a list of the notations following the dates and the sources of the information.

Thief = Thief in the Night by William Sears, George Ronald press, 1977

99R = 99 Reasons Why No One Knows When Christ Will Return by B.J. Oropeza, InterVarsity Press, 1994

SSA = Soothsayers of the Second Advent by William M. Alnor, Fleming H. Revell Company, 1989

Doom = Doomsday Delusions by C. Marvin Pate and Calvin B Haines, Jr., InterVarsity Press, 1995

TEOT = The End of Time by Damian Thompson, University Press of New England, 1996

Armada = The Armada by Garrett Mattingly, Houghton Mifflin Company, 1959

DISP = Dispensational Truth by Clarence Larkin, Rev. Clarence Larkin Est—publisher, 1918

Apoc = Apocalypses by Eugen Weber, Harvard University Press, 1999

Bury = Bury My Heart at Wounded Knee by Dee Brown, Holt, Rinehart & Winston, 1970

TSOR = The Sleep of Reason by Derek Jarrett, Harper and Row, 1989

TEOTW = The End of the World by Otto Friedrich, Coward, McCann & Geoghegan, 1982

Hand = Handbook of Denominations in the United States—New Eighth Edition by Frank S. Mead, Abingdon Press, 1985

Brit = Encyclopaedia Brittanica

APPENDIX 2

Close Planet Configuration

The year 2000 began with the naked-eye planets dispersed over 160° of sky and all but Mercury visible. Venus was prominent in the morning sky while Mars, Jupiter and Saturn were in the evening sky. Mercury moved to the evening sky and became visible early in February. All planets were then moving eastward (none were in retrograde) and their spread was decreasing. On February 28, 2000 their span had decreased to 90°. A few days later Mercury swung back to the morning sky. Keep in mind that this configuration only involved the bright planets. The planets whose brightness are below naked-eye visibility, Uranus, Neptune and Pluto were not anywhere near the bright planets in the sky during this time.

The first conjunction of many occurred when Venus passed Mercury on March 15, and the two inner planets were 2.1° apart at their closest. Times here are of closest approach, not conjunction in Right Ascension or ecliptic longitude. At the same time Saturn, Jupiter, and Mars span 20° in the evening sky. These three outer planets continue to converge. Mars was overtaking Jupiter which in turn was overtaking Saturn. On April 6, 2000 Mars passed Jupiter with Saturn 6° to the east. This conjunction happened while Mars and Jupiter were 30° from the Sun and was easily visible. The prettiest evening sight of the suite of planetary groupings came at about 7 pm EST on Saturday night, April 6, for middle latitudes in the United States, when the thin crescent Moon was near Saturn and the Moon and four planets fit within a circle about 9° in diameter. A week later Mars was roughly midway between Jupiter and Saturn and the three planets fit within a circle 5° in diameter. Mars was closest to Saturn (2.2°) on April 15, 2000. Mars then left Saturn and Jupiter behind. Meanwhile, Mercury and Venus had been approaching superior conjunction and their separation with the Sun (and with the other planets) had been decreasing. On April 20, 2000 the five planets (and Sun) span 39°, with Venus and Mercury in the morning sky and Mars, Jupiter, and Saturn in the evening. In clear sky, the five planets should have been visible, although not simultaneously, to people with binoculars and clear eastern and western horizons at sunset and then the following sunrise. On April 28, 2000 Mercury passed 0.3° from Venus, but the two were less than 12° from the Sun. The five planets and Sun now spanned 30°. The Moon joined the five planets a few days later, and it remained between Venus, which was the westernmost planet, and Mars, which was the easternmost, from 3:37 am EDT on May 3 until 2:08 am EDT on May 5, 2000 as measured in ecliptic longitude. Because Venus was moving eastward faster than Mars, the grouping of the five planets plus Moon and Sun continued to compress during the time it takes the Moon to move eastward and reach the longitude of Mars. All seven *classical* solar system bodies spanned their smallest geocentric arc in ecliptic longitude on May 5, 2000. This moment was the culmination of the celestial configurations. The Sun was near the center of the grouping, so all that was visible was Mars and the crescent Moon, both 16° east of the Sun in the evening sky, and perhaps Venus, 10° west of the Sun in the morning sky. The five classical planets plus the Sun and Moon span 26°, their closest separation since 1962 and their closest until 2675. Only Venus in the morning and Mars and the crescent Moon in the evening might be visible. Ecliptic grids are 5° apart. On this date, as seen from the Sun. The five naked-eye planets span 50°. The Earth is in the opposite direction. Jupiter and Saturn are nearly aligned. Ecliptic grids are 5° apart. After passing Mars on the 5th of that year, the Moon left the Sun and planets behind, but the five planets continued to converge (and to become even less-easily visible). In sequence, Jupiter was in superior conjunction, Mercury passed Jupiter, Mercury was in superior conjunction, Saturn was in superior conjunction, and Venus passed Jupiter. This last conjunction, which took place on May 17, 2000, determined the smallest geocentric spread in longitude of the five classical planets (and the Sun, but not the Moon), which spanned 19° 25'. Note however that the planets were not in an exact straight line! After this moment, Jupiter's slower eastward motion caused it to lag behind the others and the planets begin to spread out. A notable feature of the May 17 minimum span is that

Venus and Jupiter were separated by only 42 arcseconds! Venus almost occulted Jupiter. It would have been a wonderful sight were they not less than 7° from the Sun. Conjunctions continue as Mercury passed Mars with a minimum true angular separation of 1.1° on May 19. They were 12° from the Sun and possibly visible. Jupiter passed 1.1° from Saturn at on May 27, 2000. Venus was in superior conjunction with the Sun on June 11 (and literally behind it), by which time both Jupiter and Saturn had become visible in the morning sky, where they rose 2° apart. Venus passed 0.2° from Mars at on June 21 of that year (both were far too close to the Sun to be seen). Another interesting configuration (and a last chance for astrologers whose earlier predictions of disaster were not fulfilled) came on July 1 and 2 when, for 11 hours, the Moon, Sun, Mercury, Venus, and Mars fit within a circle 8° in diameter. This configuration was not visible, of course, due to the brightness of the Sun, so it was missed by dooms day prophets. Further groupings of lesser interest continued on and on . . . Every astrologer and psychic put their own spin on these alignments. They occurred over so a wide a span of time that there were many opportunities to link at least a few natural and political disasters to planetary positions. When did this last happen? The short answer to the question, "prior to 2000, when was the last time the five planets plus Sun and Moon were this close," is 1962—when there was a solar eclipse at the same time! Can the Planets Ever Exactly Line-Up? To answer this question it is necessary to get a full understanding of the structure of the solar system. In astronomy, the plane of the solar system is defined as the ecliptic—the apparent path that the Sun makes on the sky as the Earth orbits it—the ecliptic is nothing more than a projection of the Earth's orbit on the sky. All of the planets orbit the Sun (except Pluto which we now know is not a planet) *nearly* in this same plane—however, not exactly in this same plane! To figure out the probability that all of the planets will be in a straight line out from the Sun (with the Moon in line too), which is the real meaning of the word alignment, we must determine the odds of all the superior planets falling on the same celestial coordinates on the ecliptic while at opposition, the inferior planets on the same coordinates while at inferior conjunction while on the ecliptic, and the Moon at one of its two node points (the position in its orbit that intersects the Earth's orbital plane) during either a solar or lunar eclipse (note that the Moon's orbit is tilted by 5° with respect to the ecliptic).

The period is the time it takes the planet to complete one orbit around the Sun, the semi-major axis is the average distance the planet is from the Sun as it orbits, the eccentricity is how flattened the orbit is (e=0 means a perfectly circular orbit, e=1 means a parabolic orbit), the inclination is the angle that the orbital plane of the planet makes with the Earth's orbital plane (i.e., ecliptic), and finally the node precession (explained below) is measured in arcseconds (=1/3600°) per century. Let's say we first wanted to determine what the probability would be for all the superior planet's to be at the same right ascension (RA) (*i.e.*, conjunction) and the inferior planets to be exactly 12 hours in RA (=180°) away at the same time. First, we must decide on the span of time we will allow for the planets to be at that location. Instead of setting this to one second, let's allow a little slop and say that the planets have to be at the above mention location within a minute of each other. To do this, we merely multiply the periods of the planets *in minutes* together (excluding the Earth). This gives: <u>Probability (planets at same RA at same time) = 1.8 x 10^{14} minutes = 3.4 x 10^8 years</u> Hence, there is one chance in 340 million years that the planet's will all be at the same RA in the sky (with Mercury and Venus 12 hours on the other side of the sky) within a minute of each! Now if we specify that this must occur while the superior planets are at opposition and the inferior planets in inferior conjunction (*i.e.*, the planet's are all at the same RA as seen from the Sun), then we must include the Earth's orbit in the calculation: <u>Probability (All planets at same RA with respect to Sun at same time) =3 x 10^{19} minutes = 1.8 x 10^{14} years</u> The final figure is a whooping once in 180 trillion years! And we are still not through, if we include the Moon in this calculation, that is, it being at either a solar or lunar eclipse during this time, we multiply its period onto this and get 6.9 x 10^{18} years! However we must continue since the astrologers and psychics claim an exact alignment. The line that marks the intersection between the two inclined planes is called the *line-of-nodes* and the projected position of this line on the sky called the nodes of the planet's orbit (which of course must lie on the ecliptic). The line-of-nodes for each planet precesses about each of the planet's orbits. So, to calculate the probability that all of the planets will line up in an *exact* straight line with the Earth included in that line, we must factor this line-of-nodes precession into our calculations. We must convert this into units of time (instead of angles per time) by realizing that there are

360° (=1,296,000") in a complete circle (*i.e.*, orbit). So the factors we are multiplying together to get the probability are $1,296,000/T_i$, where T is the node precession rate per year for each planet "i" (hence T_i is 1/100 of the value listed in the table above). Carrying out this calculation in conjunction with our calculations above, we get: <u>Probability (ALL planets in straight line out from the Sun) = 8.6×10^{46} years</u> Since the solar system is only 4.6×10^9 (4.6 billion) years old, and will only be in existence for a grand total of 10^{10} (10 billion) years, the calculated probability for an exact planetary alignment to occur is once in 86 billion-trillion-trillion-trillion years! (That's a 86 followed by 45 zeros years!) The odds strongly favor that an exact planetary alignment will *never* occur throughout the entire history of the solar system. What of tidal and gravity effects? At first glance, the claims that planetary alignments or groupings will cause earthquakes, floods, solar eruptions, and perhaps even the destruction of the Earth do seem interesting. Gravity is a long reaching force, and the planets are big. Can their influence reach across the solar system and cause all sorts of headaches here on Earth? As always, it is not a bad idea to run a sanity check first. We have pretty good evidence that the Earth has been around a long time, approximately 5 billion years, without being split in two. As it turns out, close planetary configurations are fairly rare on a human time scale, but not on a geologic time scale. Getting more than three to go into conjunction is difficult; getting them all to be in close conjunction is rare indeed. But 5 billion years is a *long* time! Close configurations may be rare, but given enough time they do occur, and the Earth is still here. Even more, what most doomsayers say is an alignment is really more of a confluence, or loose gathering, of planets. Some say it is enough to just have them all on the same side of the Sun, which happens pretty often! This is a hallmark of crackpot science: Using inflammatory words when cornered, they start being very vague and loose with terms. "Alignment" sounds much better than "loose collection" or "a pattern somewhat weighted towards one side of the Sun", which are more accurate. I think we can rest assured that the Earth will not be destroyed any time soon. A web page constructed by Brian Monson's contains data where he has worked out the positions and times of several past alignments and shows that better "alignments" in recent history than the one in May of 2000 have occurred with no ill effects. There is also an excellent page giving great detail about the upcoming "alignment" constructed by the Griffith Observatory. Yet another page has been set up by Truman Collins. Much of the information here was constructed by the data supplied by these pages and by the Bad Astronomy Web pages. But just how strong is the influence of the planets? This turns out to be a relatively easy calculation. First, to clarify: there are two effects a planet can have. One is simply gravity, which basically means how hard that planet can pull on us. The other influence is tidal force, which is more complicated, but you can think of it as a stretching force rather than a simple pull. Think of it this way: a strong enough gravity could pull the Earth from its orbit, while a strong enough tide could rip it in half. Can the planets do this to us? Could they possibly send Earth flying into space, or rend us asunder (quick answer: no). Let's start with gravity, and then show why tides are even less important. Gravity depends on two things: the mass of the object pulling on you, and the distance from that object. The bigger an objects mass, the stronger it pulls, and the farther away it is, the less it pulls. As a matter of fact, for gravity the strength depends on the square of the distance. If you double the distance, the force of gravity drops by 2 x 2 = 4. If you put something ten times farther away, the gravitational force drops by 10 x 10 = 100. You can see that gravity gets weak pretty quickly with distance. The tidal force is much like gravity, but it drops with the *cube* of the distance. This makes it much less important in our case! Say you double the distance to an object. Its tidal force on the Earth drops by 2 x 2 x 2 = 8. If you increase its distance by a factor of ten, the tidal force drops by 10 x 10 x 10 = 1000! So tides are in fact much weaker than gravity. So if we know the mass of an object and its distance, we can calculate the forces of both gravity and tides. It shouldn't be too much of a surprise to find out that the overwhelming winner in this game is the Earth's own Moon. Its mass is small in comparison to the other planets (only about 1/80 of the Earth), but it is very close (Venus, the closest planet to the Earth, is at best 150 times farther away!). To make matters easier on us, let's say that the Moon's gravitational force on the Earth is equal to 1 in whatever units gravity is measured in. That way we can see right away how strong the other planets are; a gravity of 10 means the planet pulls on the Earth 10 times as much as the Moon does. We can do the same with tides; assume that the tidal force is equal to 1 in tidal force units and see how the other planets fare. So, in units of Moon gravity and tides, below are the forces on the Earth from rest of the planets The masses are in units of 10^{22} kilograms (the Earth masses 6×10^{24} kilograms, or 600 on this scale), and the distances in millions of kilometers. By the way, the distances of closest approach to the Earth are used to maximize the effect. Realistically, the force will be smaller than what is listed. Let's look at gravity first. Right away you can see that even mighty Jupiter, king of the planets, only pulls about 0.01 (= 1%) as hard as the Moon does (just to show how this was done, Jupiter mass is 27,000 times the Moon, but is 1640 times farther away. The square of 1640 is about 2.7 million, and 27,000/2.7 million=0.01). Venus is next, with only 0.6% of the Moon's force. After that, the numbers drop a lot. The total pull of all the planets combined is 0.017, not even 2% of the Moon's pull! That ain't much. But is it enough to destroy the Earth? No, it isn't. Think of it this way: the Moon orbits the Earth in an ellipse, which means that sometimes in its orbit it is closer to the Earth than others. At perigee, or closest approach, it is about 363,000 kilometers away, and at apogee, or farthest point, it is about 405,000 kilometers away. If you use these numbers like we did above, you see that the Moon's own gravitational effect on the Earth fluctuates by about 25% every orbit! The Moon orbits the Earth in about a month, incidentally, so it goes from apogee to perigee every two weeks. So every 14 days we see a change in gravitational effects from the Moon more than 10 times greater than all the other planets combined! To put this in even more perspective, the force of the Moon on you is only about 0.000003 times the Earth's. For me, that means I weigh an extra 0.4 grams (0.0009 pounds) more when the Moon is under my feet versus when it's on the horizon (and therefore not contributing to the downward pull of the Earth). Not much! Now consider the tides. Venus stretches us the most of the planets, simply because it is the closest on average. But look! Even Venus only stretches us 5 hundred thousandths as much as the Moon does! This is completely negligible, and the other planets have even less effect. The change in tidal force due to the Moon's elliptical orbit is hugely larger than the combined tides of all the planets. It's worth mentioning that the "alignment" in 2000 has all the planets on the far side of the Sun. This means that you can add 300 million kilometers to the above distances, and the numbers will drop even an enormous amount more! For example, Jupiter's gravity drops from 0.02 to 0.005, and Venus' tides drop by a factor of 500!

APPENDIX 3

Some Scriptural References to Christ

The Divine Heritage of Christ:

Ps 2:7 I will declare the decree: the Lord hath said unto me, Thou art my Son; this day have I begotten thee.

Acts 13:33 God hath fulfilled the same unto us their children, in that he hath raised up Jesus again; as it is also written in the second psalm, Thou art my Son, this day have I begotten thee.

Heb 1:5 For unto which of the angels said he at any time, Thou art my Son, this day have I begotten thee? And again, I will be to him a Father, and he shall be to me a Son?

Heb 5:5 So also Christ glorified not himself to be made an high priest; but he that said unto him, Thou art my Son, today have I begotten thee.

The Incarnation:

Ps 40:6 Sacrifice and offering thou didst not desire; mine ears hast thou opened: burnt offering and sin offering hast thou not required. 7 Then said I, Lo, I come: in the volume of the book it is written of me, 8 I delight to do thy will, O my God: yea, thy law is within my heart.

Heb 10:5 Wherefore when he cometh into the world, he saith, Sacrifice and offering thou wouldest not, but a body hast thou prepared me: 6 In burnt offerings and sacrifices for sin thou hast had no pleasure. 7 Then said I, Lo, I come (in the volume of the book it is written of me,) to do thy will, O God. 8 Above when he said, Sacrifice and offering and burnt offerings and offering for sin thou wouldest not, neither hadst pleasure therein; which are offered by the law;

9 Then said he, Lo, I come to do thy will, O God. He taketh away the first, that he may establish the second.

Connection to David:

Ps 110:1 The Lord said unto my Lord, Sit thou at my right hand, until I make thine enemies thy footstool.

2 Sam 7:12 And when thy days be fulfilled, and thou shalt sleep with thy fathers, I will set up thy seed after thee, which shall proceed out of thy bowels, and I will establish his kingdom.

13 He shall build an house for my name, and I will stablish the throne of his kingdom for ever.

Ps 89:3 I have made a covenant with my chosen, I have sworn unto David my servant,

4 Thy seed will I establish for ever, and build up thy throne to all generations. Selah.

Mic 5:2 But thou, Bethlehem Ephratah, though thou be little among the thousands of Judah, yet out of thee shall he come forth unto me that is to be ruler in Israel; whose goings forth have been from of old, from everlasting.

Matt 22:44 The Lord said unto my Lord, Sit thou on my right hand, till I make thine enemies thy footstool 45 If David then call him Lord, how is he his son??

Mark 12:36 For David himself said by the Holy Ghost, The Lord said to my Lord, Sit thou on my right hand, till I make thine enemies thy footstool.

Luke 20:43 Till I make thine enemies thy footstool. 44 David therefore calleth him Lord, how is he then his son?

John 7:42 Hath not the scripture said, That Christ cometh of the seed of David, and out of the town of Bethlehem, where David was?

Christ's Conception:

Isa 7:14 Therefore the Lord himself shall give you a sign; Behold, a virgin shall conceive, and bear a son, and shall call his name Immanuel.

Matt 1:21 And she shall bring forth a son, and thou shalt call his name JESUS: for he shall save his people from their sins.22 Now all this was done, that it might be fulfilled which was spoken of the Lord by the prophet, saying,23 Behold, a virgin shall be with child, and shall bring forth a son, and they shall call his name Emmanuel, which being interpreted is, God with us.

Oh Little Town of Bethlehem:

Mic 5:2 But thou, Bethlehem Ephratah, though thou be little among the thousands of Judah, yet out of thee shall he come forth unto me that is to be ruler in Israel; whose goings forth have been from of old, from everlasting.

Matt 2:6 And thou Bethlehem, in the land of Juda, art not the least among the princes of Juda: for out of thee shall come a Governor, that shall rule my people Israel.

John 7:42 Hath not the scripture said, That Christ cometh of the seed of David, and out of the town of Bethlehem, where David was?

Escape to Egypt:

Hos 11:1 When Israel was a child, then I loved him, and called my son out of Egypt.

Matt 2:13 And when they were departed, behold, the angel of the Lord appeareth to Joseph in a dream, saying, Arise, and take the young child and his mother, and flee into Egypt, and be thou there until I bring thee word: for Herod will seek the young child to destroy him. 14 When he arose, he took the young child and his mother by night, and departed into Egypt: 15 And was there until the death of Herod: that it might be fulfilled which was spoken of the Lord by the prophet, saying, Out of Egypt have I called my son.

Death in Ramah:

Jer 31:15 Thus saith the Lord; A voice was heard in Ramah, lamentation, and bitter weeping; Rahel weeping for her children refused to be comforted for her children, because they were not.

Matt 2:16 Then Herod, when he saw that he was mocked of the wise men, was exceeding wroth, and sent forth, and slew all the children that were in Bethlehem, and in all the coasts thereof, from two years old and under, according to the time which he had diligently inquired of the wise men. 17 Then was fulfilled that which was spoken by Jeremy the prophet, saying, 18 In Rama was there a voice heard, lamentation, and weeping, and great mourning, Rachel weeping for her children, and would not be comforted, because they are not.

Home Again:

Matt 2:19 But when Herod was dead, behold, an angel of the Lord appeareth in a dream to Joseph in Egypt, 20 Saying, Arise, and take the young child and his mother, and go into the land of Israel: for they are dead which sought the young child's life. 21 And he arose, and took the young child and his mother, and came into the land of Israel. 22 But when he heard that Archelaus did reign in Judaea in the room of his father Herod, he was afraid to go thither: notwithstanding, being warned of God in a dream, he turned aside into the parts of Galilee: 23 And he came and dwelt in a city called Nazareth: that it might be fulfilled which was spoken by the prophets, He shall be called a Nazarene.

A Voice From the Wilderness John as Elijah

Isa 40:3 "The voice of him that crieth in the wilderness, Prepare ye the way of the Lord, make straight in the desert a highway for our God. 4 Every valley shall be exalted, and every mountain and hill shall be made low: and the crooked shall be made straight, and the rough places plain: 5 And the glory of the Lord shall be revealed, and all flesh shall see it together: for the mouth of the Lord hath spoken it.

Matt 3:1 "In those days came John the Baptist, preaching in the wilderness of Judaea, 2 And saying, Repent ye: for the kingdom of heaven is at hand. 3 For this is he that was spoken of by the prophet Esaias, saying, The voice of one crying in the wilderness, Prepare ye the way of the Lord, make his paths straight.

Mark 1:2 "As it is written in the prophets, Behold, I send my messenger before thy face, which shall prepare thy way before thee.3 The voice of one crying in the wilderness, Prepare ye the way of the Lord, make his paths straight.4 John did baptize in the wilderness, and preach the baptism of repentance for the remission of sins.

Luke 3:4 As it is written in the book of the words of Esaias the prophet, saying, The voice of one crying in the wilderness, Prepare ye the way of the Lord, make his paths straight. 5 Every valley shall be filled, and every mountain and hill shall be brought low; and the crooked shall be made straight, and the rough ways shall be made smooth; 6 And all flesh shall see the salvation of God.

John 1:19 And this is the record of John, when the Jews sent priests and Levites from Jerusalem to ask him, Who art thou? 20 And he confessed, and denied not; but confessed, I am not the Christ. 21 And they asked him, What then? Art thou Elias? And he saith, I am not. Art thou that prophet? And he answered, No. 22 Then said they unto him, Who art thou? that we may give an answer to them that sent us. What sayest thou of thyself? 23 He said, I am the voice of one crying in the wilderness, Make straight the way of the Lord, as said the prophet Esaias.

John Before Jesus:

Mal 4:5 "Behold, I will send you Elijah the prophet before the coming of the great and dreadful day of the Lord: 6 And he shall turn the heart of the fathers to the children, and the heart of the children to their fathers, lest I come and smite the earth with a curse."

Matt 11:12 "And from the days of John the Baptist until now the kingdom of heaven suffereth violence, and the violent take it by force.13 For all the prophets and the law prophesied until John.14 And if ye will receive it, this is Elias, which was for to come."

Matt 17:12 "But I say unto you, That Elias is come already, and they knew him not, but have done unto him whatsoever they listed. Likewise shall also the Son of man suffer of them."

Mark 9:12 "And he answered and told them, Elias verily cometh first, and restoreth all things; and how it is written of the Son of man, that he must suffer many things, and be set at nought.13 But I say unto you, That Elias is indeed come, and they have done unto him whatsoever they listed, as it is written of him."

Luke 1:17 "And he shall go before him in the spirit and power of Elias, to turn the hearts of the fathers to the children, and the disobedient to the wisdom of the just; to make ready a people prepared for the Lord."

Temper in the Temple

Ps 69:9 "For the zeal of thine house hath eaten me up; and the reproaches of them that reproached thee are fallen upon me."

John 2:13 "And the Jews' passover was at hand, and Jesus went up to Jerusalem,14 And found in the temple those that sold oxen and sheep and doves, and the changers of money sitting: 15 And when he had made a scourge of small cords, he drove them all out of the temple, and the sheep, and the oxen; and poured out the changers' money, and overthrew the tables; 16 And said unto them that sold doves, Take these things hence; make not my Father's house an house of merchandise.17 And his disciples remembered that it was written, The zeal of thine house hath eaten me up."

Capernaum

Isa 9:1 "Nevertheless the dimness shall not be such as was in her vexation, when at the first he lightly afflicted the land of Zebulun and the land of Naphtali, and afterward did more grievously afflict her by the way of the sea, beyond Jordan, in Galilee of the nations. 2 The people that walked in darkness have seen a great light: they that dwell in the land of the shadow of death, upon them hath the light shined."

Matt 4:14 "That it might be fulfilled which was spoken by Esaias the prophet, saying, 15 The land of Zabulon, and the land of Nephthalim, by the way of the sea, beyond Jordan, Galilee of the Gentiles; 16 The people which sat in darkness saw great light; and to them which sat in the region and shadow of death light is sprung up."

Deut 18:15 "The Lord thy God will raise up unto thee a Prophet from the midst of thee, of thy brethren, like unto me; unto him ye shall hearken; 16 According to all that thou desiredst of the Lord thy God in Horeb in the day of the assembly, saying, Let me not hear again the voice of the Lord my God, neither let me see this great fire any more, that I die not. 17 And the Lord said unto me, They have well spoken that which they have spoken. 18 I will raise them up a Prophet from among their brethren, like unto thee, and will put my words in his mouth; and he shall speak unto them all that I shall command him. 19 And it shall come to pass, that whosoever will not hearken unto my words which he shall speak in my name, I will require it of him."

Jesus the Compassionate

Isa 61:1 "The Spirit of the Lord God is upon me; because the Lord hath anointed me to preach good tidings unto the meek; he hath sent me to bind up the brokenhearted, to proclaim liberty to the captives, and the opening of the prison to them that are bound; 2 To proclaim the acceptable year of the Lord, and the day of vengeance of our God; to comfort all that mourn;"

Isa 42:1 "Behold my servant, whom I uphold; mine elect, in whom my soul delighteth; I have put my spirit upon him: he shall bring forth judgment to the Gentiles.2 He shall not cry, nor lift up, nor cause his voice to be heard in the street.3 A bruised reed shall he not break, and the smoking flax shall he not quench: he shall bring forth judgment unto truth.4 He shall not fail nor be discouraged, till he have set judgment in the earth: and the isles shall wait for his law."

Luke 4:18 "The Spirit of the Lord is upon me, because he hath anointed me to preach the gospel to the poor; he hath sent me to heal the brokenhearted, to preach deliverance to the captives, and recovering of sight to the blind, to set at liberty them that are bruised,19 To preach the acceptable year of the Lord.20 And he closed the book, and he gave it again to the minister, and sat down. And the eyes of all them that were in the synagogue were fastened on him.21 And he began to say unto them, This day is this scripture fulfilled in your ears."

Matt 21:17 "And he left them, and went out of the city into Bethany; and he lodged there. 18 Now in the morning as he returned into the city, he hungered.19 And when he saw a fig tree in the way, he came to it, and found nothing thereon, but leaves only, and said unto it, Let no fruit grow on thee henceforward for ever. And presently the fig tree withered away.20 And when the disciples saw it, they marvelled, saying, How soon is the fig tree withered away! 21 Jesus answered and said unto them, Verily I say unto you, If ye have faith, and doubt not, ye shall not only do this which is done to the fig tree, but also if ye shall say unto this mountain, Be thou removed, and be thou cast into the sea; it shall be done."

Acts 3:22 "For Moses truly said unto the fathers, A prophet shall the Lord your God raise up unto you of your brethren, like unto me; him shall ye hear in all things whatsoever he shall say unto you.23 And it shall come to pass, that every soul, which will not hear that prophet, shall be destroyed from among the people."

2012 The Real Story

Acts 7:37 "This is that Moses, which said unto the children of Israel, A prophet shall the Lord your God raise up unto you of your brethren, like unto me; him shall ye hear."

Jesus Christ, M.D.

Isa 53:4 "Surely he hath borne our griefs, and carried our sorrows: yet we did esteem him stricken, smitten of God, and afflicted.

Matt 8:17 "That it might be fulfilled which was spoken by Esaias the prophet, saying, Himself took our infirmities, and bare our sicknesses."

Christ as Priest

Ps 110:4 "The Lord hath sworn, and will not repent, Thou art a priest for ever after the order of Melchizedek."

Heb 6:6 "If they shall fall away, to renew them again unto repentance; seeing they crucify to themselves the Son of God afresh, and put him to an open shame."

Heb 7:17 "For he testifieth, Thou art a priest for ever after the order of Melchisedec."

Heb 7:21 "(For those priests were made without an oath; but this with an oath by him that said unto him, The Lord sware and will not repent, Thou art a priest for ever after the order of Melchisedec:)"

They Just Won't Listen

Isa 6:9 "And he said, Go, and tell this people, Hear ye indeed, but understand not; and see ye indeed, but perceive not. 10 Make the heart of this people fat, and make their ears heavy, and shut their eyes; lest they see with their eyes, and hear with their ears, and understand with their heart, and convert, and be healed."

Isa 53:1 "Who hath believed our report and to whom is the arm of the Lord revealed?"

Matt 13:14 "And in them is fulfilled the prophecy of Esaias, which saith, By hearing ye shall hear, and shall not understand; and seeing ye shall see, and shall not perceive: 15 For this people's heart is waxed gross, and their ears are dull of hearing, and their eyes they have closed; lest at any time they should see with their eyes, and hear with their ears, and should understand with their heart, and should be converted, and I should heal them."

Mark 4:12 "That seeing they may see, and not perceive; and hearing they may hear, and not understand; lest at any time they should be converted, and their sins should be forgiven them."

Luke 8:10 "And he said, Unto you it is given to know the mysteries of the kingdom of God: but to others in parables; that seeing they might not see, and hearing they might not understand."

John 12:37 "But though he had done so many miracles before them, yet they believed not on him:38 That the saying of Esaias the prophet might be fulfilled, which he spake, Lord, who hath believed our report? and to whom hath the arm of the Lord been revealed? 39 Therefore they could not believe, because that Esaias said again, 40 He hath blinded their eyes, and hardened their heart; that they should not see with their eyes, nor understand with their heart, and be converted, and I should heal them. 41 These things said Esaias, when he saw his glory, and spake of him."

Your King Comes

Isa 62:11 "Behold, the Lord hath proclaimed unto the end of the world, Say ye to the daughter of Zion, Behold, thy salvation cometh; behold, his reward is with him, and his work before him."

Zech 9:9 "Rejoice greatly, O daughter of Zion; shout, O daughter of Jerusalem: behold, thy King cometh unto thee: he is just, and having salvation; lowly, and riding upon an ass, and upon a colt the foal of an ass."

Matt 21:5 "Tell ye the daughter of Sion, Behold, thy King cometh unto thee, meek, and sitting upon an ass, and a colt the foal of an ass."

John 12:14 "And Jesus, when he had found a young ass, sat thereon; as it is written, 15 Fear not, daughter of Sion: behold, thy King cometh, sitting on an ass's colt."

Rejected by his own people

Ps 118:22 "The stone which the builders refused is become the head stone of the corner. 23 This is the Lord's doing; it is marvellous in our eyes."

Isa 8:14 "And he shall be for a sanctuary; but for a stone of stumbling and for a rock of offence to both the houses of Israel, for a gin and for a snare to the inhabitants of Jerusalem."

Matt 21:14 "And the blind and the lame came to him in the temple; and he healed them. 15 And when the chief priests and scribes saw the wonderful things that he did, and the children crying in the temple, and saying, Hosanna to the Son of David; they were sore displeased,"

Matt 21:42 "esus saith unto them, Did ye never read in the scriptures, The stone which the builders rejected, the same is become the head of the corner: this is the Lord's doing, and it is marvellous in our eyes?"

Mark 12:10 "And have ye not read this scripture; The stone which the builders rejected is become the head of the corner: 11 This was the Lord's doing, and it is marvellous in our eyes?"

Luke 20:17 "And he beheld them, and said, What is this then that is written, The stone which the builders rejected, the same is become the head of the corner?"

Acts 4:10 "Be it known unto you all, and to all the people of Israel, that by the name of Jesus Christ of Nazareth, whom ye crucified, whom God raised from the dead, even by him doth this man stand here before you whole. 11 This is the stone which was set at nought of you builders, which is become the head of the corner."

1 Peter 2:7 "Unto you therefore which believe he is precious: but unto them which be disobedient, the stone which the builders disallowed, the same is made the head of the corner, 8

Everybody hates me:

Ps 35:19 "Let not them that are mine enemies wrongfully rejoice over me: neither let them wink with the eye that hate me without a cause."

Ps 69:4 "They that hate me without a cause are more than the hairs of mine head: they that would destroy me, being mine enemies wrongfully, are mighty: then I restored that which I took not away."

John 15:25 But this cometh to pass, that the word might be fulfilled that is written in their law, They hated me without a cause."

Christ must suffer:

Ps 22:1 "My God, my God, why hast thou forsaken me? why art thou so far from helping me, and from the words of my roaring? 2 O my God, I cry in the daytime, but thou hearest not; and in the night season, and am not silent. 3 But thou art holy, O thou that inhabitest the praises of Israel. 4 Our fathers trusted in thee: they trusted, and thou didst deliver them.5 They cried unto thee, and were delivered: they trusted in thee, and were not confounded. 6 But I am a worm, and no man; a reproach of men, and despised of the people. 7 All they that see me laugh me to scorn: they shoot out the lip, they shake the head saying, 8 He trusted on the Lord that he would deliver him: let him deliver him, seeing he delighted in him. 9 But thou art he that took me out of the womb: thou didst make me hope when I was upon my mother's breasts. 10 I was cast upon thee from the womb: thou art my God from my mother's belly. 11 Be not far from me; for trouble is near; for there is none to help. 12 Many bulls have compassed me: strong bulls of Bashan have beset me round.13 They gaped upon me with their mouths, as a ravening and a roaring lion. 14 I am poured out like water, and all my bones are out of joint: my heart is like wax; it is melted in the midst of my bowels. 15 My strength is dried up like a potsherd; and my tongue cleaveth to my jaws; and thou hast brought me into the dust of death. 16 For dogs have compassed me: the assembly of the wicked have inclosed me: they pierced my hands and my feet. 17 I may tell all my bones: they look and stare upon me. 18 They part my garments among them, and cast lots upon my vesture."

Isa 53:3 "He is despised and rejected of men; a man of sorrows, and acquainted with grief: and we hid as it were our faces from him; he was despised, and we esteemed him not.4 Surely he hath borne our griefs, and carried our sorrows: yet we did esteem him stricken, smitten of God, and afflicted. 5 But he was wounded for our transgressions, he was bruised for our iniquities: the chastisement of our peace was upon him; and with his stripes we are healed.6 All we like sheep have gone astray; we have turned every one to his own way; and the Lord hath laid on him the iniquity of us all. 7 He was oppressed, and he was afflicted, yet he opened not his mouth: he is brought as a lamb to the slaughter, and as a sheep before her shearers is dumb, so he openeth not his mouth. 8 He was taken from prison and from judgment: and who shall declare his generation? for he was cut off out of the land of the living: for the transgression of my people was he stricken. 9 And he made his grave with the wicked, and with the rich in his death; because he had done no violence, neither was any deceit in his mouth. 10 Yet it pleased the Lord to bruise him; he hath put him to grief: when thou shalt make his soul an offering for sin, he shall see his seed, he shall prolong his days, and the pleasure of the Lord shall prosper in his hand. 11 He shall see of the travail of his soul, and shall be satisfied: by his knowledge shall my righteous servant justify many; for he shall bear their iniquities."

Mark 9:12 "And he answered and told them, Elias verily cometh first, and restoreth all things; and how it is written of the Son of man, that he must suffer many things, and be set at nought.:"

Luke 18:32 "For he shall be delivered unto the Gentiles, and shall be mocked, and spitefully entreated, and spitted on: 33 And they shall scourge him, and put him to death: and the third day he shall rise again."

Luke 24:25 "Then he said unto them, O fools, and slow of heart to believe all that the prophets have spoken: 26 Ought not Christ to have suffered these things, and to enter into his glory?"

The disciples run:

Zech 13:7 "Awake, O sword, against my shepherd, and against the man that is my fellow, saith the Lord of hosts: smite the shepherd, and the sheep shall be scattered: and I will turn mine hand upon the little ones."

Matt 26:31 "Then saith Jesus unto them, All ye shall be offended because of me this night: for it is written, I will smite the shepherd, and the sheep of the flock shall be scattered abroad."

The traitorous Zelot:

Ps 109:4 "For my love they are my adversaries: but I give myself unto prayer. 5 And they have rewarded me evil for good, and hatred for my love. 6 Set thou a wicked man over him: and let Satan stand at his right hand. 7 When he shall be judged, let him be condemned: and let his prayer become sin. 8 Let his days be few; and let another take his office."

John 13:18 "I speak not of you all: I know whom I have chosen: but that the scripture may be fulfilled, He that eateth bread with me hath lifted up his heel against me."

John 17:12 "While I was with them in the world, I kept them in thy name: those that thou gavest me I have kept, and none of them is lost, but the son of perdition; that the scripture might be fulfilled."

Judas' death

Zech 11:12 "And I said unto them, If ye think good, give me my price; and if not, forbear. So they weighed for my price thirty pieces of silver. 13 And the Lord said unto me, Cast it unto the potter: a goodly price that I was prised at of them. And I took the thirty pieces of silver, and cast them to the potter in the house of the Lord."

Matt 27:5 "And he cast down the pieces of silver in the temple, and departed, and went and hanged himself."

Matt 27:6 "And the chief priests took the silver pieces, and said, It is not lawful for to put them into the treasury, because it is the price of blood. 7 And they took counsel, and bought with them the potter's field, to bury strangers in."

Matt 27:9 "Then was fulfilled that which was spoken by Jeremy the prophet, saying, And they took the thirty pieces of silver, the price of him that was valued, whom they of the children of Israel did value; 10 And gave them for the potter's field, as the Lord appointed me."

The Messiah is arrested:

Zech 13:7 "Awake, O sword, against my shepherd, and against the man that is my fellow, saith the Lord of hosts: smite the shepherd, and the sheep shall be scattered: and I will turn mine hand upon the little ones."

Matt 26:54 "But how then shall the scriptures be fulfilled, that thus it must be? 55 In that same hour said Jesus to the multitudes, Are ye come out as against a thief with swords and staves for to take me? I sat daily with you teaching in the temple, and ye laid no hold on me.56 But all this was done, that the scriptures of the prophets might be fulfilled. Then all the disciples forsook him, and fled."

Matt 26:57 "And they that had laid hold on Jesus led him away to Caiaphas the high priest, where the scribes and the elders were assembled."

Mark 14:48 "And Jesus answered and said unto them, Are ye come out, as against a thief, with swords and with staves to take me? 49 I was daily with you in the temple teaching, and ye took me not: but the scriptures must be fulfilled."

Christ the transgressor:

Isa 53:12 "Therefore will I divide him a portion with the great, and he shall divide the spoil with the strong; because he hath poured out his soul unto death: and he was numbered with the transgressors; and he bare the sin of many, and made intercession for the transgressors."

Luke 22:37 "For I say unto you, that this that is written must yet be accomplished in me, And he was reckoned among the transgressors: for the things concerning me have an end."

The Gentiles get in on the act:

Luke 18:32 "For he shall be delivered unto the Gentiles, and shall be mocked, and spitefully entreated, and spitted on:"

There's a conspiracy afoot:

Ps 2:1 "Why do the heathen rage, and the people imagine a vain thing? 2 The kings of the earth set themselves, and the rulers take counsel together, against the Lord, and against his anointed, saying,"

Acts 4:25 "Who by the mouth of thy servant David hast said, Why did the heathen rage, and the people imagine vain things? 26 The kings of the earth stood up, and the rulers were gathered together against the Lord, and against his Christ. 27 For of a truth against thy holy child Jesus, whom thou hast anointed, both Herod, and Pontius Pilate, with the Gentiles, and the people of Israel, were gathered together,"

Gambling for garments:

Ps 22:18 "They part my garments among them, and cast lots upon my vesture."

John 19:24 "They said therefore among themselves, Let us not rend it, but cast lots for it, whose it shall be: that the scripture might be fulfilled, which saith, They parted my raiment among them, and for my vesture they did cast lots. These things therefore the soldiers did."

Christ on the cross:

Thrist: Ps 22:15 "My strength is dried up like a potsherd; and my tongue cleaveth to my jaws; and thou hast brought me into the dust of death."

John 19:28 "After this, Jesus knowing that all things were now accomplished, that the scripture might be fulfilled, saith, I thirst."
Broken Bones: Ps 34:20 "He keepeth all his bones: not one of them is broken."

Ex 12:46 "In one house shall it be eaten; thou shalt not carry forth ought of the flesh abroad out of the house; neither shall ye break a bone thereof."

Num 9:12 "They shall leave none of it unto the morning, nor break any bone of it: according to all the ordinances of the passover they shall keep it."

John 19:32 "Then came the soldiers, and brake the legs of the first, and of the other which was crucified with him. 33 But when they came to Jesus, and saw that he was dead already, they brake not his legs:"

Pierced: Zech 12:10 "And I will pour upon the house of David, and upon the inhabitants of Jerusalem, the spirit of grace and of supplications: and they shall look upon me whom they have pierced, and they shall mourn for him, as one mourneth for his only son, and shall be in bitterness for him, as one that is in bitterness for his firstborn."

John 19:34 "But one of the soldiers with a spear pierced his side, and forthwith came there out blood and water.35 And he that saw it bare record, and his record is true: and he knoweth that he saith true, that ye might believe.36 For these things were done, that the scripture should be fulfilled, A bone of him shall not be broken."